Indian Architecture

[Hindu, Buddhist, Jain and Islam (3000 B.C.E to 1750 C.E)]

(For Degree, Diploma, AMIE students, Practicing architects, Archeologists, Heritage societies, Historians and Competitive examinations)

VEDULA V.L.N. MURTHY
B. Arch., AIIA, ISTE

STANDARD PUBLISHERS DISTRIBUTORS
1705-B, NAI SARAK, POST BOX No.: 1066, DELHI-110006
Phone : 23262700, 23285798, Fax: 011-23243180
Email:stpub@vsnl.com www.standardpublishers.com

Published by:
A.K. Jain
For Standard Publishers Distributors,
1705-B, Nai Sarak, Delhi-110006.
Showroom:
4581/15 G.F., Near, LIC, Ansari Road,
Daryaganj, New Delhi-110002.
Ph.: 011-23281159

First Edition : 2011
Reprint : 2014
Second Edition : 2023

Price Rs : 400-00

ISBN : 978-81-8014-179-9

Laser Typesetting by: Ajesh Bhargave
Printed by: Prabhat Offset Press.

PREFACE

India has great historical and architecture heritage ever inspiring and emotive. Architecture and the structures speak the culture, traditions and believes of the people. Architecture is the matrix of civilization and is a mirror that reflects the aspirations and achievements of a society. Indian Architecture mainly developed and persisted as religious architecture. Elegant and astonishing temple structures were built in which decorative and sculptural elements form the main part of the structure.

Early religious hermitages of Hindus, Buddhists and Jains are found in rock cut caves in I millennium C.E at Ajanta, Ellora, Elephanta and Khandagiri hills which exhibit both utility and applied decoration. Early temple structures are found mainly from 5th century C.E during Guptas regime.

Increase in temple activities, rituals festivals and other users' needs made Dravidian temples spread horizontally in concentric oblong rings. Exquisitely sculpted pillars, corridors, pillared halls, flat roofs, lotus carved ceilings, golden Sikharas, step lined tanks, multiple small shines and soaring gopurams are the common features well exhibited in temples of Tamilnadu state. Gopurams which are the entrance pylons stand tall ever inspiring, inviting and greeting the visitors. The temples are saturated in figure sculptures making of which require inborn natural talent and knowledge of Anatomy. These structures stand on columns, beams and brackets and have flat roofs all over and stepped Sikhara over Sanctum.

On other hand, Indo Aryan temples especially Khajuraho, Rajputama and Gujarat were high raised structures often with no enclosure walls and having less number of pillars. The roofs of these structures are Sikharas or pyramidal type. North Indian and south Indian temples developed different Sikhara forms.

In Deccan and north of India, temples earlier to 13th century only are seen, as the period after this came under the influence of Islam, hence the structures of Islam faith came into existence.

Islamic Architecture: It is a change in the historical era from 12th century C.E in India and it was the impact of Islamic ideas and their building techniques on the well-established civilization of kingdoms in India. It is a synthesis between the two divergent building systems that of Hindus and Muslims. Indo-Islamic architecture is a blend of local sculptural traditions of Hindu architecture and the structurally advanced techniques of Islam builders producing a result of unique Indo-Islamic style. Hence Indo-Islamic architecture is Hindu Muslim venture.

This period had produced great range of buildings like simple, ornamental, artistic, monumental, fine and royal. Mosques, tombs, palaces, forts and gardens were mainly built. Though these structures are different, but they consist of same architectural forms and elements. They stand on columns, arches, beams and brackets and have domical cupola or flat roofs. Additionally they have geometrical inlaid designs, stucco carvings and stone traceries.

Hence Indian craftsmen had become conversant in working both in sculpture images and geometrical works. Hence, different and distinctive style is the outcome.

Indian historical heritage structures are great manifestations which indeed show the subtle features (feelings) like sentiments, emotions, superstitions, faith, values, super imaginative minds, patronage and above all hardship of artisans. In this book, the description of structures is made based on regions and the kingdoms, which naturally changes the style. It gives information on brief political background, architectural characters, nomenclature, contemporary structures in other areas and important examples. Matter is in simple language with subtitles and is well illustrated in diagrams and photographs.

The book is written as per the latest curriculum of degree, diploma students of architecture. It is also useful to practicing architects, Archeologists, Heritage societies, Historians and Competitive examinations. In spite of every care taken to ensure accuracy, some errors might have crept in. The author will be grateful to readers for bringing such error to his notice. Suggestions for improvement of the text will be acknowledged with thanks.

Gratitude:

My reverences are to great Architectural book writers Sir Banister Fletcher and Percy Brown who created great everliving books in Architecture and whose books motivated and made me to write this book in other words. Also I pay my Pranams to all my teachers and friends at college of Fine Arts and Architecture, Hyderabad which is now called School of Planning and Architecture under whose guidance and help I came to this level.

Mahavir Jayanti, 16.4.2011

—VEDULA V.L.N. MURTHY

CONTENTS

FACTORS AND INFLUENCES

(An Over view of Resources and Development)

INTRODUCTION

India is a land of endless sagas. The land is continuously inhabited since time immemorial. Evidences of 50000 years back activity of Homo sapiens (Human like species) and Hominids (Resembling humans) who lived 5 lakhs years ago were found in India. Indian culture is the highest among world cultures. Ancient Indian scriptures discussed much on the matters like importance of human life, sustaining power of the universe, chain of births and deaths and many more. Numbers of festivals are celebrated all over the year with religious and social fervor. India is also called Hindustan and Bharat. The word India is a changed form of Sindhu to Indu, Hindu, Hindi, Indi and India. There are number of languages spoken. Some important languages have their own distinction. The language did not create any barrier for the people's movement. The ancient classical language of India is Sanskrit, which is spoken all over by educated. Common people spoke in Prakrit and Pali language in some areas of north India.

As the country is vast in size, hence the factors like the Land, its resourses, Climate, Believes of people, Social Cultural setup, Economics, Political position etc influences much on the life of people, which in turn reflects on the Design and development of structures. These are described here under briefly.

FACTORS

Geographical

Indian continent is situated on earth in a potentially prominent position. The land is pushed and pressed on southwest and southeast, as it naturally happens due to geological and seismological earth pressures and also by wave currents in oceans. India was bordered on three sides by the seas- on east by Bay of Bengal sea, on south by Hindu ocean and on west by Arabian sea, on northeast it was walled by mighty Himalayan mountains. The only land access available is on north-west side, from where the foreign intruders ventured often. Due to its vast size, almost all kinds of natural land resources like seas, mountains, hilly areas, desert, forests, rivers, river plains, lakes, springs, snow and cool places exist. Important mountains are the western ghats, eastern ghats, Nilagiri mountains, Vindhya mountains and Himalayas. The sprawling Vindhya mountains and the rivers Narmada and Tapti crossing across in the center of India in east west direction are separating north and south India. The land of India encompasses the present India, Bangladesh on east, Pakistan and Afghanistan on northwest.

Geographical factors and the vastness of area naturally influence architecture and make necessary changes and innovations.

Geological

India is rich and abundant in all resources available some where in some form. Alluvial soils in river plains, black soils in coastal regions, sandy soils near sea coasts, red earths and muram soils in Deccan plateau are plentifully available. Stones of different kinds like sandstone, lime stone, granite, marble, slate and quartzite are available all over the country.

Rajasthan is the main source for different coloured marble. Laterite stone was available in Orissa and Karnataka. Basalt is plenty in Karnataka, Maharashtra and Gujarat.

Use of stone is much in the areas of Rajasthan, Gujarat and in south. Raw stone blocks were used in foundation, walls, floor slabs, pillars, lintels, beams, roof slabs and so on. Stone was also used for making household items like grind stones, pots, oil lamps etc.

Clay was in use extensively all over India. Black earths and smooth alluvial soils were used in making bricks. Large number of utility items and artifacts were made in terracotta almost all over India. Especially Rajasthan, Uttar Pradesh and Gujarat were famous for special art terracotta items. Mud houses and tile roofs are common in villages every where as clay is available. And in some areas of Deccan, slate stone in slices are plenty and hence are used for complete construction including walls, lintels, shades and roof.

To build structures of permanent nature, religious structures and some forts were built in stone. Sometimes stone was transported laboriously on bullock carts or carried on elephants from distant places if the stone required to build the structure was not available nearby. Top portions of Sikharas, Gopurams in temples, some forts and palaces were built in brick.

Climatic

In general the climate of India is hot and humid. In the coastal regions the climate is humid and sultry due to heavy evaporation of sea waters. In the Deccan central regions the climate is hot and dry. The winter season from November to March months is cool and dry.

The high altitude hilly areas in the states of Tamilnadu, Karnataka in south and Uttarakhand, Himachal Pradesh, Jammu and Kashmir in north are cool all the year due to their high altitude position. Jammu and Kashmir and Himalayan mountains experience snow, frost and avalanches in winter. Due to snow fall and heavy rains the roofs of the structures in these hilly areas require a slope.

In north, climate is extremely hot and cool in summer and winter seasons respectively. Hence closed structures were preferred which resulted to closed temple compartments. In South, the climate is humid and sultry in sea coasts. Hence open living preferred here and it resulted to pillared halls in temples.

Religious

Hindu religion is the oldest religion of the world. India was completely a Hindu religion state. Buddhism and Jainism were raised and flourished for some time. Though these religions are different by their names they have some homogeneity and similarities. Their Gurus (teachers) and the worshiping deities are different. From 3rd cent. B.C.E to 8th cent. C.E Buddhism was much flourished and later declined. Hindu religion was the outcome of an undergoing process of culture and civilization. Hence religion and culture are interwoven. It was strengthened and consolidated much by great teachers like Shri Sankaracharya and Shri Ramanujacharya. Hindus worshiped multiple Gods in different forms and also worshipped nature. It created rituals, festivals and religious gatherings. It taught human values, ethics, morals and behaviour. Vedas described elaborately the supreme Reality which is the vital essence of universe. Hindu religion taught supreme philosophy (Vedanta) to make the mind elevated and equanomous.

After 12th century C.E Islams raised and forced their religion into India. And after 17th century, Christianity appeared and came into existence by the influx of British. Islam and Christianity are exotic and different to the culture already in practice in India. By this India became a country of multiple religions and Hindus being the majority.

The deep religious faith made construction of many large temples dedicated to god. Buddhist, Hindu and Islam structures were built as schools of religion.

Social and Cultural

India's social fabric is much united by its deep rooted culture. There are number of festivals, Birthdays of Gods (great personalities), Astronomical days which are being celebrated with religious fervour and geity. India lives in villages. Hence harvest festivals, decorating the dwellings, bullock carts and animals especially the cows and bulls are celebrated. Piligrimages, dip in river waters, visiting holy places is believed a must in one's life. And all this is soley linked with strong belief.

The great epics Ramayana, Mahabharata and others influence the value system forever. Indian Astronomical days and calculations match to the modern scientific calculations. People lived by different jobs and occupations especially Agriculture. All this made an inter-woven society. Vastness of place made diversity and strong culture made unity. Its culture and civilization influenced other lesser cultures.

Historical

India had many kingdoms piece by piece ruled by kings of different dynasties. These kingdoms were sometimes united and sometimes divided by conquest and waging wars. There are many epoch making historical events like Ramayana and Mahabharata. Suryavamsh King Srirama in ancient times and Yadava king Srikrishna in recent time around 3600 B.C.E lived and stood as ever lasting great kings and heroes. Hindus pay reverences to these great masters and worship them.

Indian history is a mix of many varieties like - Great Sagas, great Sages, great kings, culture, traditions, strong faith, worshipping, festivals, literature, classical music, dancing, devotion, Mathematics, Science, Astronomy, Astrology, Vastu Sastra, Sacrificing, Innocence, Righteousness Coexistence, Integration and so on.

During the period of Mauryan King Chandragupta Mauraya under the minister Kautilya (Chanukya), the country established much power. Arth sastra written by Chanukya was a great treatise containing the matter on economics, politics, administration, foreign affairs, military, war, religion, town planning etc. And during Asoka's reign around 2nd century B.C.E it attained largest country status encompassing whole of north India, Bangladesh, Pakistan and Afghanistan. The same status occurred during the rule of Mogul king Akbar and Auranzeb in 16th Century C.E and it included all south India except Madurai and Kerala region. The Vindhya mountains restricted the movement of people and hence the mountains became the natural border separating north and south India kingdoms.

During Gupta dynasty ruling in 4th and 5th centuries political administration, economic stability and security reached great heights. This period is known as Golden age.

The following are the names of important Hindu dynasties that established kingdoms and ruled in India.

Maurya, Satavahana (Andhras), Sunga, Gupta, Kushan, Kalinga, Bhaumakara, Somavamsi, Ganga, Pallava, Chola, Pandya, Chera, Hampi Vijayanagar (Rayala), Nayak, Gajapati, Kakatiya, Chalukya, Hoysala, Rastrakuta, Maratha, Solonki, Gurjar, Chauhan and Rajputs.

Islams came and entered as traders into India through Kerala. Earlier Muslim intrusion began in 712 C.E in India, when Muhammad Bin Qasim an Arab general conquered Sindh and Multan in Punjab. And after 12th century Islams from Afghanistan ventured into India and captured areas in north India one by one and the whole country except some kingdoms came under their control by 17th century.

The Islam dynasties who ruled India were mainly Sultans and Moguls. The sultan dynasties were Slave, Khalji, Tughlaq, Sayyid and Lodi.

The British merchants in the name of East India Company began pouring into India in 17th century C.E. from sea routes by navigation and spread their business across the country. They were producing and selling machine made products and making huge profits and established a firm base in business in India. They introduced tea into India and were purchasing cashew, scents, honey and spices from India. Indian situation made them and encouraged them to sell Arms and Ammunition like canons, guns, bullets, gunpowder etc. to the native kings. The native quarreling neighbour kings used to approach the British to get their help to defeat or to eliminate their neighbour opponent kings by using modern gunpowder warfare system. Opportunistic British took the advantage of the fragile and unrest political situation prevailed in India and started capturing the kingdoms one by one by their political litigacy of Divide and Rule. The kingdoms one after the other had been captured by British including the Mogul empire with the capital city of Delhi. All the country had gone into the power of British.

During two millenniums of Indian history, empire after empire rose and fell. It is quarrels, capturing and politics for the supremacy of empire one over the other. It is rise and fall of empires.

Hindu supremacy was captured by Islams, who in turn drawn by British (Christians). British rule in India became tyrannical and peace was lacking. Huge wealth, artifacts were transported to England. East India Company became a transport company.

To stop this tyranny and injustice one Mahatma (Great soul) rose who fought with British not with arms and ammunition, but by using peace methods like protests, dialogues, discussions, sacrifices and exhibiting patience. He is lean, not strong bodied and weaponless. But he is fearless, will powered and silent. He led the struggle through protests and sacrifices. His war is aimed towards independent India free from the clutches of British. His weapon was Non-violence (Ahimsa). He is not a single individual. He became the total nation of Bharat. From 1920, a nation wide struggle was led by Mahatma for independence launched by Indian national congress against British colonial rule.

The strong mighty British who captured countries like Africa, parts of Europe and India could not suppress the freedom struggle in India. Finally British quit India in 1947 leaving ill effected and worn India to Indians. Pakistan and east Bengal which were integral part of Hindustan since millenniums were parted from free India by the reason of religion and formed into a separate nation Pakistan. Seven and half centuries of foreigners' ruling ended by one leader Mahatma whose name is Mohandas Karamchand Gandhi. He is called Mahatma, which is one and only greatest title awarded to only one person in the whole world. Gandhi is also called Father of modern India (Father of nation). Independent India became a democratic secular state.

During this period of history forts and religious structures of permanent nature were built to which the rulers' patronage was ever available.

Architectural characters

In early years, it was the practice in India to use simple natural materials like bamboo, timber, mud, palm leaves, grass and reeds to build dwellings. Forts, palaces and riches' houses were built in brick, mud or lime and timber.

Making Rock-cut caves and hermitages was in practice before this current era. Early Hindu temples were rudimentary and were built in timber and bamboo. Construction of temples in stone came in practice somewhere near 5th century C.E during Guptas' regime. Early temple examples built in stone were found at Tigawa in Jabalpur district in Madhya Pradesh (Fig. 2) and others were found at Ran in Rajasthan state. Everlasting stone temple structures were built in India than any other structures to perform rituals, festivals and for religious gatherings.

Indian temple contains mainly two compartments namely an Assembly hall and a Sanctuary. The Assembly hall contains pillars, beams and a flat roof above. The pillars and the ceilings were lavishly ornamented and the designs change from place to place and time to time. The sanctuary is a square hall accommodating the idol of the god (deity). A decorative and sculpted Spire (Sikhara) takes place over the sanctuary and it has attained a distinctive and complex form by a series of projections and recesses.

To the main core of this temple building additions were made at a later stage. These additions were like thousand pillared halls, marriage halls, cloisters, Nat mandir (dancing hall), Bhog mandir (offering hall), enclosure walls containing Gopurams (Pylons), Pushkarini (Water pool) and so on.

Differences in North and South Indian temples

North Indian temples are: Mostly high rised, Closed and limited in compartments, Small or medium in size, Less number of pillars, Nagara type Sikhara and Pyramidal type roofs.

South Indian temples are: Normal in Plinth height and horizontally spread, Open pillared halls, Large size temples, More number of pillars, Stepped Sikhara in storeys and Flat roofs .

Every part of the temple structure is so richly and profusely decorated, carved and sculpted that they became the pulsating fire and energy ever inspiring the people.

Exuberant decoration, carvings, figure sculptures and embellishments are too heavily loaded in temple buildings. The figure subjects exhibit great mythological events, religious practices and culture. Temple structures were utility oriented and luxury was not found. However, this flourishing great temple architecture was restricted or rather not allowed to continue after the rise of Islams from 12th century especially in north, central and Deccan areas of India.

Islam Structures

By the rise of Islams at Delhi, a new movement in architecture is seen. Along with religious structures, other buildings like forts, palaces, tombs, gardens, water pools, fountains, fame towers came into existence. These new structures were built in different varieties of coloured stones like red sand stone, marble, granite and other varieties. Geometrical elements like arches, domes, ornamental parapets, inlaid geometrical patterns, kiosks, balconies were found in these structures. Figure carvings and sculptures are absent and avoided in Islam buildings. There is strong contrast in between Hindu temple structures and Islam structures. But yet, both schools of architecture had exhibited great variety and excellence in their work.

Surfaces Islam structures show ornamental decoration containing geometrical pattern designs, leafs, flowers, which were either carved in stone or inlaid or in stucco. Importance was given to build tomb structures which are treated as permanent abode to the mortal body to stay during everlasting void life after death. Hence more tomb structures are found emphasizing personal cult. Luxury, ornamentation and beautification were often found.

The built structures in India may be distinguished broadly into two parts.

Part I. Hindu, Buddhist and Jain

The structures are Rock cut caves, Monolithic shrines and Structural temples. These are religious temples and institutions.

Part II. Islam

Islam structures built in India are mainly Mosques, Forts, Palaces and Tombs.

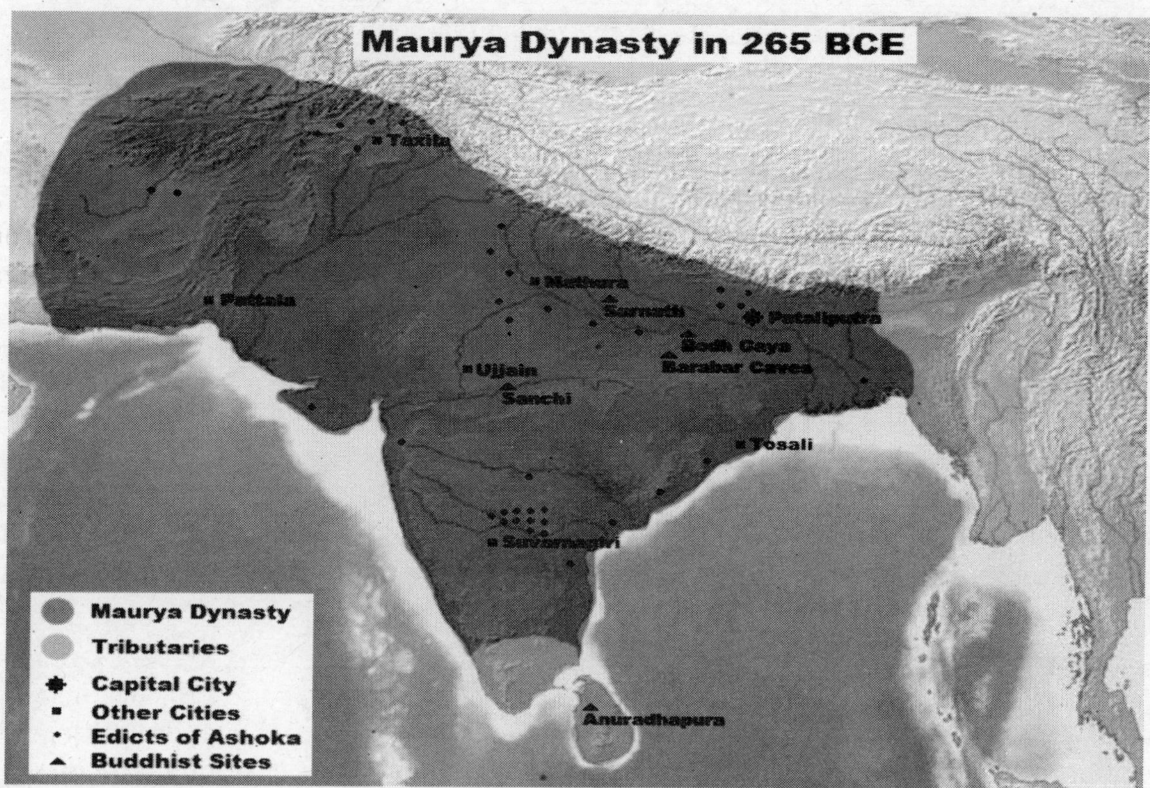

Fig 1. Maurya Dynasty empire in 265 BC

Fig 2. Temple at Tigawa

PART—1

Hindu, Buddhist and Jain

(3000 B.C.E to 1750 C.E)

1

Sindhu Valley Civilization

(3000 B.C.E to 1700 B.C.E)

1.1. INTRODUCTION

Groups of people lived in northwest lands of India more than 5000 years ago. The urban life flourished during this period was the first ever known matured civilizations of the world. The resources were abundant and the climate was generous. The community had the knowledge of cultivation, agriculture, irrigation, industries, artifacts and trade. Bronze was the main metal in use, hence it is called Bronze Age civilization.

This Bronze Age civilization flourished from 3300 B.C.E to 1300 B.C.E. The main matured period of development took place from 2600 B.C.E. to 1900 B.C.E. Number of excavations and discoveries are still in progress. This civilization was developed in between the rivers of Sindhu and Saraswathi. The Sindhu name was altered and spelt as Indu and Hindu. This civilization also is called Sindhu-Saraswathi civilization.

The first excavations made after 1920 C.E near Harappa revealed great urban settlements in Punjab region of present Pakistan. Hence this is also called Harappa civilization. Early Harappa period is centered on Ravi river developed from 3300 B.C.E to 2800 B.C.E.

Mohenjodaro is a different site located in Sindh region of Pakistan situated on Sindh river. The civilization exists from 2600 B.C.E on par with other ancient civilizations like Egypt, Mesopotamia and Crete. Mohenjodaro is now UNESCO's world Heritage site.

1.2. GEOGRAPHICAL

These settlements extended over considerable large areas. They encompassed the areas of Baluchistan, Pakistan, Southeast Afghanistan and extended into Indian present states of Rajasthan, Gujarat and Punjab (Fig. 1.2). These sites were found mostly on river side and some lie on sea coast. Such river valley sites flourished during this time were at–

– Shortughai in north Afghanistan on Oxus river.

– North western region in Pakistan on Gomal river.

– Manda near Jammu in India on Beas river.

– Alamgirpur near Delhi in India on Hindon river.

– Kalibangan in India on Hakra river.

Also many sites have been discovered along Ghaggar-Hakra dry river beds which were tributes to Sindhu river. Ghaggar-Hakra river is believed to be the Saraswathi river which was completely dried at the time of close of this civilization. Research findings revealed that Saraswati river dried because of certain geological events, which blocked the flow of Himalayas waters into it and instead fed it to Ganga and Yamuna rivers. Satellite images on Haryana and Rajasthan region showed the existence of underground river and Archeological excavations found ancient towns by the side of this river.

1.3. THE CITIES

Sindhu valley cities showed the evidence of sophisticated and technologically advanced urban culture. The three sites explored are Mohenjodaro in Sind (Sindi—the place of the dead), Harappa in southern Punjab and Chanudaro in Baluchistan situated some 120 kilometres from Mohenjodaro. (Fig. 1.1) The excavations revealed the foundations of cities in well-defined form. They showed that these cities have flourished for a long period and established a firm culture. The planning of buildings and civic administration of the principal cities constitute a great achievement of the people. There was efficient municipal government system having the knowledge of urban planning.

The main urban centers were— Harappa, Ganeriwala and Mohenjodaro in Pakistan.

— Dholavira, Kalibangan, Rakhigarhi, Rupar and Lothal in India.

In total 1052 settlements were found.

1.4. TOWN PLANNING

The towns were geometrically designed and had fortifications for protection against intruders. With in the town there are several residential quarters, assembly halls, public baths and manufacturing units of various types. Both Mohenjodaro and Harappa were nearly a square mile in area set within defensive walls. The layout of the town was a gridiron pattern of narrow streets of about 2.7 metres wide running in north-south and east-west directions. The streets divided the city into 12 blocks, each measuring 365 metres long by 244 metres wide approximately. From the main streets the residents approached the individual houses through irregular, narrow and shaded walkways. The residential unit invariably had no entrance opening directly into the main streets and even no windows towards the subsidiary walkways. The same principle was followed by Le Corbusier in the city of Chandigarh, where no access is made from dwellings in to the expressways.

There are large and small houses, which predominate in the town. Other large structures probably may be market hall, storerooms or offices. Some others were arranged around two spacious courtyards, which may have been the palace and several halls possibly for religious purpose. A very complete bathing establishment was found at Mohenjodaro. (Fig. 1.5)

1.5. WATER SUPPLY AND DRAINAGE

High priority was given to hygiene and sanitation. This was the world's first known urban sanitation systems. Sewerage through underground drains and efficient water management with numerous reservoirs and wells were managed. Mohenjodaro had over 700 wells. They were 15 metres deep built with trapezoid bricks.

Each house or groups of houses had a common well for their water usage. But each house had its own separate bath. The entire city was served by an extensive system of drainage. A sophisticated drainage system had existed here. The waste water from the houses was connected to drains running under the walkways, which in turn were connected to large sewers laid under the main street. These small drains were covered by brick slabs. Corbelled brick arches spanned the larger main sewers. Manholes were located at regular intervals along the main sewer for inspection and cleaning purposes. This elaborate drainage system took care also of the abundant rainfall in the region. Dholavira town had separate drains to collect rain water. Six or seven dams were built across over nearby rivers. The sewerage and drainage system developed and used in these cities was far advanced than the present contemporary systems available in towns of India and Pakistan.

1.6. PLANNING OF HOUSES

The houses of Harappa and Mohanjodaro were completely 'utilitarian'. The house was planned as a series of rooms around an open to sky central court. The central court ventilates all the rooms surrounding it, keeping privacy and security. It also provided a space for open air living within the house. The surrounding rooms are opened into this open courtyard. No openings were provided on outside walls except an entrance door openinig into the side lanes (Fig. 1.4). Houses of varying sizes and storeys were built in brick and roofed by clay tiles laid over timber rafters. The efficiency of this planning system is such that right up to 19th century, this was the accepted system of house building planning in India.

The upper storeys were built largely in wood. The roofs are flat and built of stout beams covered with planks finished with a top-dressing of beaten earth. Openings are spanned by wooden lintels. But there are traces of use of corbelled arch made by over-sailing courses of brick. The houses are barely utilitarian.

1.7. CITY CITADEL

Sindhu valley cities were ruled by religious group rather than by kings (Fig. 1.8). The priestly citadel was located always in the central blocks on western side. It was built over a platform of backed bricks over 15 metres high than the general level of the city. Within it were located a palace, a bathing tank and a massive granary shed. Within the citadel are the ruins of a vast hall measuring 70 by 24 metres, which could have been a palace or place of worship. A tank obviously for ceremonial bathing measuring 7 metres long 12.2 metres wide and 2.4 metres deep was meticulously waterproofed with asphalt hving a system for filling and draining water. Surrounding it were series of cells, may be for priests. Circular brick paved flour-making platforms and barracks for labourers were located near the granaries. The granary is a timber shed stood on the steep verge of the citadel for safe storage of grain. It has a huge unloading platform. But this structure is now completely disappeared.

Advanced architecture of Harappans was seen in the construction of Granaries, Brick platforms, Warehouses, Protective walls and Dock yards. But strangely there are no evidences of construction of large monumental structures like temples and palaces. (Fig. 1.6, 1.7)

1.8. USE OF BRICKS

Mud bricks and some times burnt bricks were used in construction of walls. These bricks are larger in size than the size of the present day bricks. They were laid in mud mortar in courses of English bond. Bricks had a standard ratio of 4:2:1. They were of varying sizes used separately for houses, fortifications or so. Stones were used for fort walls. The walls have a slope for stability.

1.9. TRADE, TRANSPORT AND AGRICULTURE

Self-sufficiency in basic needs encouraged growth of industries like pottery, brick making, carpentry and weaving of cotton textiles. Consequently a prosperous mercantile class emerged and they also engaged in overseas trade.

The economy of the people seems to have depended on trade and agriculture. The goods were transported on bullock carts on land and in boats on seas. Canal network was used for trade and irrigation. The trade was extended to far places including Afghanistan, Persia, Mesopotamia and India. Most city dwellers were traders or artisans. Some bigger cities had furnaces for production of copper, tools, weapons and ornaments.

Food production was indigenous. Wheat, Barley, Cereals and cotton were cultivated.

1.10. SCIENCE

Great accuracy was developed in measuring length, mass and time. They had a system of uniform and precise measures and weights. They produced bronze, copper, lead and tin. Iron was not yet known. From discoveries it is found that they had the knowledge of photo dentistry. An astonishing fact is that evidence of drilling human teeth in a living person was found in Mehrgarh, Pakistan dating back to around 8000 years. Testing the purity of gold was also found. Using the same techniques is still in practice in many parts of India.

1.11. ARTS AND CULTURE

Various sculptures, seals, pottery, stone, gold jewelry, terracotta and bronze items were found in excavated sites. Figures of dancing girls, (Fig. 1.9) make up and toiletry items like special kind of combs were also found. Craft items in ceramics, agate, shell work and glazed steatite beads were used in making bangles, necklaces and other ornaments. These techniques are still in practice in India and Pakistan.

Seals depicting figures like sitting cross legged and another figure standing on its head that were found at Mohenzodaro site show the practice of subjects like yoga.

String musical instruments (Harp like instrument) on seal were found at Lothal. They also made various toys and games instruments like cubical dice.

1.12. RELIGION

Harappan people worshiped mother goddess symbolizing fertility. Some seals showed Swastika symbols, Siva lingam and animals. Terracotta female figures had red colour applied to the line of partition of hair (Sindhuram). These symbols are related mainly to Hinduism.

In initial periods Harappans buried their dead. Later they cremated the dead and buried the ashes in burial urns.

1.13. SYMBOLS

Large numbers of non linguistic symbols were found on seals, small tablets, ceramic pots and trade transportations. Writing was in the form of symbols. (Fig. 1.10)

1.14. THE DECLINE

The reason for decline of such great civilization is not fully known. A probable natural reason may be due to climate and ecological changes. The climate grew significantly cooler and drier from about 1800 B.C.E. and might have weakened the monsoon. Another factor was the disappearance of large portions of Gaggar-Hakra river system.

QUESTIONS

1. What is Sindhu Valley civilization and briefly explain its geographical position.
2. Explain the town planning developed in the cities of Sindhu valley civilization and mention names of any five such cities.
3. Describe briefly the following:
   (*i*) Water supply and Drainage system developed in Sindhu valley cities
   (*ii*) Planning of Houses
4. Explain the Trade and Economy of the people of Sindhu valley and how Science, Arts and culture were developed.

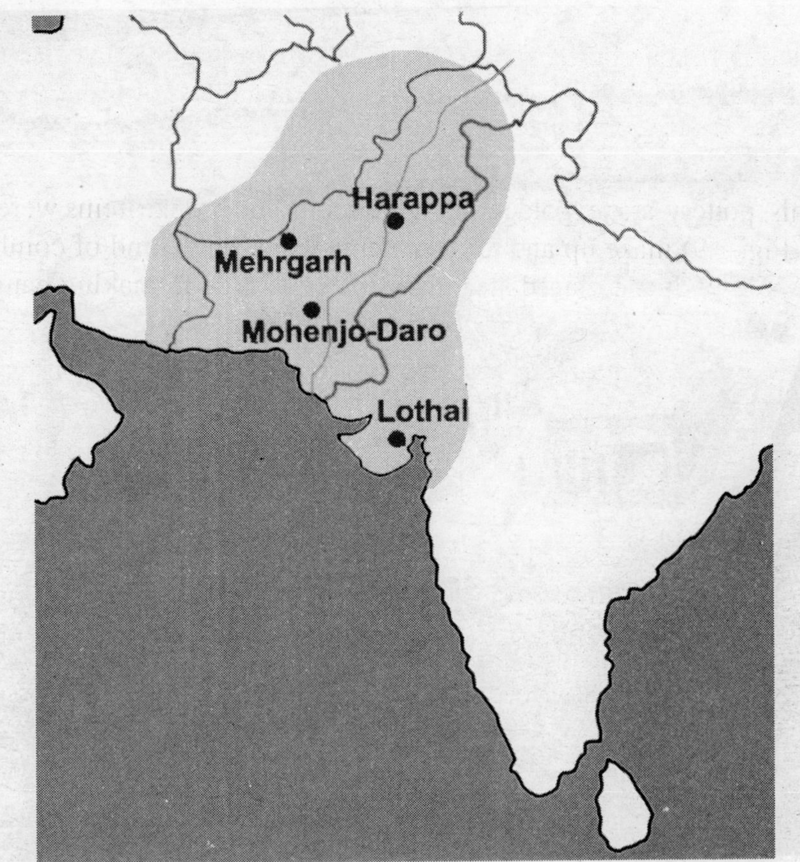

Fig. 1.1. Sindhu Valley civilization-Area map

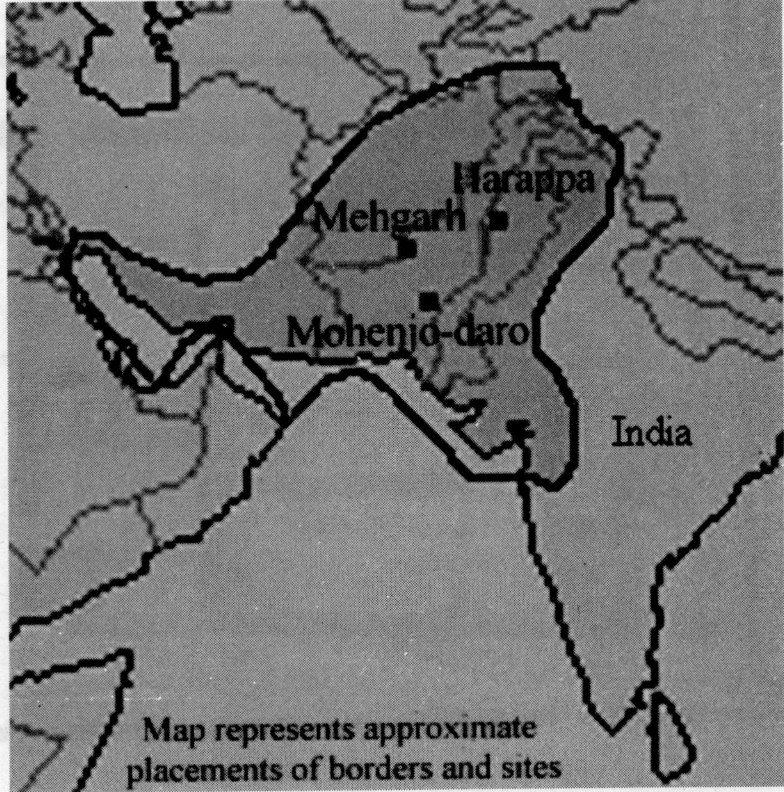

Fig. 1.2. Sindhu Valley civilization-Map showing boarders and sites

Fig. 1.3. Lothal, Gujarat-Aerial view

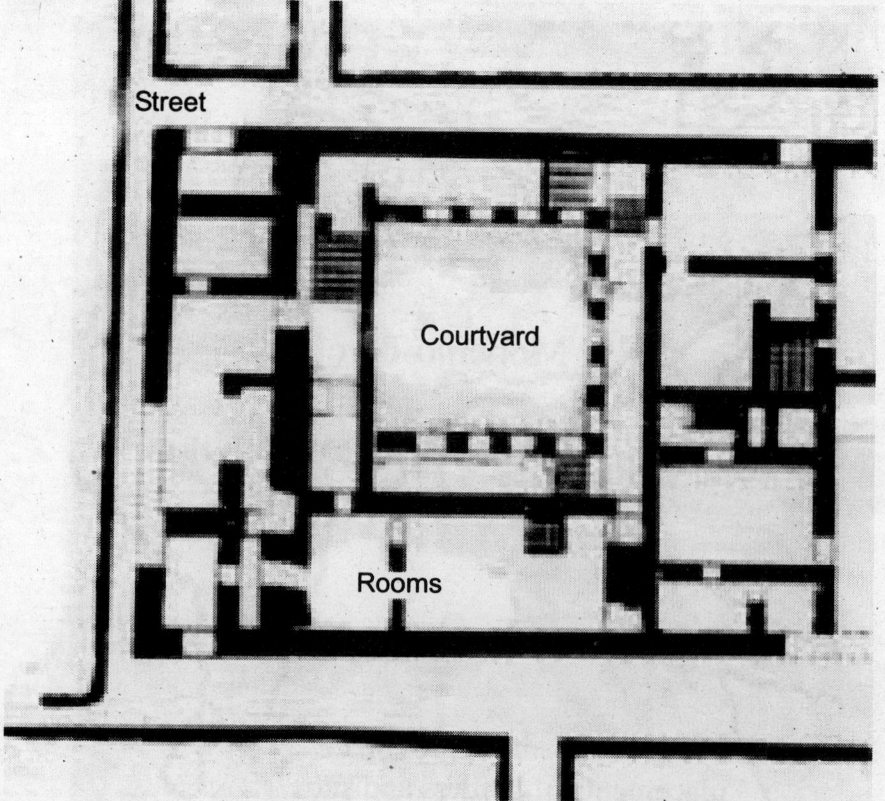

Fig. 1.4. Harappan house-Plan

Fig. 1.5. Great bath at Mohenjodaro

Fig. 1.6. Mohenjodaro remains

Fig. 1.7. Sindhu valley remains

Fig. 1.8. Mohenjodaro-Priest king statue

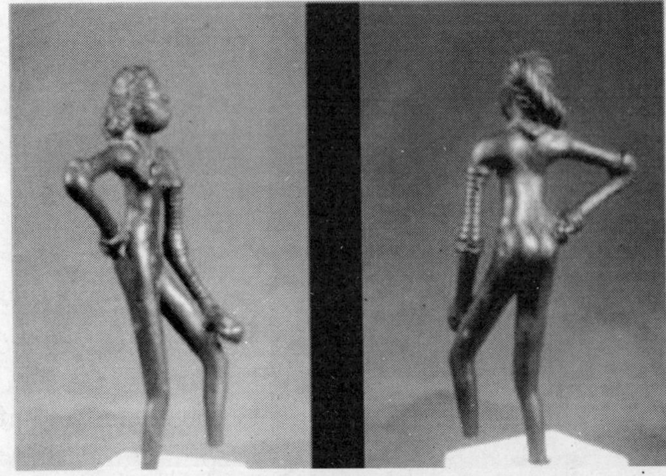

Fig. 1.9. Mohenjodaro-Metal statues of Dancing girl

Fig. 1.10. Indus script symbols

2

Vedic Civilization

(1500 B.C.E to 1800 B.C.E)

2.1. INTRODUCTION

It is believed that some group of people who conquered the civilization of Sindu valley were calling themselves 'Aryas', whose original home was somewhere in central Asia. Groups of Aryans in search of more favourable places had been moving to the places eastward from Pakistan region and finally descended into the Ganga river plains in about 1500 B.C.E. The natural wealth of the area had attracted these nomads and Aryan immigration into this area began at a fast pace. They were termed as Aryans by historians. Aryans attacked the aboriginals with their military superiority. They had spread themselves out in the lands between the two rivers of Ganga and Yamuna and foothills of Himalayas and Vindhya mountains. The nomads were gradually accustomed, settled and established the life of an agriculturist. The territory stretched from modern Afghanistan to Bangladesh. (Fig. 2.1)

Rig-Veda was the first text made and brought by Aryans. Later they made other three Veda texts namely Yajurveda, Samveda, Atharvanveda. Hence the period after this is called Vedic period in India. Hence the settled Aryans are called Indo Aryans or Vedic people.

Agriculture is the main source of economy and livelihood. They made ox drawn ploughs and canal system for irrigation. Money and coins were not known. Exchange and trade were done through Barter system. Weaving, pottery, carpentry, smithy were in practice. Iron was known and iron implements were made. Hence this age is called Iron Age.

Basic unit of Aryan social life is the family. Women excelled in education and enjoyed equal status with men and participated in public life.

Aryans personified the forces of nature and worshiped them. Rig-Veda written in Sanskrit contains hymns on creation, death, sacrifice, ritual and various gods.

2.2. VEDIC VILLAGE

Though the early Aryans had seen the use of brick in the cities of Harappans, their descendants choose to build their village settlements in timber, bamboo and thatch, which were readily and abundantly available in nature. Timber and bamboo dwellings were simple and easy to maintain or rebuild in case of damage by rains, winds or floods. The early Aryan village was a combination of timber and thatch huts of different types.

Village Boundary: The village was defined and bounded by a timber fence to get secured from the wild life of surrounding forest. The fence is simple containing horizontals and verticals. This took the form of a railing with upright wooden posts (Thabha) fixed into the ground. And the rectangular wooden posts were strung by threading them into holes in the verticals. In the early days this fence was made with bamboos. Three horizontal bars called suchi (needles) were threaded through the holes in the uprights. This type of protection became universal after sometime and used widely.

Gateway: At points of entry a portion of the fence was projected out. It contained a gateway (Gramadwara) in it to provide a controlled entry, through which the people and the cattle passed. This was built much like the fence with its horizontal ties rose high enough. The shape of this primitive gateway was later transformed into the famous Toranas of Buddhists built in stone later. (Fig. 2.2)

2.3. VEDIC HOUSES

Most houses in villages were huts built with temporary materials. The elementary huts were circular in plan. The wall was made of upright bamboos tied together with twigs. The roof made with bent bamboos took a domical or conical shape was covered by overlapping thatch or grass.

As this circular hut is not enough to serve all the purposes, therefore an addition was made in the form of a rectangular hut in the front. Lengths of bamboos were bent into semi-circular shape and tied then with a string at the base to form a vaulted roof. This tunnel-like roof was covered either with palm leaves, cane or grass. The huts were arranged in groups of threes or fours around an open courtyard. A group of such huts formed a typical Aryan village.

Apart from this in towns some houses were built in brick and mud in towns and they had upper floors containing a traditional central open to sky court. The roof is a vault having an ogee curve at top ending with graceful gable ends. This arch form is named 'Chaitya arch' later after it's much use in Chaitya halls by Buddhists.

2.4. TOWN PLANNING

Ultimately about 450 B.C.E. the three kingdoms of Kashi, Koshala and Magadha were manoeuvred. The towns of these kingdoms were Sharavasti, Champa, Rajagriha, Ayodhya, Kaushambi and Kashi. Unlike the cities of Harappa and Mohanjodaro, the foundations of which were left once they had been abandoned, the most cities of Ganga river plains in India have been continuously inhabited and constantly rebuilt.

The ideal town of this period was laid out as a square with a gridiron pattern. Three main streets would run north-south and another three in the east-west direction as prescribed in the book 'Arthasastra', the Indian manual of town planning written by the great Minister Kautilya also called Chanukya.

Excavations at Kaushambi near Allahabad have revealed that this town was built with baked bricks of immense size. The city was protected with ramparts over 9 metres high built in mud. Rectangular towers were erected on the bastions. Even the excavated site of today reveals many methods and principles. The town was also served by a rudimentary sewage system equipped with soak pits with perforated bases. The Aryans had established a comfortable urban life in the plains of Ganga river.

QUESTIONS

1. Explain Vedic village, its Boundary and Gateway.
2. Describe the design of Vedic Houses.
3. Explain the Town planning developed during Vedic period. Mention any two names of such towns.
4. Sketch the view of Gateway of an Vedic village.

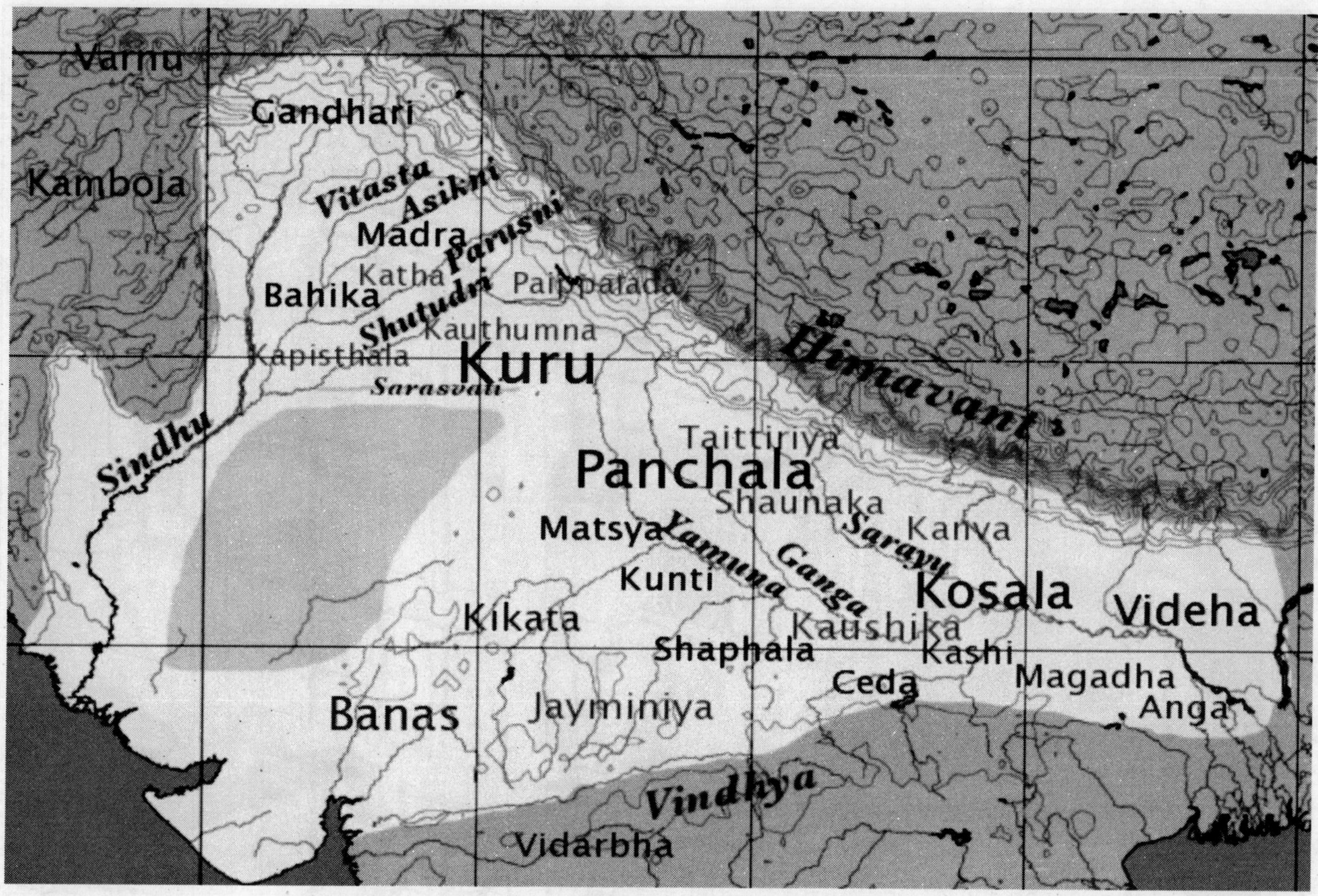

Fig. 2.1. Vedic Civilization period, India-Map

Fig. 2.2. Vedic Village- Fence, Gateway and houses

3

Asoka's Pillars, Early Rock Cut Caves and Early Temples

(250 B.C.E to 700 C.E)

3.1. INTRODUCTION

Asoka was an independent emperor of Mauryan dynasty who ruled almost all India including present Pakistan, Afghanistan and Bangladesh. After the severe war over Kalinga (the present state of Orissa) and after witnessing huge number of deaths Asoka adopted Buddhism and started propagating the message of Buddha by inscriptional writings on stones and construction of everlasting structures like free standing pillars.

During this time art of making rock cut caves was also developed by Buddhists and Jains.

3.2. FREESTANDING PILLARS

These freestanding pillars are remarkable and notable of Asoka period. There are a series of pillars erected throughout north India during 3rd century B.C.E. These pillars are not isolated monuments, but they are part of a complex of stupas and other buildings of Buddhist settlements.

Each pillar circular in section is like a palm tree plain and unadorned measuring 9 meters to 12 meters in height rising straight from the ground without having any base or pedestal. There is gentle tapering towards top, the diameter at which is 0.60 metres. At the top was mounted a large Lion capital. Inscriptions were carved on the pillars. These pillars were built at intervals along the road leading to Buddhist pilgrim places.

The columns averaging between 12 metres to 15 metres long and weighing some 50 tons were carved out of a single block of sandstone from the now famous quarry at Chunnar in present Bihar state. These massive columns were carried unbroken and intact to the sites far away on a specially designed huge timber bullock carts. The column was varnished and polished to give a unique and unbelievable mirror-like luster fantastic finish indeed. (Fig. 3.1)

Iron pillars were also made and erected at some places. The quality of iron in these pillars is such that they were not rusted even today and are still lying. Muslim rulers later replaced these iron pillars and erected them in their building compounds. Such of these examples are one at Qutb mosque, Delhi and the other at Purana quila at Delhi.

Lion capital: The pillar has a capital containing a large sculptured figure of an animal usually the lion. And in some cases four different animals like elephant, horse, bull and lion were placed looking into four cardinal directions reflecting a theme of guarding the kingdom in all directions in righteousness. (Fig. 3.2).

Lion capital at Saranath: It bears an inverted bell shaped or a lotus flower. Over this the disc has the figures of a bull, horse, a lion, elephant and the Asoka chakra (Dharma chakra). Above this disc the four lions are standing back to back. The chakra (wheel) was chosen to place it in the center of Indian national flag. The lion capital is adopted as national emblem of India. The famous capital of four lions at Saranath had acquired great popularity after it being adopted as a national emblem of independent India. This Lion capital weighing five tones and about 2.10 metres in height was joined to the pillar by a 0.60 metres long cylindrical copper dowel inserted accurately into the pillar and the capital without the use of any binding material.

Examples of important Pillars:

1. *Sanchi:* Pillar at Sanchi is similar to Saranath example having a lion capital.
2. *Rampura:* There are two pillars at Rampura, one with a bull and the other with a lion as crowning capital.
3. V*aishali:* Pillar at Vaishali had a single lion. A Buddhist monastery and a sacred coronation tank exist here. Inscription on the pillars were in Prakrit or Brahmi script.

As works of art these Asoka pillars had high place. They are finely proportioned and well balanced. The purpose of these pillars was solely monumental, as they are just freestanding pillars.

3.3. EARLY ROCK-CUT CAVES

The foremost and earlier Rock-cut caves in India are found in following places- Barabar hills and Nagarjuna hills situated to north of Gaya in Bihar state made during 250 B.C.E.

- Udayagiri and Khandagiri hills in Orissa state, 2nd century B.C.E.
- Ajanta caves in Maharastra state, 2nd century B.C.E (Described in Chapter 4- Buddhist Architecture)

1. Barabar Hills, 3rd cent. B.C.E

These were the oldest surviving rock cut caves in India dating back to 3rd century B.C.E. These were hewed in a low raised large boulder of granite stone in Babarbar hills near Gaya in Bihar state. On the order of Asoka these caves were made for the use of Ajivika sect, who were the followers related to Jain religion. These chambers are exact copies of existing wood and thatch structures. These caves are situated adjacent to each other.

The configuration of the whale-backed hill has prevented the excavation being made axially. The caves contain two chambers with highly polished stone surfaces with echo effect. The two chambers are:

- A barrel-vaulted hall of 10 metres by 6 metres and 3.7 metres high meant for worshipers to congregate.
- At the end of this chamber a separate circular cell 5.8 metres in diameter with a hemispherical domical roof 3.70 metres high at the center

Externally the cave was made to imitate like a thatch hut. It has overhanging shade and perpendicular grooves in imitation of upright posts of wood or bamboo. It is surprising to see that the stone surface has been rubbed until it resembles glass.

The ornamentation that surrounds the doorway of Lomas Rishi is remarkable. It is an exact copy of the gable end portion of a wooden structure chiseled in rock-face. In appearence it looks like carpenter's work. A doorway of 2.30 metres high is recessed within a semi-circular archway. Above this is a fanlight with two lunettes. The elephants in the lower lunette and a pattern of latticework in the second lunette were carved exquisitely. Surrounding the gable is a finial of terracotta. Every detail is sharply chiseled and still retains its high polish.

Names of Caves: Lomas Rishi and Sudama. (Fig. 3.3)

2. Udayagiri and Khandagiri Hills (Jain Rock cut Caves), 2nd cent.B.C.E

These are the earliest group of Jain Rockcut shelters of 2nd century B.C.E situated near Bhuvaneswar city in Orissa state. Udayagiri and Khanadagiri are situated opposite each other divided by a highway road. The caves were patroned and carved for Jain monks as dwellings and worshiping shelters during the reign of emperor Karavela or Karabela of Cheti dynasty who called themselves Maha Meghavahana dynasty of Kalinga kingdom. Thse are partly cut in rock and partly built.

These hills are lower in height situated in plain grounds. Hence the caves were excavated on top of the hill access to which is provided through steps. The height of the caves is too low less than the height of a human being. The caves open directly into a verandah.

Udayagiri and Khanadagiri has 18 and 15 caves respectively. The caves are now called by local names based on the carvings on the walls of the cave and were numbered by Archeological Survey of India. (Fig. 3.4, 3.5)

Following are important caves in Udayagiri hill.

- Ranigumpha (Queen's cave): Cave No. 1
- Hathigumpha: Cave No. 14
- Ganeshagumpha: Cave No. 10

Decoration was applied in the form of figures, reliefs and sculptural friezes. Extensive inscriptions in Brahmi script of Prakrit language revealed the information of the name of the king, the time of carving of caves, expeditions and victories of king Kharavela, political and other information. Some inscriptions were made in Devanagari letters of Sanskrit language.

Ranigumpha: This is the largest and well preserved cave excavated on three sides of a quadrangle having fine wall friezes. The figures depict the images of Dwarapalas (Door keepers), Royal couple with folded hands, Female dancers etc. (Fig. 3.4)

In Khandagiri hill a cave contains images of 24 Jain Apostles on monolith stones. Some additions were made during restoration work.

3.4. EARLY TEMPLES IN INDIA, 400 TO 700 C.E

Early temples in north India were built during Guptas' regime from 400 to 700 C.E in Madhya Pradesh and some in Rajputana. Temples consisting of basic elements like Square Sanctum and a pillared porch were emerged. These were built in stone masonry and usually had monolithic flat roof slabs. Portico was supported on 4 pillars having more intercolumnation in the middle than the sides. Ornamentation in pillars is seldom found. But in later temples decoration in geometrical patterns and Vase and foliage motif came to appear.

Examples: Temple No. 17, Sanchi

Temple at Tigawa in Madhya Pradesh and at Ran in Rajputana

Gradually temples having Sikharas (Nagara style) over the Sanctum and pyramidal roof over Mandapa appeared.

Early Examples of Nagara Sikhara are: Gurjar Pratihara temples in Rajputana, 8th century C.E

Temples at Aihole of 5th century C.E. built during the rule of Chalukyas were the earliest temples in south India. These are described in Chapter No. 5 Early Chalukyas Architecture.

QUESTIONS

1. Explain the structure of Asoka's free standing pillars. Mention names of any two such examples.
2. Briefly explain the early Rock cut caves of Barabar hills in Bihar state including examples.
3. Sketch the Lion capital of Asoka pillar.
4. Explain the Jain caves of Udayagiri and Khanadagiri Caves of Orissa. Mention any two names of examples of these caves.
5. Describe briefly the early temples built in India.

Fig. 3.1. Asoka pillar at Vaishali, 250 B.C.E

Fig. 3.2. Asoka pillar capital

Fig. 3.3. Early Rock cut caves-Lomasrishi Entrance arch, 250 B.C.E

Fig. 3.4. Udayagiri caves, Ranigumpha

Fig. 3.5. Udayagiri Caves, 2nd cent. B.C.E.

4

Buddhist Architecture

(185 B.C.E to 600 C.E)

4.1. INTRODUCTION

Buddhism was spread in India as a new spiritual faith and a system of spiritual learning and living. In early years, Viharas (Buddhist Monasteries) were built as temporary shelters for the wandering monks and later developed into learning institutes. Such example is at Nalanda in Bihar state where a University was found which was unfortunately destroyed during Islam ruling.

Initially Stupas were built as memorials and monuments containing Buddhist relics. Later Chaitya temples were added built mostly in timber, hence destroyed. Then cave-temples came into existence. These were established by making caves in hills away from normal habitations.

The caves are good in climate inside. They were cool in summer and warm in winter. Water is served from waterfalls, narrow streams, ponds and ground water. An appropriate place where the need of water is served was choosen to make these habitations. Influence of place served much here.

Monks, learners and aspirers continued and migrated to these peaceful and solitary places. Increase in temple activities and influx of inmates pressed for additional accommodation for learning, sleeping, eating, food making and storage and others.

Early Buddhist period from 2nd century B.C.E to 1st century C.E is called Hinayayana period, in which the images of Buddha were not presented. They were presented as symbols like footprints, trees and elephants. Later in Mahayana period the images of Buddha were carved and painted.

Three types of structures that are associated here are:

- Stupas
- Chaityas (temples)
- Viharas

4.2. STUPAS

Stupas are the symbolic monuments of Buddhists. They are the brick mounds in the shape of a hemisphere rising to a height approximately equal to its radius. In the bottom center of this domical mound Buddha's relics were kept preserved making it sanctified and sacred. Stupa contains the following elements.

- A hemispherical mound
- Harmika
- Chatrayasti (Umbrella)

The brickwork surface of the mound was plastered thick and recesses were provided at intervals for the reception of small lamps for lighting. A railing was also built encircling the Stupa.

On the summit of the mound is a Harmika which is a stone railing enclosing a small square area. This was made in polished stone in some Stupas. Within this Harmika, a stone umbrella (Chatrayasti) is placed.

Decoration on Stupas was made in the form of tablets, friezes including human figures. Images of Buddha were not presented until 1st century C.E and the same were introduced in Mahayana period.

Sanchi monuments

Sanchi is a historical site where Buddhist institutions and monuments are found. This is now UNESCO's world heritage site. Out of many Stupas existing in India the following two important examples are selected for description. (Fig. 4.1)

4.3. EXAMPLES

1. Stupa at Sanchi, 1st cent. B.C.E:

Earlier Stupa: Sanchi stupa is the earliest surviving example. It is the largest and famous at Sanchi on a hilltop near Bhopal close to Vidisha, the centre of Sunga dynasty rulers. An old Stupa existed here built during the reign of Asoka. This was a masonry hemisphere of some 21.34 metres in diameter and rising to a height equal to its radius approximately. A small space was usually left for keeping the relic of the Buddha in the center of the domical mound. On the top of the mound was an umbrella (Chatrayasti) made in polished stone. The brickwork was plastered thick. Recesses were provided at intervals for the reception of lamps for lighting.

Enlarged Stupa: The existing Stupa was enlarged by building another mound increasing the diameter to 36.5 metres and the height to 16.4 metres. An elevated processional passage (Pradakshina Patha) was built at 4.8 metres high above the ground level, perhaps made for priests. Access to this is made by a double stairway (Sopana) on south side. The whole of this structure was finished with hammer-dressed stones laid in fairly even courses.

Harmika: The top of the mound was made flattened to make place for Harmika. This encloses a square area by a stone railing with horizontals and verticals. From the center of this rose the three tiered circular stone umbrella (Chatrayasti). The tiers reduce in diameter above. This is the earlier form of Chatri (Umbrella). In the later structures the tiers were reversed and were expanded above tier by tier resembling an inverted stepped pyramid.

Enclosure: The whole of this structure was enclosed and surrounded by a massive stone railing of 3.3 metres high with an entrance at each cardinal point. The railing was the copy of the wooden railing of Vedic villages, but built in stone. Its uprights consist of octagonal posts 2.7 metres high from the ground and placed at close intervals of 0.60 metres gap between each. Connecting these posts are three horizontal bars, each 0.60 metres wide and separated only by a narrow gap of 8 centimeters. On the top of the railing was placed a large beam, its upper side rounded forming a coping stone. (Fig. 4.1 to 4.4)

Torana: Ornamental entrance gateways took the form of a 'Torana', a special kind of entrance archway made similar to wood and bamboo gates of early Vedic village. There are four gateways each facing the cardinal points. These sandstone gateways consist of two upright posts prolonged vertically and connected above by three separate lintels. Between these lintels is a row of ornamental balusters. The total height is 10.3 metres with a width of 6 metres. The thickness of these upright posts is only 0.60 metres. They had no struts or similar supports. Carpentry types of joints were employed here in the railings. The two uprights and the cross beams bore the figures of dwarfs, elephants, lions and other symbolism. A portion of the railing was projected to accommodate the Toranas. The entrance access was staggered here to make a controlled entry and privacy. It is surprising that these gateways lived and withstood the time of over two thousand years and remained intact. (Fig. 4.1 to 4.4)

2. Stupa at Amaravathi (3rd cent.C.E)

Amaravathi was the capital town of Satavahana Andhras at around 300 C.E situated in Guntur district of Andhra Pradesh state. The Stupa is a hemispherical mound of 49 metres diameter. It contains a 4.5 metres wide-open processional passage on the ground around the Stupa. A stone railing with horizontals and verticals encloses this. A processional passage on the Stupa at height of 6 metres from the ground was built, to which flight of steps were provided on four sides of the Stupa. On the wall adjoining this flight of steps four Aryaka pillars were placed.

The whole of the Stupa was cladded with glazed marble stone slabs. The facing surfaces were overlaid, ornamented and decorated hiding the inner masonry work. But today nothing remains of this grand Stupa except the irregular marking of the brick mound. It was the practice of the Buddhists to carve the designs of the structure in bas-reliefs. A bas-relief is carved on the wall adjoining to the stairway.

4.4. ROCK CUT CAVES (2ND CENT. B.C.E . TO 7TH CENT. C.E)

Buddhist monks continued to live a peaceful and spiritual life away from urban habitations. To live any type of human life some shelter is required. The thatch shelter dwellings are not permanent and were affected by climate and fire. Hence caves were made in living rock on the hillsides by means of cutting and carving. The design of these caves was a copy and prototype of structural work. Carpentry joints were shown in stonework. It was a succession of worshipping halls and other living quarters in mountains. Buddhist rock-cut carvers made wondrous caverns in granite hillsides and this may be termed as Cave architecture. In other words this may be treated as sculpture rather than architecture as it involved cutting and carving of stone instead of construction.

The cave settlements of Buddhists are mainly divided into two types.

1. Chaitya halls or worshiping halls
2. Viharas or the hostels

1. Chaitya halls

Chaitya hall is the worshipping place and temple of Buddhists. In accordance with growing religious practice Buddhist temples (Chaitya grihas) were made containing stupas inside. The Chaitya halls were cut into the living rock on hillsides by cutting and removing a portion of the hill to make worshiping halls. Excavation was done from top to bottom so that formwork or centering can be avoided. Cutting a portion of the hill produced these caves. These caves date from 2nd century B.C.E to 7th Century C.E.

Group of such examples are found in Western Ghats at Bhaja, Kondane, Pithalkora, Bedsa, Nasik, Ajanta, Karli and Ellora all existing in the present state of Maharashtra. (Fig. 4.5 to 4.9)

Plan

The Chaitya hall consists of a rectangular hall, the dimensions of which vary from one to other and from place to place. As this is carved in the hill portion, hence there is only one opening in the front and the crust of the hill closes other three sides. The hall contains a central nave and single aisle on either side divided by row of pillars. The three entrance doorways in the front wall are symmetrically arranged. The central door is the main door, which is meant for scholars, teachers and elders opens into the nave of the hall. The two side doors, which open into the aisles, are meant for disciples and latecomers. On the other side opposite to the entrance is usually an apsidal end where the Stupa stands which is a monolith and is part of the remains after cutting the unrequisites. The Stupa is a vertical cylindrical solid having its height more than its diameter. On either side of the rectangular hall columned aisles were formed. The aisles were carried behind the Stupa through the apsidal end making a processional pathway. The hall of Karli measures 38 metres long, 14 metres wide and 14 metres high. (Fig. 4.12)

In front of side entrance doorways the floor was sunk to form shallow cisterns filled with water to wash the feet before entering into the sacred hall.

Pillars

Columns divide the nave and the aisles. They were placed very closely and followed the shape of apsidal curve behind the Stupa. Pillars have pot shaped bases, octagonal shafts and a capital with inverted stepped pyramidal mould surmounted by a group of fine statuary. In the Karli Chaitya hall there are thirty-seven pillars closely placed leaving a narrow space in between, which is little more than the width of the pillar itself. The fifteen pillars on each side were richly carved and decorated, while the seven pillars encircling the apse have plain octagonal shafts. (Fig. 4.8, 4.9)

Ceiling

The ceiling is the central hall is made into a vaulted roof to which closely set wooden ribs were added making it appealing, aesthetic and inspiring. The aisles have a curved or vaulted roof and in some instances it has only a flat roof. (Fig. 4.8, 4.9)

Stupa

Stupa was placed in Chaitya hall on the other end opposite to entrance. It is elongated and contains a domical top, over which a Harmika and inverted pyramid type umbrella were placed resembling a crown. The portion of the Stupa above the mid-level was recessed inside making an edge to resemble the processional pathway. In the early Hinayana period the display of Buddha images was not practiced, hence there were no images of Buddha. In the later Mahayana period the image of Buddha was introduced and was carved in a recess within the Stupa. (Fig. 4.8, 4.9)

Chaitya arch window

As the chaitya halls are closed on all other three sides by the hill, hence scope of ventilation is only from front side. A large arched window was placed over the main central door. The shape of this Chaitya arch was differed from one to one. The earliest shape of Chaitya arch is a horseshoe type found in the Chaitya hall at Bhaja in western ghats in Maharastra state. In the later examples the lower curves of the arch were turned inwards making the arch highly aesthetic in appearance. The Chaitya arch window had ribs carved in rock itself. The window was covered by wooden trelliswork, which is now disappeared. (Fig. 4.6, 4.7, 4.14, 4.15).

Chaitya arch form was derived from vaulted roofs of Vedic houses. The form became more popular after its use by Buddhists inside Chaitya halls and also as a decorative motif. Hence the ogee-vaulted shape attained the name of 'Chaitya Arch'. It became a popular beauty element and was used for several purposes in- Chaitya arch motif (Kudu) in cornices, pillars, and gable of Gopurams, Roofs of Pallava Rathas etc.

Exterior

Chaitya grihas were recessed deep into the hill leaving a space in the front. The projected hill top portion in the front created a canopy giving shade. In some examples a portico containing two decorated pillars was made in front of main door. The exterior portions of the rock is richly decorated containing horizontal bands, exquisitely carved cornices, Pilasters, Chaitya arch motifs, railing motifs, elephants and other figure carvings. Karli Chaitya hall contains two large Simha Sthambhas (Lion pillars) in front of the central doorway. A freestanding stone column was placed asymmetrically on one side in Karli Chaitya hall, which resembles Asoka pillar. (Fig. 4.6, 4.7)

In the process of cutting, the requisite elements and their shapes are to be well planned and the portion of stone should be kept remained without its cutting to make the preconceived elements like vaulted ceilings, pillars, stupa, apsidal portion, front wall, portico etc. These were meticulously executed keeping into consideration the main theme.

Best Example: Chaitya hall at Karli, 1st cent.C.E in Borghat hills in Maharastra state carved in Basalt stone.

Other Examples: Group of Chaitya halls at Bhaja, Kondane, Pithalkora, Bedsa, Ajanta, Nasic, Karli and Ellora in Western ghats in Maharashtra state.

2. Viharas

Viharas are the hostels for Buddhist monks, disciples and preachers. Many Viharas are rock-cut except some structural examples at Takht-i-Bahai near Taxila and at Sanchi. (Fig. 4.11)

Plan

The rock-cut Vihara mainly consists of the following compartments.

– a front verandah

– a central hall

– cells on three sides of the hall

In front of the Vihara a verandah takes place containing pillars giving access into the hall. The front wall of the hall contains a central door and two windows symmetrically placed ventilating the hall. Central hall is a common hall giving access to the cells on three sides. The cells are small rooms for reading, rest and sleep. In the cells a portion of the rock was left uncut to form a raised platform useful for sleeping and sitting. The cells contain a small recess for its use as a locker. The rooms are small averaging to 2.7 Metres Square. The doorway to the rooms is not in the centre, but kept to one side for inside convenience of space to accommodate the bed. The roof of the halls and the cells is plain and horizontal.

Pillars

The central hall contains plain octagonal pillars making a colonnade. Number of pillars and their arrangement vary from Vihara to Vihara depending on the need and space. The pillars of the verandah consist of a base, shaft and capital. The base is vase type and the pillars are octagonal in section. Vase and inverted pyramid are the features of the capital, which contains figures of elephants and horses intricately carved.

In the famous Hinayana Buddhist settlement at Ajanta, group of Vihars were found. As the Buddhist community was growing, hence more numbers of Viharas were found necessary and were proceeded in the adjacent rock.

Examples: Group of Viharas at Ajanta, Kondane, Nasik, Bhaja.

4.5. AJANTA CAVES, 200 B.C.E TO 650 C.E

Ajanta in India is a celebrated name for its Buddhist cave hermitages. Actual name of Ajanta is Ajunthi. It is a village in Budhana district of Maharashtra state. It is located 99 kilometres from Aurangabad. Location by the side of a vertical gorge in Sahyadri hills where water falls from upper hill into a pool so that the need of water is served. Ajanta has 29 rocks cut caves carved from 200 B.C.E to 650 C.E. Four are Chaitya halls and the others are Viharas. These caves are not known till 19th century until British discovered them on a hunt. (Fig. 4.5)

The artisans carefully carved the rock and made the columns, sculpture figures, stairs, benches, screens and decorative elements from out of the rock. They also painted the pictures and patterns. After 7th century these caves were abandoned due to the decline of Buddhist religion.

4.6. ELLORA CAVES, 6TH TO 12TH CENTURY C.E

Ellora is also a celebrated name for caves of Buddhist, Hindu and Jain religions made from 6th to 12th century C.E as per Archeological Survey of India (ASI). This is located about 30 kilometres from Aurangabad in Maharashtra state. Here the caves were initiated by Buddhists about 400 C.E. Later it was followed by Hindus and Jains. (Fig. 4.10)

Hindu Rock cut caves were made during Rastrakuta rulers. There are 34 important caves, which are numbered by Archeological Survey of India as detailed below.

Buddhist caves: 1 to 12 – 12 Nos.

Hindu caves: 13 to 29 – 17 Nos.

Jain caves: 30 to 34 – 5 Nos.

Exact period of making of caves of each religion is not possible as the caves of these religions were made simultaneously as the religions were progressing in parallel. The rooms of Ellora are comparatively smaller and simpler than Ajanta caves. Some important caves and their dedication is mentioned here

– Cave No. 10: Visvakarma

– Cave No. 15: Dasavatara

– Cave No. 16: Kailasa

– Cave No. 21: Rameswara

Both Ajanta and Ellora are UNESCO's world heritage sites.

4.7. OTHER IMPORTANT BUDDHIST SITES

– Bodh Gaya, Patna, Sravasthi, Vaisali in Bihar state

– Saranath, Kushinagar in Uttar Pradesh state

– Nagarjuna Konda in Andhra Pradesh state

– Kanheri caves at Borivali near Mumbai

– Bagh caves in Vindhya Mountains in Dhar district in Madhya Pradesh

Conclusion

The Art and Architecture of Buddhists spread throughout India and East Asia. But Buddhism disappeared in India after 10th century C.E.

QUESTIONS

1. What are Buddhist Stupas? Explain their structure in detail. Mention any two important names of such Stupas made in India.
2. Describe the planning, interior, pillars and other elements of a Buddhist Chaitya hall. Mention any three names such Chaitya halls.
3. What is a Buddhist Vihara and explain its plan and other features.
4. Explain Ajanta and Ellora caves and what they contain.
5. Sketch the plan of a Chaitya hall and name the parts. Mention the names of any two best examples.
6. Draw the plan of a Vihara and name its parts.
7. Sketch and describe any one Chaitya Arch window.

Fig. 4.1. Sanchi Stupa, 1st cent. B.C.E

Fig. 4.2. Sanchi stupa gate

Fig. 4.3. Sanchi stupa northern Gateway

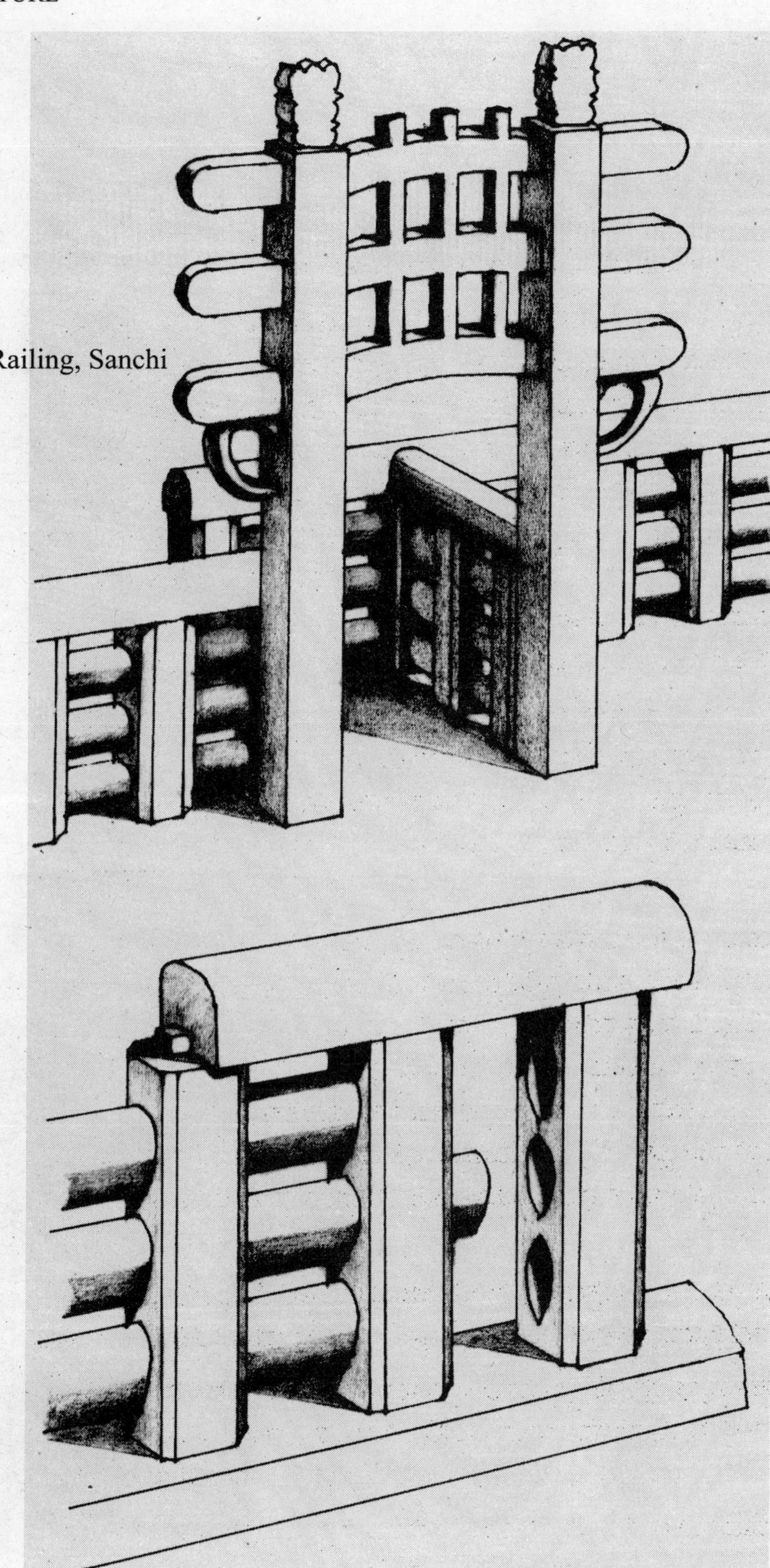

Fig. 4.4. Buddhist Torana and Railing at Sanchi

Fig. 4.5. Ajanta caves, 200 to 650 B.C.E-Total view

Fig. 4.6. Chaitya hall at Bhaja-facade

Fig. 4.7. Ajanta-Chaitya cave No. 9 Facade

Fig. 4.8. Karli Chaitya Hall-Interior

Fig. 4.9. Ajanta Chaitya hall-Interior illuminated now for tourists

Fig. 4.10. Ellora cave 33

Fig. 4.11. Vihara at Nasik

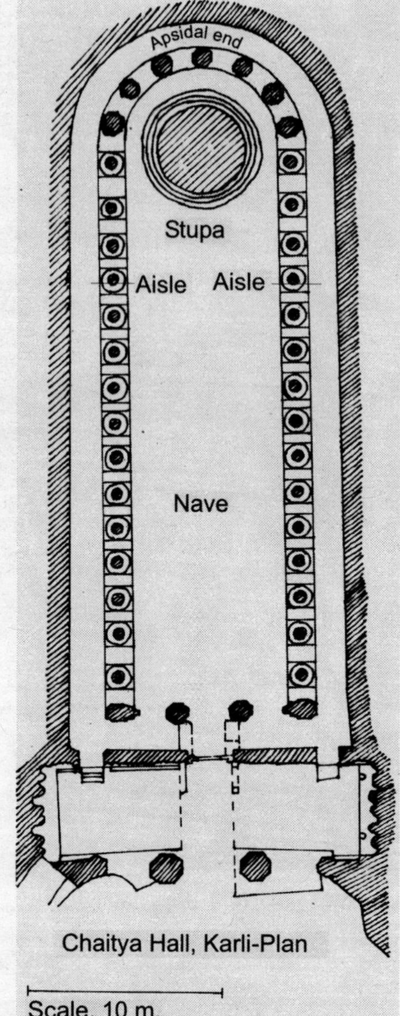

Fig. 4.12. Chaitya hall, Karli-Plan

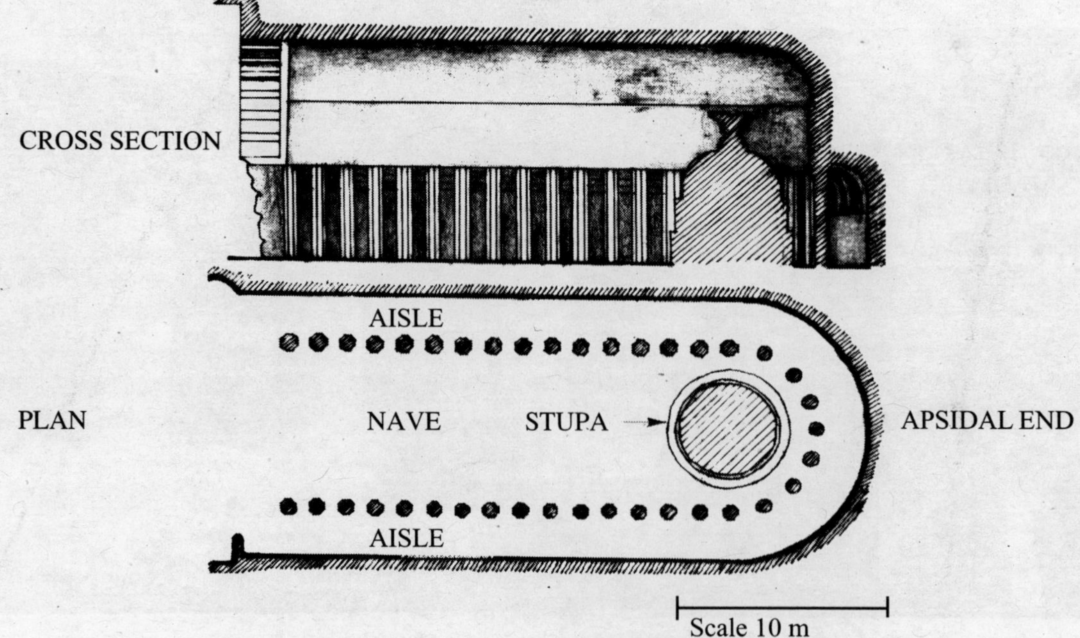

Fig. 4.13. Chaitya hall at Ajanta-Plan and Cross section

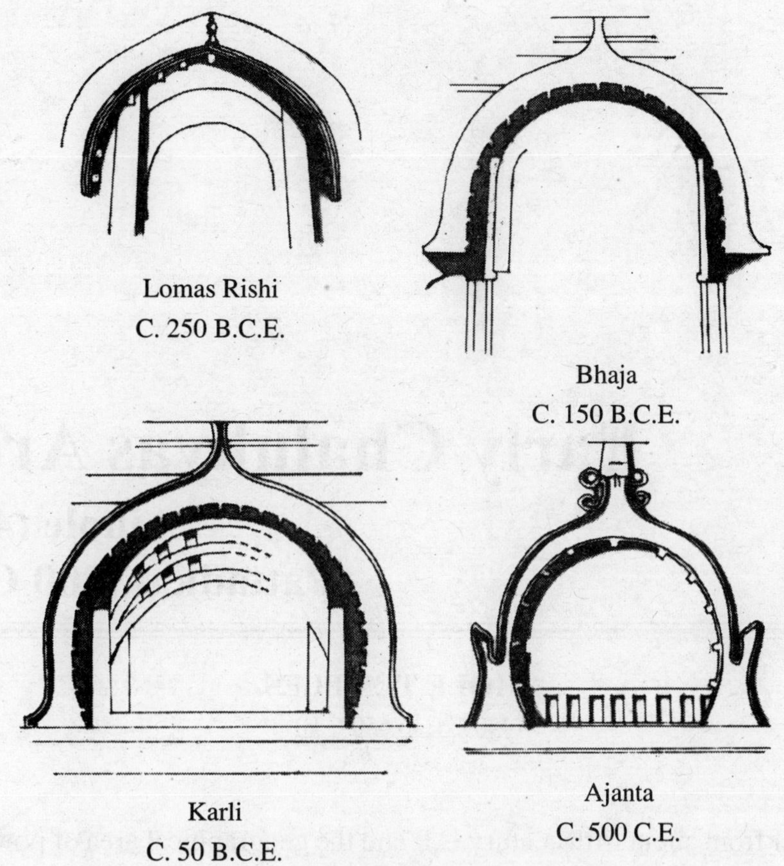

Fig. 4.14. Chaitya Arches, C. 250 B.C.E. to 9th cent. C.E.

Fig. 4.15. Chaitya arch-Visvakarma cave at Ellora

5

Early Chalukyas Architecture

Aihole (450 to 650 C.E.)
Pattadkal (600 C.E. to 750 C.E)

AIHOLE TEMPLES
(450 C.E to 650 C.E)

5.1. INTRODUCTION

Chalukyas rose to power from about fifth century C.E and the geographical area of power extended over Deccan region in central India. Aihole is now a small decayed village in the district of Bagalkot in Karnataka state.

Aihole temples were the first originated Hindu structural temples in south India. At this time in north India Gupta's supremacy was ending and some earlier forms of temples were taking shape at Tigawa, Jabalpur district in Madhya Pradesh state and in Ran in Rajasthan state, which are primitive and smaller. In south India, Pallavas were the contemporaries who initiated Rock cut Mandapas and built Shore temple at Mamallapuram after some time. Chalukyas built both rock cut and structural temples.

5.2. ROCK CUT CAVES OF BADAMI, 6TH TO 8TH CENT.

There are some series of rock-cut pillared halls in the neighbouring town of Badami carved in sixth century C.E in sandstone hills. Rock cut halls consisted of a pillared verandah, a columned hall and a sanctum. There are 4 caves here. Caves 1 to 3 belong to Hindus and the others to Jains. The stone columns and Brackets are the distinctive features. (Fig. 5.1)

5.3. TEMPLES

The groups of structural Hindu temples built here were the earliest showing their beginning with their introductory form.

The Aihole village consists of some seventy temples and about thirty of them are lying inside a walled and bastioned enclosure while the remaining were scattered in the vicinity. It means that the art of temple building must have been carried with utmost fervour and energy. Later in the middle of 7th century this activity was moved to the neighbouring town of Pattadkal which became the new capital.

The temple contained mainly a sanctuary and a pillared hall (Mandapa). Aihole temples have flat or slightly sloping roofs. But in the later examples an upper story or a tower (Sikhara) has emerged over the sanctuary. A definite decision was not yet reached in the design of the temple building. The builders and the priests were seeking for a formula for fulfilling their requirements.

EXAMPLES: Out of many temples, the following two important examples are selected, as the design of these temples is clear and specific.

1. Ladh Khan temple, Aihole, 450C.E
2. Durga temple, Aihole, 550C.E

1. Ladh Khan temple, Aihole 450 C.E

Introduction: This is a primitive and oldest temple of the group built at Aihole in Dharwar district in Karnataka state built around 450C.E. The present appearance of the temple is not impressive. It is a low flat roofed building and its plan being 15 metres square inside.

It is believed that this edifice was originally built for secular and civic use meant for Santhagara, the village mote or meeting hall. The building originally contains an open Square hall and a front portico. At a later stage the spaces between the outside pillars were filled with masonry walls and perforated windows. Hence the pillars now look like pilasters. The rear side is completely enclosed by walls and the walls on either side are relieved by perforated stone grilles. On the fourth and front side there is a projected open-pillared porch making its eastern entrance. (Fig. 5.2 to 5.6)

Interior

The Interior is a hall of pillars containing two square groups of columns one within the other, thus making a double aisle all round. There are sixteen columns in these two squares. A large size stone effigy of a bull (Nandi) almost fills the central square bay, while at the end is the cella within the hall, in which Siva lingam was placed at a later stage.

Pillars

The pillars are simple in their design. They have plain square shaft and bracket capital. The shafts taper slightly at the upper ends above which is a cushion capital with an expanded floral abacus supporting the bracket. This design afterwards became universal in Dravidian architecture. Sloping backrest or Asana was provided in the portico. (Fig. 5.6)

Roof

The roof of this structure resembles thatch hut. The temple has two tiered roof imitating wood construction in stone logs. A flat roof with flat stone slabs covers the central nave. The surrounding aisles had a tapering stone roof laid lower than the nave roof leaving in between a clearstory for ventilation. (Fig. 5.4, 5.5)

2. Durga temple, Aihole, 550 C.E

The plan of this temple is like Buddhist Chaitya hall probably built in 6th century. This is an apsidal-ended structure measuring externally 18 metres by 11 metres. There is an addition of portico on its eastern front 7.2 metres in depth making the total length to 25.2 metres. (Fig. 5.7 to 5.9)

It is believed that this temple was once used as a military outpost (Durg- meaning fort). It is not known to which god the temple was originally built.

Interior

The temple consists of a hall of 13.4 metres long and divided into two rows of four pillars into a nave and two aisles with an apsidal shaped cella at the far end. The aisles are continued round the cella as processional passage (Pradakshina patha). Inside is a pillared vestibule within which a door was located. Light is admitted to the hall and passages through stone grilles elegantly carved with perforated patterns.

Exterior

The structure was raised on a high and heavily moulded plinth. The height of the structure up to the flat roof of the aisles is 9 metres from the ground. A passage was carried round the building joining with similar pillars comprising the portico. The portico is approached by two flights of steps, one on each side of the front. Pillars of the temple show fine figure carving. The roof of the nave is higher than the side aisles. A straight-sided pyramidal Sikhara was added over the cella at a later stage, which is significant and earliest mark of a Sikhara. (Fig. 5.7, 5.9)

Other temple Examples: Huchchimalligudi, Aihole, 7th cent.C.E

Jain temples, Aihole

PATTADKAL TEMPLES

(600 C.E TO 750 C.E)

5.4. INTRODUCTION

Pattadkal is located on the banks of Malaprabha river in Bagalkot district in Karnataka state. The next stage of development of Chalukyan architecture is found in the buildings of Pattadkal, the new capital of Chalukyas 25 kilometres from Badami. The Chalukya dynasty reached its height of power under the kings Vijayaditya (696 – 733 C.E) and Vikramaditya (733 – 736 C.E).

Here in this part of the country a separate form of temple architecture developed, which contains both Dravidian and Indo Aryan temple characters.

The building art was undergoing a course of reformation and evolution especially in the design of Sikharas, where two types of Sikharas- a stepped lined one and a curved one were markedly developed denoting the Dravidian (South Indian) type and Indo-Aryan (North Indian) type Sikharas. Dravidian Sikhara evolved in horizontal layers like multiple storeys. And Indo-Aryan Sikhara developed into a sky raising structure. This change is seen only in the Sikharas. The plans and arrangement of compartments is truly Dravidian type. Pattadkal is now UNESCO's world heritage site. (Fig. 5.11 to 5.15)

5.5. EXAMPLES

There are about ten temples built at Pattadkal but for study purpose the following important and large temples are selected.

1. Papanath temple (Indo Aryan type), Pattadkal, 680 C.E
2. Virupaksha temple (Dravidian type), Pattadkal, 740 C.E

1. Papanath temple, Pattadkal, c.680 C.E

Papanath temple dedicated to Lord Mukteswara is a long and low height temple of some 27.4 metres long. This is a north Indian type (Indo Aryan) of temple.

Plan: It consists of the following in its axis from east to west.

– Entrance porch - Mukha mandapa
– Assembly hall - Sabha mandapa
– Supplementary hall - Ardha mandapa
– Cella - Garbhagriha

The Mukha mandapa is a simple portico having two pillars in front of Sabha mandapa. The Sabha mandapa is a large hall with window openings on three sides. There are sixteen pillars arranged in four squares each square containing four pillars slightly set aside to corners thus making the central bay wider and spacious. The hall gives access into Ardha mandapa which is a square room containing four pillars. This is an anti chamber. There is no separate vestibule. It seems that during construction there were some modifications in the structure of Ardha mandapa. Hence the external walls of Garbhagriha (Vimana) are concealed and obscured into Ardha mandapa. The last one is the cella having a narrow processional passage surrounding it.

There is no Nandi (Bull) mandapa. But image of an ornate Nandi is placed in east wall of Sabha mandapa. (Fig. 5.13).

Exterior

The lower part of the structure is a substantial basement formed by bold stringcourses decorated with animal motifs, floral designs and Kudu. Above this, the central broad space of the wall is decorated with niches, each niche carrying two pillars, a cornice and a traceried canopy of Indo-Aryan type repeated through out. These niches housed Siva and Vishnu deities depicting episodes from Ramayana. There is much solidity in the overall treatment of the walls.

The Sikhara is separated from its substructure. It is the simplest form of Indo-Aryan spire (Rekha nagara) appearing over the flat roof. It has the convex type curve turning inward and has horizontal grooves and contains elaborately carved Chaitya arch enshrining Nataraja on its front. Amalaka and Kalasa are missing. (Fig. 5.11)

2. Virupaksha temple, Pattadkal, C.740 C.E

Virupaksha temple was built at Pattadkal by queen Lokamahadevi to commemorate her husband's (Vikramaditya 2) victory over Pallavas of Kanchi. The temple has a walled enclosure entered by an appropriate gateway from eastern side. It measures about 36.5 metres long.

Plan

It consists of the following usual compartments

– Detached Nandi Pavilion in front

– Mandapa having three elegant porches

– Garbhagriha on the rear side having a processional passage

Mandapa has 16 square pillars symmetrically laid inside and there are two more pillars in line in front of vestibule. (Fig. 5.14)

Exterior

It is much pleasing owing to its balanced composition. There is of course still solidity in its appearance and it was partly relieved by the sculptured ornamentation. The temple contains the mouldings, pilasters, cornices, brackets, the floral scrollwork, perforated windows and ornamental carvings.

Embellishment was mainly concentrated in the main wall between the basement and the cornice. The wall was divided by means of pilasters into well-proportioned spaces alternating with perforated windows. The intervening panels were enriched by the introduction of niches. The niches contain full size statuary. Lavish ornamentation and figure sculptures are skillfully coordinated in the entire building. The canopy parapets and the sikhara were ornamented with Chaitya-arch motif. Elegant Dravidian sikhara in three tiers is separated from its substructure and having a prominent projecting gable front. (Fig. 5.12)

Pillars

The upper end of the shaft of the pilaster was narrowed where it joins with the capital.

Earlier form of Gopuram

A notable structure that is rising above the parapet at the back of its porches is an embryo Gopuram. Inspired

from this small monumental gate head further new designs were evolved, developed, modified and had attained remarkable shapes and sizes into large Gopurams which have dominated all the approaches of the Dravidian temple complexes built later.

5.6. NAMES OF OTHER IMPORTANT EXAMPLES AT PATTADKAL

Dravidian type:	Sangameswara temple, 720 C.E
	Mallikarjuna temple, 733-45 C.E
Indo Aryan type:	Jambulingeswara temple,7th cent.C.E
(Rekha Nagara)	Kadasiddheswara temple, 7th cent.C.E
	Kasi Visweswara temple, 8th cent.C.E
	Jain temples:
	Galagnath temple, 750 C.E

QUESTIONS

1. **Sketch and describe Ladhkhan temple of Aihole.**
2. **Sketch and describe Durga temple of Aihole.**
3. **Mention the names of any two important temples of Early Chalukyas period of Aihole and describe the architectural features of any one temple.**
4. **Explain briefly Geographical and Political position of Pattadkal and describe architectural features of one important temple.**
5. **Sketch and explain architectural features of Pattadkal temple which is a prototype of Indo Aryan.**
6. **Describe Virupaksha temple of Pattadkal and sketch its plan and elevation.**
7. **Mention two names each of Dravidian type and Indo Aryan type of Pattadkal temples and explain architectural features of any one temple. Sketch the plan and elevation.**
8. **Sketch the plan of Ladkhan temple, Aihole and name the parts.**
9. **Sketch the plan of Durga temple, Aihole and name its parts.**
10. **Sketch the elevation of Sikhara of Papanath temple, Pattadkal.**

Fig. 5.1. Badami-3rd Cave

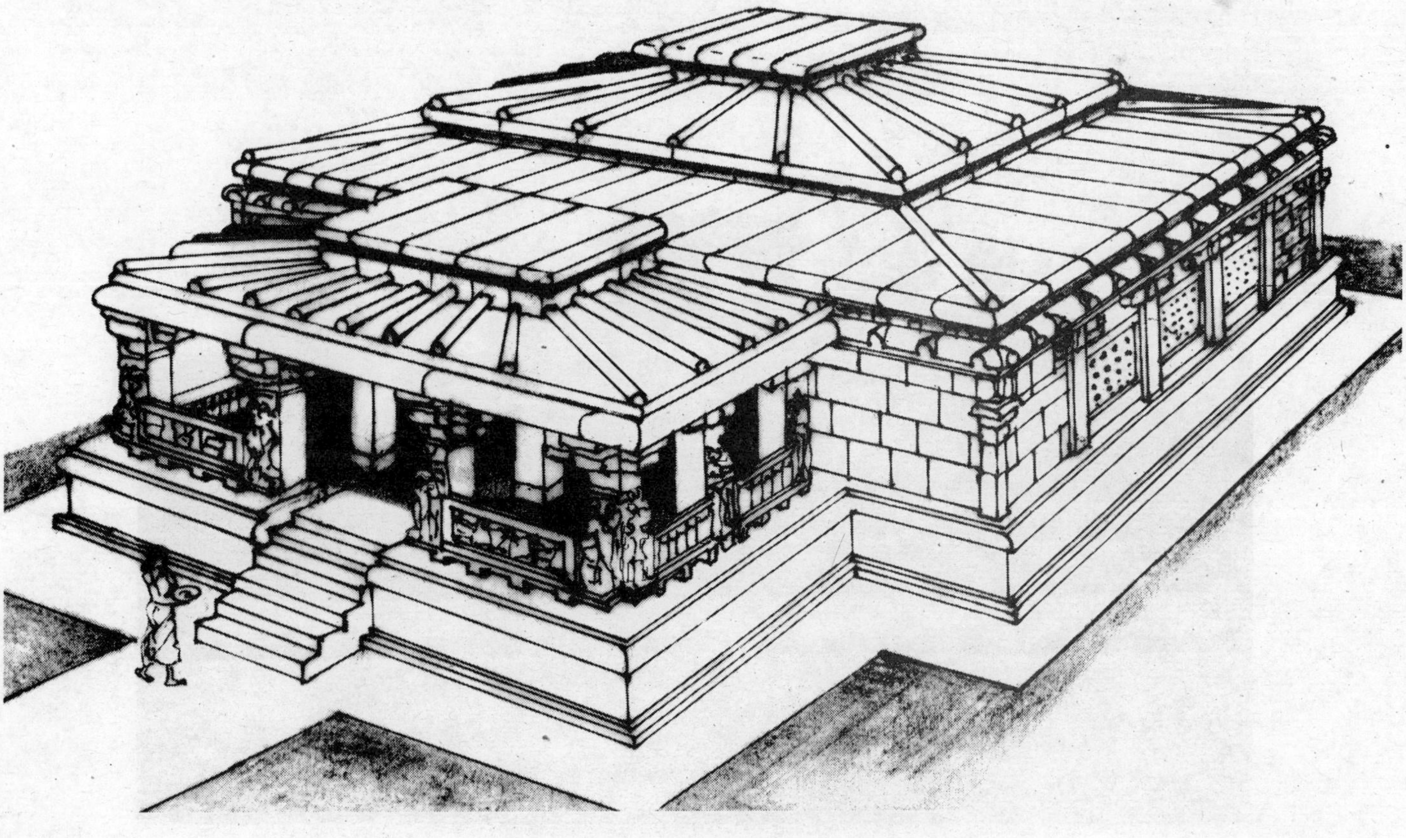

Fig. 5.2. Ladh Khan temple, Aihole

Fig. 5.3. Ladh khan temple,450 C.E-Front

Fig. 5.4. Ladh khan temple-Side view

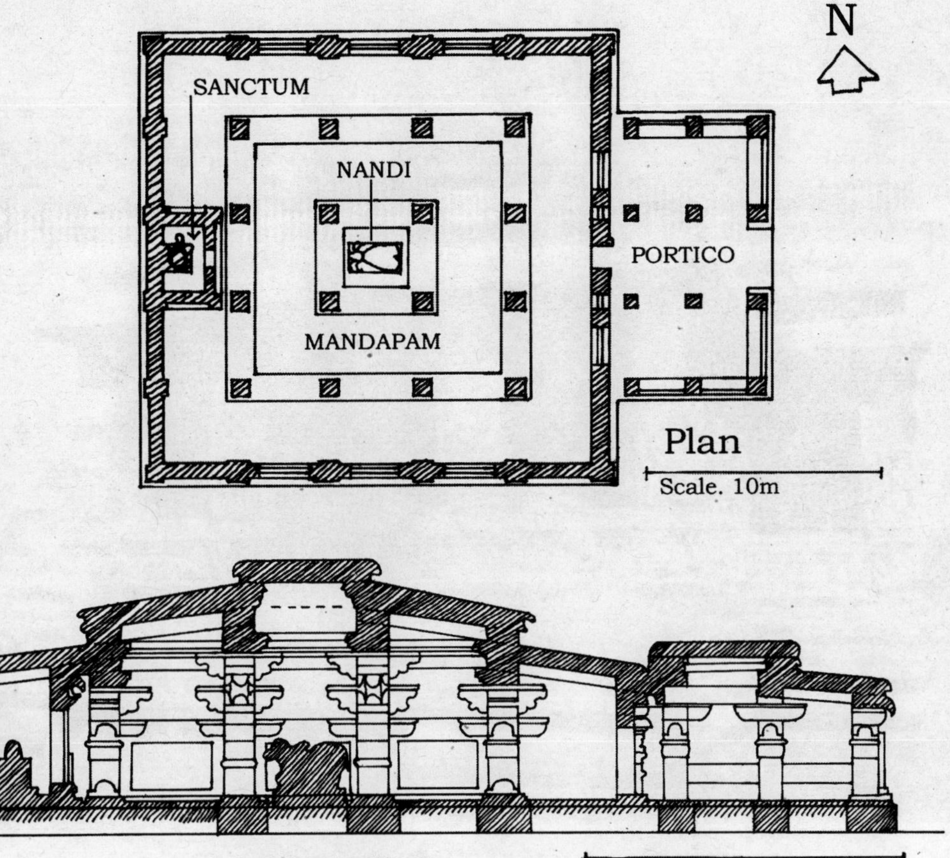

Fig. 5.5. Ladh Khan temple, Aihole-Plan and cross section

Fig. 5.6. Ladh Khan temple, Aihole, Pillar capital

Fig. 5.7. Durga temple, Aihole Front porch

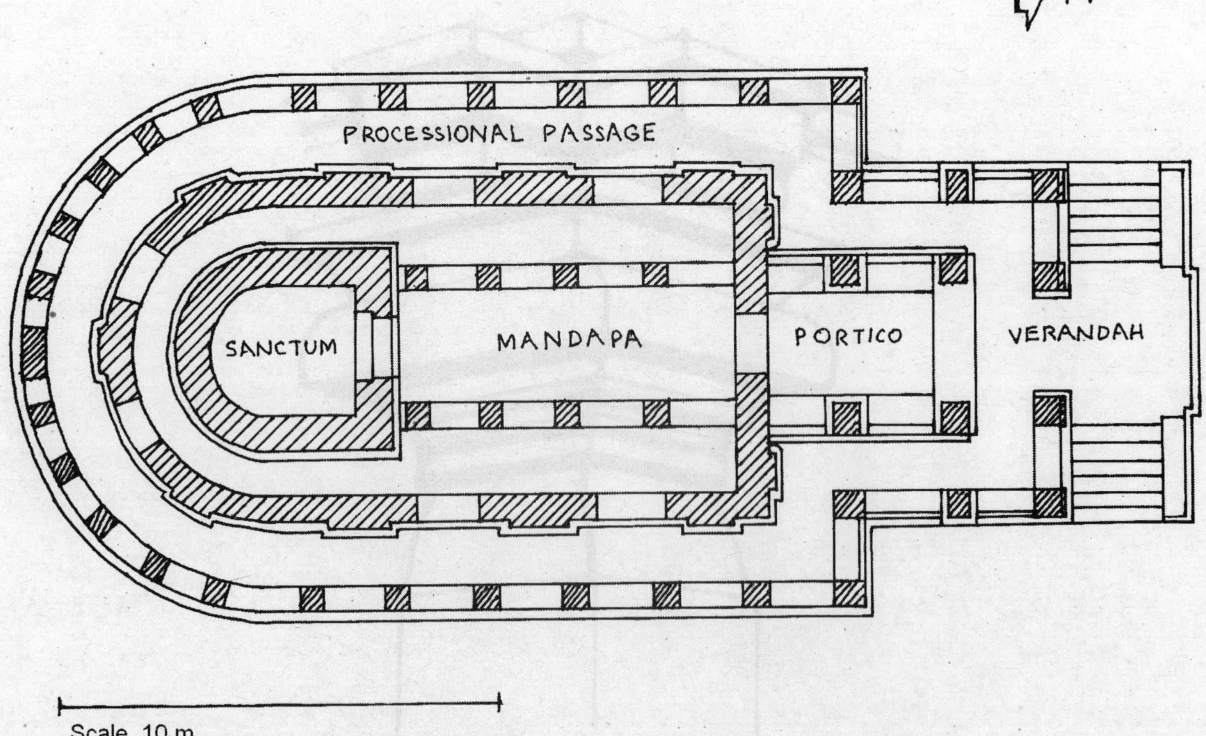

Fig. 5.8. Durga temple-plan

Fig. 5.9. Durga temple Aihole, 550 C.E

Fig. 5.10. Durga temple Aihole-Column

Fig. 5.11. Papanath temple, Pattadakal, 680 C.E

Fig. 5.12. Virupaksha temple, Pattadakal, 740 C.E

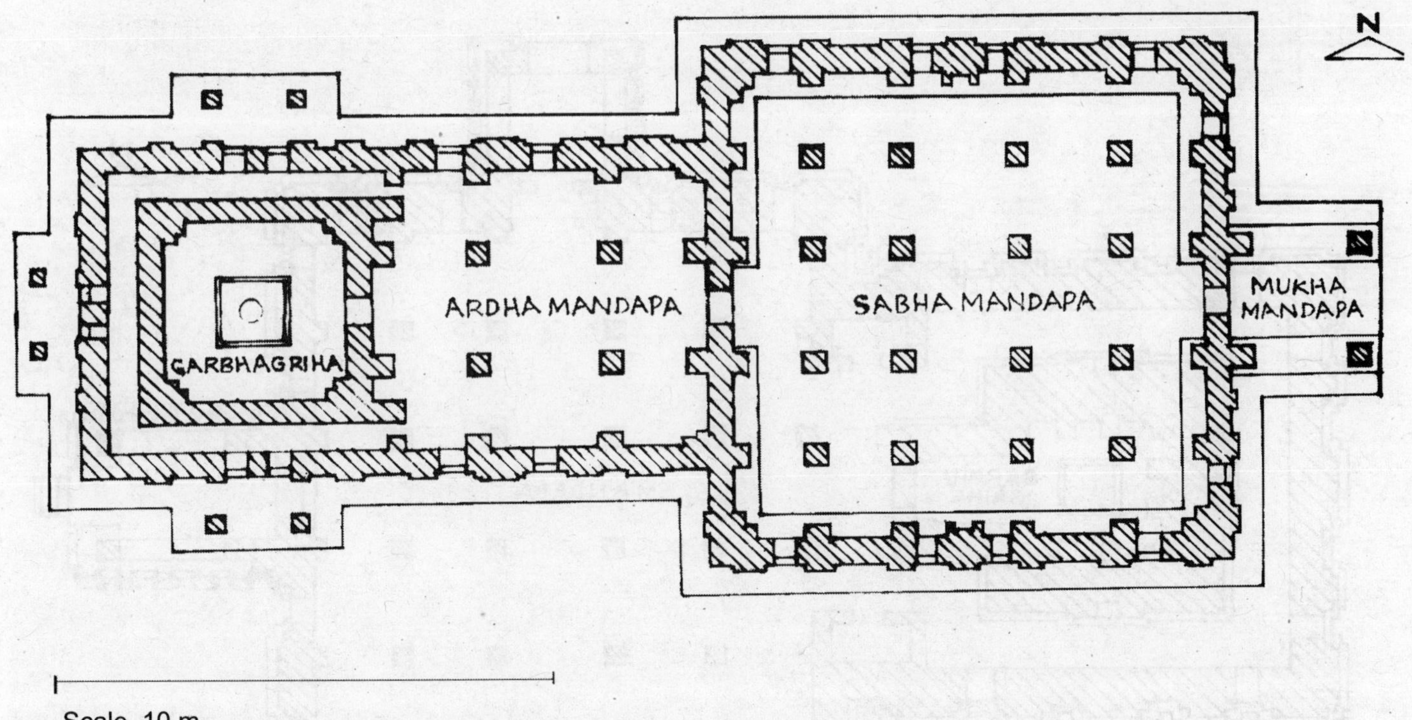

Fig. 5.13. Papanath temple, Pattadkal C. 680 C.E,- Plan and Side elevation

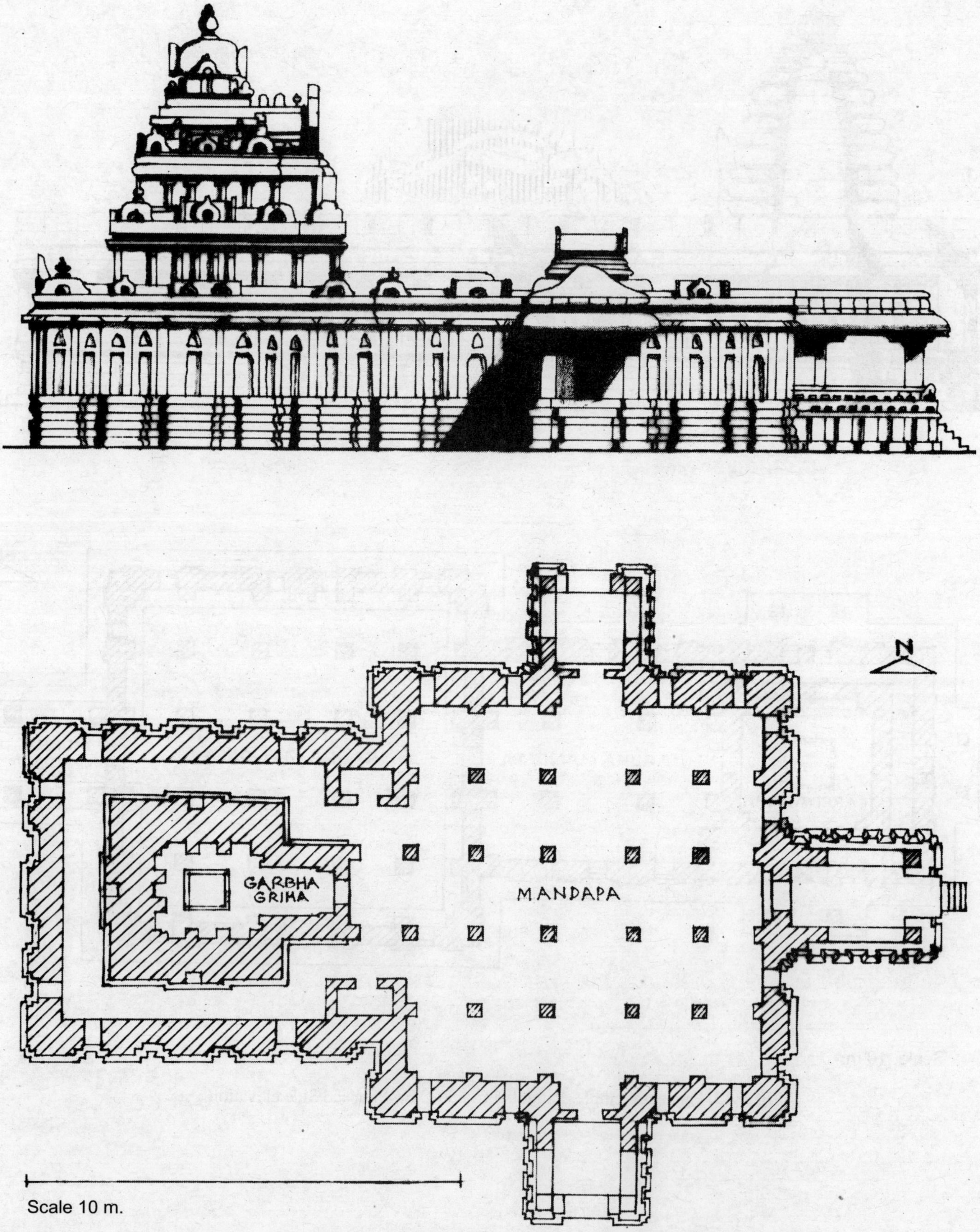

N

GARBHA GRIHA

MANDAPA

Scale 10 m.

Fig. 5.14. Virupaksha Temple, Pattadkal, C. 740 C.E.-Plan and side elevation

Aihole temple Sikhara
6th cent. C.E.

Pattadkal temple Sikhara
7th cent. C.E.

Fig. 5.15. Aihole and Pattadkal Sikharas

6

Hindu Rock-Cut Architectrue

Kailasa (Siva's Paradise) at Ellora (8th cent. C.E)

6.1. INTRODUCTION

Living in Rock cut hermitages away from busy habitations is common in India, especially to the people who want to live a total spiritual life. Hilly areas were preferred for this, where cave shelters were made, which are permanent in nature. This need developed Rock cut art. Such caves were made by religion groups like Hindus, Buddhists and Jains. These cave settlements are not totally separated as per their religion. They were coexisting in some sites. They are compatible and religious harmony prevailed. Hence exact division of these is not possible.

Some important Hindu rock cut settlements are briefly described here.

6.2. IMPORTANT HINDU ROCK CUT CAVES

Udaigiri caves at Vidisha, 320-600 C.E: Udaigiri situated 6 km. from Vidisha, which is 15 km. distant from Sanchi in Madhya Pradesh state. The caves were made during Gupta's reign from 4th to 6th century C.E and belong to Hindus and Jains. The rock formation in this hill is sandstone. Out of total of 20 caves 2 belong to Jain group and the rest are Hindu caves. Some of the walls in these caves show fine intricate figure carvings. The caves were numbered by Archeological Survey of India. Some of the important carvings are 4 metres tall image of Varaha Vishnu (Boar) in cave No. 5 along with images of river goddesses Yamuna and Ganga and the other is Reclining Vishnu.

Elephanta caves, 6th to 7th cent. C.E: Elephanta is more popular for its situation as an island in Arabian sea near Mumbai city. It consists of Buddhist and Hindu caves hewn in Basalt rock. Basalt rock is more ideal for rock hewing. The popular cave here is Mahesamurthi cave. This is UNESCO's world heritage site.

Badami caves, 600 to 800 C.E: Described in Chapter5-Early Chalukyas Architecture

Undavalli caves, 4th to 5th cent. C.E: Undavalli situated near Tadepalli in Guntur District near Vijayawada in Andhra Pradesh. There are several caves made in granite hills and a large cave has 4 storeys containing a huge statue of Lord Vishnu in reclining posture in second floor.

Mamallapuram Mandapas, 600 to 900 C.E: Described in Chapter 7-Dravidian Architecture under Pallavas

Ellora caves, 6th to 10th cent. C.E: Described in Chapter 4-Buddhist Architecture

The best and outstanding example of Hindu rock cut Architecture at Ellora is Kailasa (Siva's Paradise). Hence it is described in detail below.

6.3. KAILASA AT ELLORA, 8TH CENT C.E

Introduction: Kailasa or Kailasanatha is a unique and unrivaled rock cut temple at Ellora located about 30

kilometres from Aurangabad in Maharashtra state. There are 17 Hindu temple caves situated in these hills out of 34 caves and other caves belong to Buddhists and Jains. Kailasa is number 16 at Ellora which is unique example of Indian rock-cut architecture. The temple is dedicated to Lord Siva. Ellora caves including this Kailasa are now UNESCO's world heritage site. (Fig. 6.1 to 6.7)

This was produced in 8th century C.E during the reign of Monarch Krishna I of Rastrakuta dynasty that ruled from Manyakheta in Gulbarga district in Karnataka state.

This is not a constructed temple. A part of the rocky hill was choosen at top of the hill and was made into a temple by cutting and removing carefully the unrequired or extra stone material. It was carefully carved and sculpted in total on a hill side. The part of the solid stone monolith after its cutting remained in the shape of a temple. Hence the temple has got the total external appearance like a structural temple.

Similar monolith examples are Rathas at Mamallapuram which were already made during Pallavas reign in 7th century C.E, but in small size made from rock boulders.

This is a free standing multistoreyed temple complex and is world's largest monolithic structure carved out from one single rock. This is more closely allied to sculpture on a grand scale than to architecture. This covered an area of double the size of Parthenon of Athens, 450 B.C.E. Excavating work was done from top to bottom. In making this temple it necessitated removal of two lakh tons of rock and it took around one hundred years to complete. This was made by hewing rock of 85000 cubic metres starting at top and working down and then hollowing out to form the temple walls, roofs, pillars, figures, decorative mouldings etc.

The main temple lies on the upper storey. The lower storey is a solid basement. Surrounding the main temple building are the ambulatory spaces cut deep into the rock. The temple was carved in Dravidian style and was modeled in the lines of Virupaksha temple of Pattadkal.

Plan: Due to its position on hillside the orientation and the axial alignment of the temple is made from west to east contrary to the convention. The place and location infuenced the orientation of the temple. The main temple was placed in the center and there is open space around the temple surrounded by multistoreyed cloisters. The plan of temple resolves into following four parts. (Fig. 6.1)

(*i*) Entrance gateway

(*ii*) Nandi shrine

(*iii*) Main temple

(*iv*) Cloisters

(*i*) *Entrance gateway*: The entrance is a fine double-storeyed gatehouse. This is approached by steep flight of steps from west side. On the opposite side it is joined to the Nandi shrine.

(*ii*) *Nandi shrine*: Nandi shrine is a two storeyed pavilion 7.6 metres square standing on a solid high plinth joined to the front entrance. The lower storey is a solid structure decorated with illustrative carvings. On the opposite side it is connected by a bridge to the main temple. There are two freestanding pillars or Dhwajasthambas, one on each side of this Nandi shrine. (Fig. 6.3)

(*iii*) *Main temple*: The main body of the temple is a two storeyed structure approximately measuring 46 metres by 30 metres with projecting sides here and there. Around the base of the Vimana there are five subsidiary shrines each an elegant reproduction of the main temple shrine to a reduced scale. The main temple consists of a pillared hall from which a vestibule leads to the cella. The pillared hall measures 21 metres by 19 metres having sixteen square pillars in groups of four in each quarter an arrangement that produced great dignity. The pillared hall leads to the cella.

(*iv*) *Cloisters* (Galleries): Encircling the courtyard are the cloisters and chambers containing colonnade of pillars. This is in three storeys. It has numerous alcoves containing figures of deities. Originally stone bridges were connecting the main temple and the galleries, but were now collapsed.

Exterior

The main body of the temple was raised on a lofty and substantial plinth. It is 7.6 metres high and is giving double storeyed appearance. Above and below of the imposing plinth is heavily moulded while the central space of the side is occupied by a grand frieze of boldly carved elephants and lions. Standing high on this plinth is the temple approached by flight of steps on western side leading to the pillared porch. Various features such as cornices, pilasters, niches and porticos are definite and sharply outlined. They have been assembled in an orderly and artistic manner to form a unified whole. Above all rises the stately tower (Sikhara) in three tiers with its prominently projecting gable-front and surmounted by a shapely cupola reaching to a height of 29 metres. The Sikhara is a work of Dravidian style.

The Nandi shrine is also standing on a high, solid and richly decorated base, the entire height being 15.2 metres. The two Dhwajasthambas on either sides of the Nandi shrine are the finished works of art gracefully proportioned, strong and stable. Each bore the Trishul or ensign of Lord Siva. (Fig. 6.2, 6.5)

The features of Dravidian order are seen on the pillars and pilasters of the entire scheme, although the vase and foliage motif of Guptas are also present in some instances. Both Siva and Vishnu deities were carved on the walls. The temple of Kailasa at Ellora as an example of rock-cut architecture is excellent and unrivalled.

6.4. NAMES OF OTHER IMPORTANT HINDU CAVES AT ELLORA

– Dasavathara (cave 15), Ellora

– Rameswara (cave 21), Ellora

QUESTIONS

1. Explain briefly the important Hindu Rock cut caves and mention any three examples.
2. Explain the location, its influence and the cutting of the temple of Kailasa of Ellora.
3. What is Kailasa at Ellora? Describe its architectural features. Sketch the important features.
4. Sketch the plan of kailasa of Ellora.

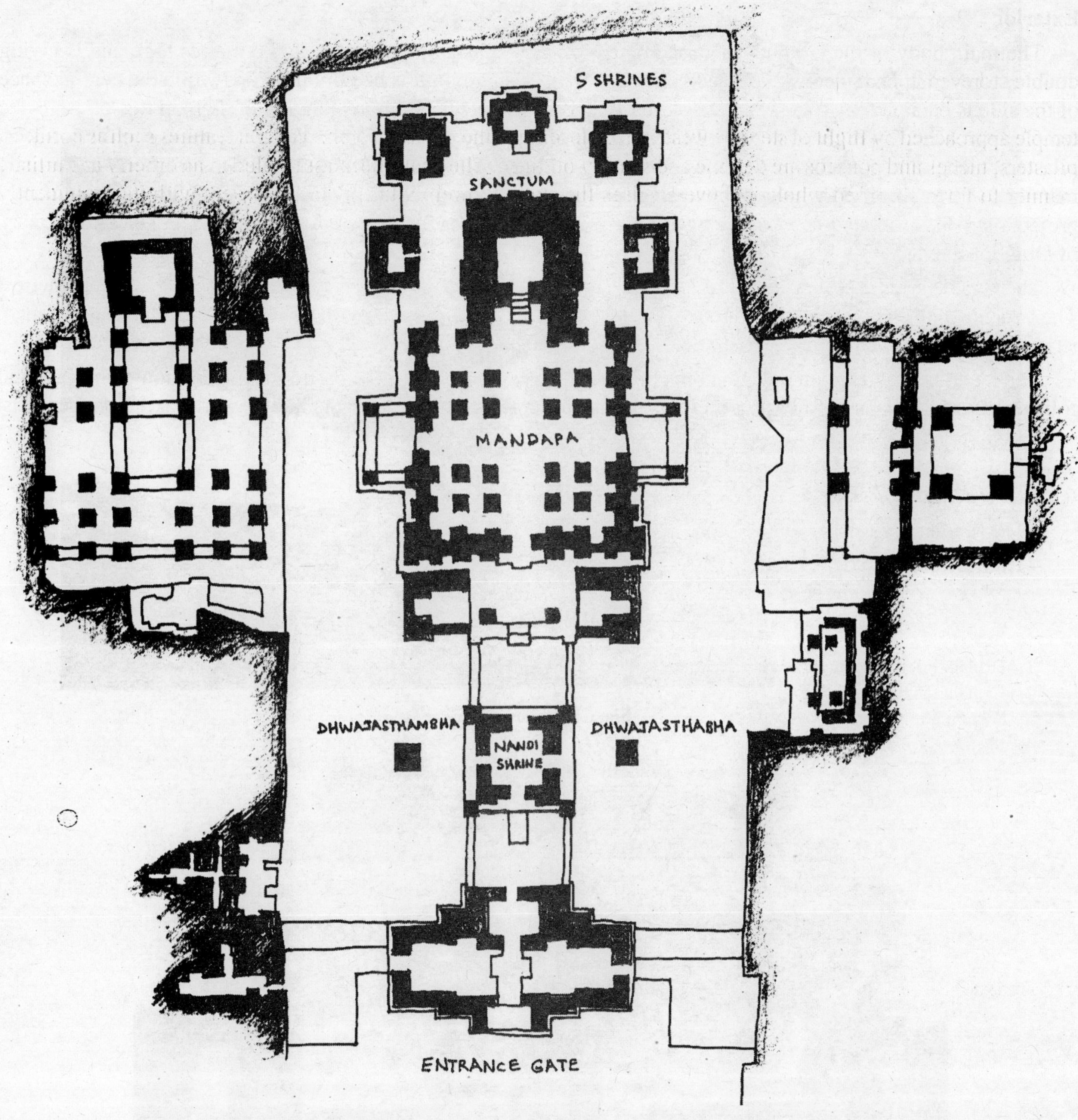

Fig. 6.1. Kailasa at Ellora 8th cent C.E.-Plan Diagram

Fig. 6.2. Kailasa-view

Fig. 6.3. Kailasa at Ellora-Nandi mandapa

Fig. 6.4. Kailasa-Close view

Fig. 6.5. Kailasa-Dwaja sthambha

Fig. 6.6. Kailsa-Close view

Fig. 6.7. Kailasa at Ellora-Shikara

7

Dravidian Architecture

Under Pallavas (600 to 900 C.E)

7.0. DYNASTICAL DIVISION

The building art in southern India had assumed a separate form. The temple development took place mostly in Tamil country known as Dravidadesha, hence has been named as Dravidian style. This southern style of architecture can be conveniently divided into following five phases corresponding to dynasties and kingdoms, which ruled south India during this time.

1. Pallavas (600 – 900 C.E)
2. Cholas (900 – 1150 C.E)
3. Pandyas (1100 – 1350 C.E)
4. Rayalas, Hampi Vijayanagar (1350 – 1565 C.E)
5. Nayaks, Madurai (from 1600 C.E)

The architectural development under these dynasties is herewith described in following chapters.

UNDER PALLAVAS

(600 TO 900 C.E)

7.1. INTRODUCTION

Pallavas are Tamil speaking people whose reign was extended over north Tamilnadu, south Andhra and north Karnataka. They came into prominence in 7th century and continued their paramount until the beginning of 10th century. The capital city was Kanchipuram which developed into a trade center in silks, spices and gems. Mamallapuram near present day Chennai city was a seaport town developed by the king Narasimha Varman I. Mamallapuram is also called Mahabalipuram. This became an export trade center to distant lands of Java, Sumatra, Combodia, Myanmar, Thailand, Vietnam and Malaysia. They had trade and cultural connections with China, Corea and Japan also. The king Mahendra Varman initiated the concept of Rock cut mandapas at Mamallapuram.

Chalukyas at Pattadkal in Karnataka state were the contemporaries and the temples at Pattadkal were in course of construction during this time. Rastrakutas in Maharastra state were the contemporaries to Pallavas. Ellora caves were in course of making especially the great Kailasa temple.

Pallava dynasty maintained its varying forms of architecture for three centuries and its productions may be resolved into two classes.

– Rock-cut examples: (*i*) Rock-cut Mandapas

(*ii*) Rathas

– Structural examples

The rock-cut examples take two forms into Mandapas and Rathas. Mandapas are rock excavated caves and the Rathas are monoliths. Now these are UNESCO's world heritage site.

7.2. ROCK-CUT EXAMPLES

1. Rock-cut Mandapas, 650 C.E

Interior

This is an open pavilion excavated in rock takes the form of a columned hall consisting of one or more cells excavated in opposite side. These halls at Mamallapuram near the city of present day Chennai are ten in number and are found on the main hill. None of these Mandapas are large. Approximate dimensions are as follows. Width of facade is 7.5 metres and cella rectangular varying from 1.5 metres to 3 metres.

Exterior

Exterior presents a facade formed of row of pillars. On the facade there is a roll cornice decorated with Buddhist chaitya-arch motif known as Kudu (Acroteria). The shape of chaitya-arch window is much reduced and converted into an object of decoration. Above is a parapet made of miniature shrines a longer one alternating with a shorter one. Images were carved in pilaster framed niches. In front of mandapa on one side a long narrow receptacle was made in the floor to keep water. (Fig. 7.6)

Pillars

Pillars are the main decorative features. The shafts have chamfered octagonal section in the middle third. The capital is an immense and heavy bracket which is an imitation of wooden beam and bracket order. Pillars are 2.1 metres high and 0.30 metres to 0.60 metres in diameter. (Fig. 7.9)

Lion Pillars

In the later examples the bottom part of the pillar is made into a sedent lion. The lion figure was reformed later into a heraldic beast and it occupied a most prominent place in Dravidian temples (Fig. 7.10). The elements in the pillar are well united to produce a notable pillar order. The features of the pillars are

- Fluted shaft (Sthambham)
- Refined necking (Tadi)
- Elegant 'melon' capital (Kumbha)
- Lotus form (Idaie) and wide abacus (Palagai)

Best Examples of Mandapas:

(*i*) Varaha Mandapa

(*ii*) Mahishasura Mandapa

2. Rathas, 650 C.E

A ratha is a chariot for taking processions of the image of the deity. But here these are a series of monolithic stone shrines, which are exact copies of certain structural prototypes in granite. The existing rock boulders were cut and made into the form of Rathas. None of their interiors is finished. (Fig. 7.1)

These rathas are not of great size, the largest is about 13 metres, the widest is 10.7 metres and the tallest is 12 metres. They are eight in all and five are Pandava Rathas. They are derived from two types of structures of Buddhishts, i.e. the Vihara and the Chaitya hall.

1. **Vihara type Rathas:** These are square in plan and contain a solid cubical portion in the center with a surrounding narrow passage consisting of front pillars. Over the solid portion the pyramidal sikhara rises.

Sikhara contains finely proportioned and well-contoured tiers, each one possessing a horizontal cornice and over this a row of solid edifices. At the top is the octagonal dome shaped finial elegantly carved. The chaitya arch motif is repeated on the cornice. The whole is perfectly proportioned and carved. The strongly moulded stylabate, the lion pillars casting their deep shadows, the pleasing forms and motifs are the architectural features of these rock-cut models.

They are five in number and varying in size. The largest of the Vihara type of Ratha is Dharmaraja ratha.

Best Examples: Dharmaraja ratha (Fig. 7.2, 7.8)
Arjuna ratha

2. **Chaitya Type Rathas:** The rathas, which followed the design of chaitya hall are oblong in plan and rise into two or more storeys. Each has a keel or barrel roof with a chaitya arch gable end. Sahadeva ratha is apsidal type. Based on these examples, those great towering pylons (Gopurams) forming the entrance gateways to the Dravidian temples have emerged later.

   Best Examples: Bhima ratha (Fig. 7.3)
   Sahadeva ratha (Fig. 7.5)
   Ganesh ratha

3. **Draupadi Ratha:** The smallest, simplest and most finished of the series is the Draupadi ratha, which is an exception in its design. This is merely a cell or Parnasala (thatched hut). Its base is carved with the figures of animals of lion alternating with an elephant. (Fig. 7.4)

7.3. STRUCTURAL EXAMPLES

Shore temple, Mamallapuram, 700 C.E

The first Pallava building to be constructed of dressed granite stone was the Shore temple at Mamallapuram so named as it stands on the foreshore of the sea of Bay of Bengal. This was built by the king Narasimha Varman II. (Fig. 7.7)

Plan

The temple is plainly visible to those approaching the harbour in ships like a lighthouse. Pallavas, the sea-faring people conducted worship of water in this temple. There are shallow cisterns on the ground, which could be flooded on occasion. Canals, conduits and receptacles were arranged to feed water to the cisterns.

The temple is a rare example having two main shrines placed asymmetrically not in axis one behind the other, one on east and the other on west. This part is surrounded by a heavy outer wall with little space between for circulation. These two shrines were built at the extreme end on east side of the complex. As there was no space in front of the cella on east side, hence all the additional structures were added on the rear side of the shrine on west. A massive enclosure wall surrounds the buildings and western side was left entirely open. Entrance through richly ornamented doorway leads to a corridor, which contains figure-subjects of striking mythological contents. Inside the enclosure foundations of an outer mandapa were found.

Exterior

In design and principle, the monolithic Dharmaraja ratha and the Shore temple are the same. There is the square lower storey and a pyramidal tower in diminishing tiers above. Sikhara of Dharmaraja ratha is short in height and the same for Shore temple is more elongated, graceful and fine.

Pillars

The most remarkable are the rampant lion pilasters, which were multiplied wherever an upright support is required. As the style progressed this Leogriff motif became more frequent and more characteristic symbol in Pallava structures. (Fig. 7.10)

Surrounding wall

The enclosure wall was an imposing structure, its parapet and coping crowned by the figures of kneeling bulls. Boldly carved lion pilasters are projected at close intervals all around the exterior of the wall.

7.4. NAMES OF OTHER IMPORTANT TEMPLES

Kailasanatha temple, Kanchipuram, 8th cent. C.E

QUESTIONS

1 Explain Rock mandapas of Mamallapuram and sketch the Mandapa column and name any two important Mandapas.
2. Describe the Rathas of Mamallapuram. Sketch the view or elevation of one Ratha.
3. What is the name of Pallavas structural temple built at Mamallapuram and explain its planning and architectural features. Sketch its Sikhara.
4. Sketch the Pallava column and name its parts.
5. Sketch the elevation of Dharmăraja Ratha, Mamallapuram.
6. Sketch the elevation or view of Bhima Ratha, Mamallapuram.

Fig. 7.4. Draupadi Ratha

Fig. 7.5. Nakula Sahadeva Ratha

Fig. 7.6. Varaha Mandapa—Cave

Fig. 7.1. Pandava Rathas, Mamallapuram,650 C.E

Fig. 7.2. Dharmaraja Ratha

Fig. 7.3. Bhima Ratha

Fig. 7.7. Shore temple

Fig. 7.8. Dharmaraja Ratha-Sketch view

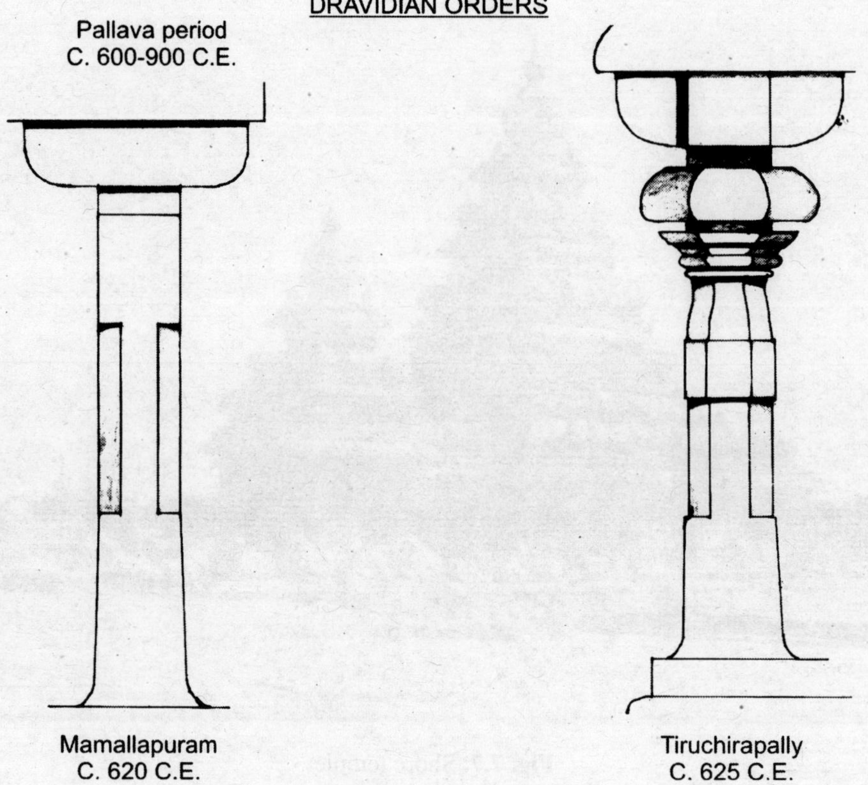

Fig. 7.9. Pallavan Columns

Fig. 7.10. Pallavan Columns-Lion pillars

8

Dravidian Architecture

Under Cholas (900 to 1150 C.E)

8.1. INTRODUCTION

Out of the struggle for power, the Cholas finally emerged triumphant and proceeded in course of time from about 900 C.E. They extended their dominion as far as Ganga river in the north and included Srilanka in south. The period of Cholas was an age of continuous improvement of Dravidian art and architecture. They made exquisite bronze statues and everlasting temples on the banks of Kaveri river. The power of Cholas is such that they built over 2300 temples in Kaveri belt between Tiruchirapally-Tanjore- Kumbhakonam. Most of the temples are small in size. But some of them are grander and monumental exhibiting the vigour and glory of Cholas.

This was the period of many temples. Many contemporary temples were taking shape especially in north India in Orissa, Khajuraho, Rajputana, Gujarat, Maharastra and Gwalior. Belur and Halebid temples were also in course of construction in Karnataka state.

8.2. EXAMPLES

Examples of large and massive temples are:

1. Brihadeswara temple, Thanjavur, 1010 C.E
2. Temple of Gangaikonda Cholapuram, 1033 C.E
3. Airavateswara temple at Darasuram, Kumbakonam, 12th cent. C.E

These are now UNESCO's world heritage sites. The first two temples are described here.

1. Brihadeswara temple, Thanjavur (1010 C.E)

Introduction: The great Brihadeswara temple of Thanjavur dedicated to Lord Siva was built and completed around the year 1010 C.E by the king Rajaraja Chola I, the great. Thanjavur also called Tanjore. The temple stands within the fort. This is the largest, highest and most ambitious production built in granite. But surprisingly granite is not available in the surroundings. It was brought from long distances. The temple is a landmark in the evolution of building art in south India. It was completed within a record time of six years.

Plan

The inner Prakaram of temple is 241 metres long 122 metres wide with a gopuram on east and three ordinary Torana entrances on other sides (Fig. 8.1). The main structure is 55 metres long and the Sikhara is 60 metres high. From these dimensions some idea of the magnitude of the work and the courage and skill required to build may be realized.

Cloisters encircle on the inner face of the enclosure wall in which number of smaller shrines are accommodated. Surrounding the main temple, subsidiary strines were built. (Fig. 8.6)

The main temple contains several structures combined axially and placed in the centre of a spacious walled enclosure from east to west. The compartments are:

– Nandi pavilion
– Pillared portico
– Assembly hall
– Inner Assembly hall
– Vestibule
– Garbhagriha

Front hall has four rows of pillars on either side closely set and the inner hall has three rows of pillars. Vestibule is opened on either side having steps down to the outer court (Fig. 8.4). Beyond the vestibule is the sanctum theholy chamber.

Exterior

The main feature of the entire temple is the grand tower of the Vimana at the western end over the sanctuary, which dominates everything in its vicinity. The massive pyramidal tower rose to some 60 metres high. This is the first highest Vimana built in India (Fig. 8.2, 8.3, 8.5). Other such high structures built later are- Jagannath temple, Puri, 1100 C.E, whose Sikhara rose to 61 metres high

– Gol Gumbaz, Bijapur, 1660 C.E, 61 metres high

Double walls were built to carry the heavy load of Vimana structure of Brihadeswara temple. These walls combine each other at third tier to support the tower. 50000 cubic metres of granite stone was used in this temple complex. Much of its dignity lies in simplicity of its parts. The body of the Sikhara may be divided into three main following parts.

– Square vertical base
– Tall tapering body
– Graceful domical finial

The vertical body covers a square of 25 metres and rises to a height of 15 metres. The plinth is extensively moulded and engraved with inscriptions. Life size statues of deities like Durga, Lakshmi, Saraswathi, Veerabhadra, Natesha, Ardha nariswara were enshrined in wall niches. Over the basement the vertical body is divided into two storeys by a massive horizontal cornice. The same cornice is repeated over the second tier also. The structure shows strong horizontal and vertical lines. The walls are superbly divided into panels by means of pilaster framing niches. Deep recesses were formed in between pilasters. Every niche was presented with a statue. Other ingenious devices and motifs were combined superbly showing great invention.

From this, the pyramidal body mounts up in thirteen diminishing tiers, until the width of its apex equals one-third of its base. On the square platform thus obtained stands the large bulbous cupola. The effect of this pyramidal mass is enhanced by the rich manner of its treatment. It has multiple horizontal lines in diminishing tiers and rows of ornamental shrines producing a marvelous visual effect of great beauty.

Finally the striking contrast on the top of Sikhara is the rounded cupola. Its winged niches on all sides relieved the solidity of dome. The monolithic octagonal dome stone is weighing 80 tons made from a single rock. The cupola has a recessed neck resting on the pyramidal tower. It is believed that this block was rolled and carried to the top on a specially built ramp of six kilometers long. The cupola appears to hang in the air. The tower resembles a human being containing body, neck and head. Either close to or from distance the upward sweep of Sikhara is supreme.

—

There are number of inscriptions on the walls and some are stating the information on the management of the temple and the society.

Unquestionably the Thanjavur Vimana (Sikhara) is the highest, finest and a daring production of both Chola king Rajaraja Chola I and the Dravidian craftsmen.

2. Temple of Gangaikonda Cholapuram 1033 C.E:

Introduction: This monumental structure was built by the king Rajendra I, the son of Rajaraja Chola I to commemorate the victory of his empire spread up to Ganga river who ruled during 1018 C.E to 1033 C.E. He commissioned this structure with an intention to excel in richness and grandeur than its predecessor structure Brihadeswara temple of Thanjavur. The temple was situated 28 kilometres from Kumbhakonam in Tamilnadu state. This temple also is called Brihadeswara temple.

Plan: The temple is large in plan than its predecessor temple, but less in height as the Vimana measures only 46 metres high. The temple building was placed in the middle of an immense walled enclosure. The plan of the temple building makes a rectangle of some 104 metres long 33 metres wide having main entrance on east. (Fig. 8.8)

The compartments in this temple are:

– Detached Nandi pavilion in the front
– Assembly hall
– Vestibule
– Garbhagriha

In front of the main temple building is a detached Nandi pavilion within the axis with a colossal image of Nandi (Bull).

The main doorway gives access to an Assembly hall, which is a low structure containing over 150 pillars of slender and simple design. The pillars are closely set on either side, but leaving a wide gap in the center axially making a spacious way to the sanctuary. In between pillared hall and sanctuary there is a vestibule or transept (Antarala) running at right angles to the axis of the building leading to north and south doorways. There are deeply recessed side entrances approached by flight of steps from outside on both sides to the vestibule. There are eight massive piers in this vestibule. Beyond this at the far end is the holy place, the Garbhagriha.

Exterior: The front mandapa bears a simple appearance with its plain pillars. The pyramidal vimana, which rises over the sanctuary on western end, is massive and superb achievement. On its plan it is a square of 30 metres side and vertically it resolves into the following three levels. (Fig. 8.7)

– Vertical ground story
– Tapering body and
– Domical finial

The tapering body is in tiers with eight diminishing zones. The contours of the tower are not strong straight lines, as was done in its predecessor example of Tanjore Vimana. But here concave curves are made making the tower smooth. The domical finial is directly placed on the square platform almost without neck. Whereas the grand finial of the Tanjore temple is separated from the tapering body and placed over a neck giving a graceful appearance of neck and head.

The main vertical body is embellished with statuary. Single figure statues occupied the niches as a whole. The figures of the god of Nataraja, Ganesh, Apsaras, Ganadevatas, Yakshas were depicted at appropriate places.

Under the supremacy of Cholas, the art and architecture in south India attained a new peak.

8.3. NAMES OF OTHER IMPORTANT TEMPLES

Sarabeswara temple (Kampahareswarar temple) at Tirubhuvanam near Kumbakonam, 12th cent. C.E

QUESTIONS

1. Describe the architecture of great Brihadeswara temple of Thanjavur.
2. Describe the temple of Gangaikonda Cholapuram.
3. List the names of UNESCO's world heritage temple sites of Cholas and describe the architecture of any one temple in detail. Sketch the Sikhara of that temple.
4. Sketch the great Sikhara of Brihadeswara temple, Thanjavur.

Fig. 8.1. Brihadeshwara temple-Entrance

Fig. 8.2. Brihadeswara temple, Thanjavur-From South east

Fig. 8.3. Brihadeshwara temple-Main temple side view

Fig. 8.4. Brihadeswara temple-Side entrance

Fig. 8.5. Brihadeswara Temple, Sikhara

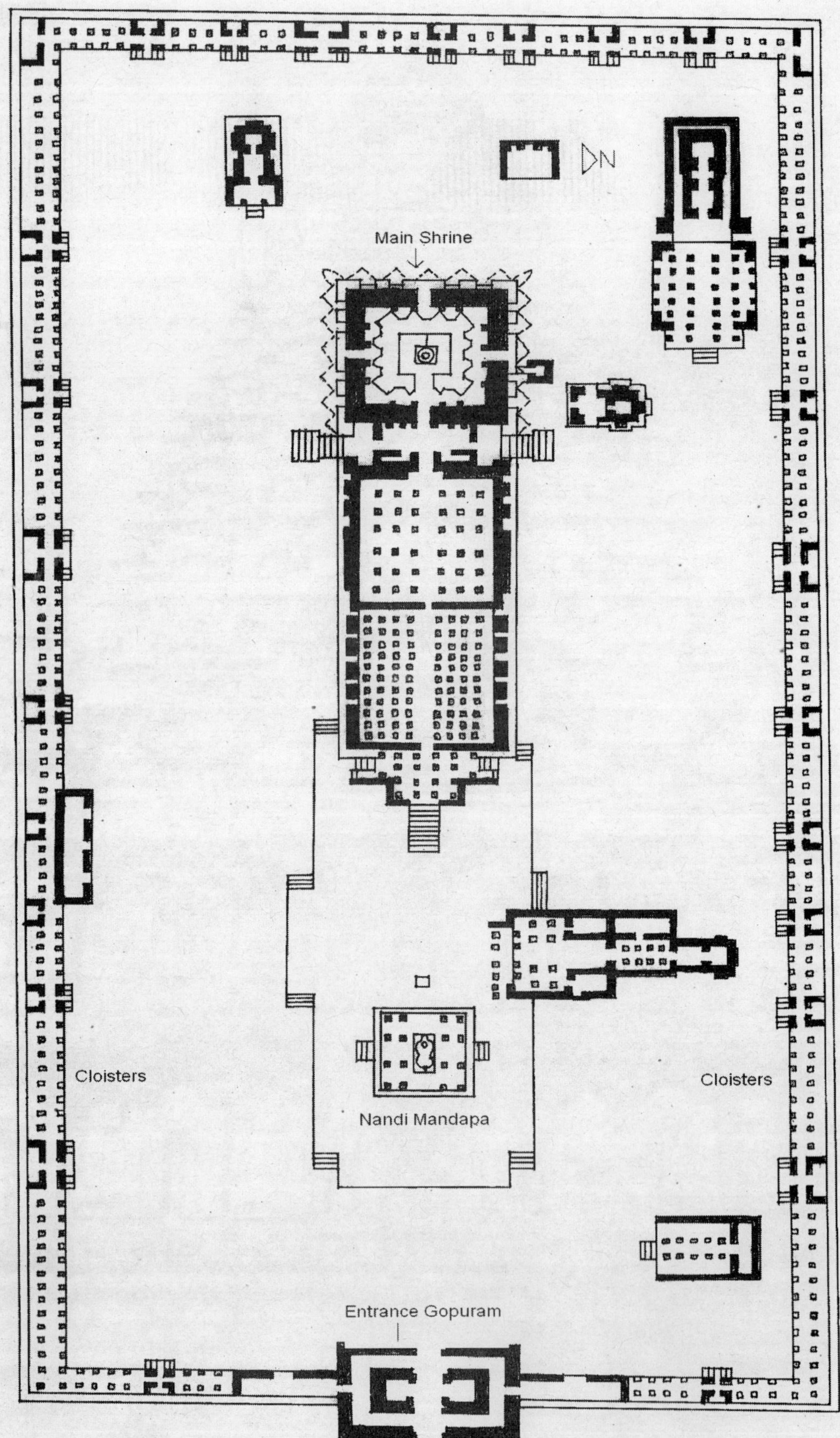

Fig. 8.6. Brihadeshwara temple—Plan

Fig. 8.7. Gangaikonda Cholapuram temple-View

Fig. 8.8. GangaiKkonda Cholapuram temple-Front

9

Dravidian Architecture

Under Pandyas (1100 to 1350 C.E)

9.1. INTRODUCTION

Pandyas dominated south India for more than two centuries after succeeding Cholas. They ruled southern Tamilnadu for long time except some breaks in between. They were the Tamil people ruling from Korkai, a seaport town on deep south and later shifted to Madurai. It is believed that Pandyas ruled from 5th century B.C.E and had connections with Roman empire. Also it is believed that Pandyas are such ancient dynasty that existed and participated in Mahabharatha war about 3000 B.C.E. They obscured for some time after their defeat by Cholas. Again they revived in 6th and 12th centuries.

Hoysala kings ruling from Halebid in Karnataka state were the contemporaries and the Hoysala temples in Hassan and Malnad districts were in course of construction at this time. At the same time, some of the important temples in north India were already built or were under construction in Rajputana, Gujarat, Maharastra, Gwalior and Orissa. Delhi came under Sultanate rule after a century and the Slaves, Khaljis and Tughlaqs were the contemporaries building mosques, tombs and forts.

Most temples were already built from early years and hence some facilities and subsidiary structures were added to the existing temples. Hence by the advent of Pandyas, instead of the sanctuary or the temple building continuing to be the architectural production, the builders' skill was diverted in order to give prominence to some of the supplementary and outlying portions of the temple complex. The main shrines and images were not altered or disturbed due to their value, sacredness and sentiment. Religious emotion however has to find some expression. Hence it was done by adding new structures like:

– High Enclosing walls surrounding the temple

– Imposing Entrance pylons called Gopuram

Higher Gopurams were built to give a long distance look of the temple.

9.2. GOPURAM

Gopuram is an imposing monumental entrance structure built in the temples of south India. These are tall and magnificent, often appearing more than one in important temples. These pylon entrances with their embellishments were introduced frequently into the temple complexes. They became the most striking structures in temples in south India. This pylon is here called the 'Gopuram'. This was derived from cow gate of early Vedic villages. Early and elementary prototypes of Gopuram were found at the entrance to Kailasanatha temple at Kanchipuram and Virupaksha temple at Pattadkal of Chalukyans.

Egyptians also built such huge pylons to their temples. Egyptian pylons are wide bodied and Dravidian Gopuram is higher bodied like a tower.

A Gopuram consists of four parts.

1. Rectangular cubical bottom containing entrance doors
2. Truncated pyramidal part rising tier by tier over the cubical base
3. Barrel vault above
4. Row of pinnacles

Plan: A typical example of Gopuram depicts a building oblong in plan. It was entered by a passage from the center of its longer side. The passage is a tall opening giving access into the temple enclosure. On either side of this passage within the structure there are either terraces or dark rooms accommodating a stairway having steep steps leading to upper floors. A huge, solid, thick paneled door made with solid wood, decorated with metal sheets and carvings having two shutters closes the passage.

Exterior: Externally the Gopuram is a solid masonry structure containing a cubical base and a truncated pyramidal portion above crowned by barrel vault and row of pinnacles. The lower storeys are vertical and were built with solid stone masonry, thus providing a stable base. The superstructure was built of light materials like brick and plaster. It is a truncated pyramid in diminishing tiers and was often raised over 46 metres in height. The average angle of slope from the vertical is 250 . The width at its apex is approximately half of its base.

In the long main side of this structure, rectangular void openings are made from front to back in the center of each upper floor. These openings are diminishing in size proportionately with the reducing mass of the pyramidal structure. These void openings in the center not only give relief in the solid mass of superstructure, but they reduce the weight and act as a devise in reducing the wind pressure and allow the air to flow through the openings.

Roof: On the summit is a kind of elongated roof with gable ends. The vaulted roof is similar to the keel roof of Buddhist Chaitya hall. The roof is more ornate and is a fantastic production with its gables. Metal Kalashas (Vases) were placed in a row on top in between the gables. The ridgeline breaking out into a row of pinnacles created an appropriate climax to the fretted mass below.

Every part of the Gopuram was moulded and sculptured with polychrome gods, Apsaras and Demons. The mystic and many weapon deities of Lord Siva were infinitely multiplied, repeated, reduced and carried in rising ranks up to the horns of the topmost roof. Over a period of time, number of such towers rising around the temple became a familiar skyline. (Fig. 9.1 to 9.4)

Gopuram may be resolved into two classes by their external appearance.

- In which the sloping sides are relatively straight, firm and rigid in their contours and appearing in their mass strictly to the pyramidal figure. (Fig. 9.1, 9.3, 9.4)
- In another class, the sloping sides are not straight but curved and concave. (Fig. 9.2)

Gopurams stood taller in Dravidian temples and became monumental ever inviting and inspiring the visitors.

9.3. EXAMPLES

1. Sundara Pandya Gopuram to the temple of Jambukeswara, Tiruchirapally built about 1250 C.E
2. Gopuram to the temple of Chidambaram
3. Gopuram to the temple of Madurai and Tiruvallur
4. Gopuram to the temple of Kumbakonam, 1350 C.E

QUESTIONS

1. Explain Pandya's contribution to Dravidian temples.
2. What is Gopuram. Explain its planning and construction. Sketch the view or elevation of a Gopuram.

Fig. 9.1. Gopuram showing close details—Tiruvannamalai temple

Fig. 9.2. Meenakshi temple—south gopuram with curved corners

Fig. 9.3. Tiruvannamalai temple—view showing Gopurams

Fig. 9.4. Tiruvanamalai temple—View of temple and Gopurams

10

Dravidian Architecture

Under Rayalas, Hampi Vijayanagar (1350 to 1565 C.E)

10.1. INTRODUCTION

The powerful and forceful Hampi Vijayanagar empire dominated entire south India for over two centuries from 1350 to 1565 C.E. This country covered entire south India extended from Krishna river to Kanyakumari with its capital city at Hampi Vijaynagar on the banks of Tungabhadra river situated near modern Hospet city in Bellary district of Karnataka state.

North India at this time was under the reign of Sultans of Tughlaq, Lodi and Sayyid dynasties ruling from Delhi. Moguls were the contemporaries during late period of Rayalas. Vijayanagar was a great stronghold and a defensive rampart against the ever-persistent menace from Bijapur Sultans from north.

It was the period when the people were encouraged in arts and given greater freedom. The architectural remains though grievously ruined and deserted, but still contain much of their beauty, richness and wonder. Hampi Vijayanagar is now UNESCO's world heritage site.

10.2. ARCHITECTURAL CHARACTERS

It was no longer to build huge structures. But on other hand, the structures of moderate proportions distinguished with exquisite character of architecture and embellishment were in course of production. All time remarkable architecture for profuseness of its applied decoration reached its extreme stage during this period. It is a record in stone of a range of ideals, sensations, emotions, prodigality, abnormalities of forms and formless and even eccentricities that only a super imaginative mind could conceive and only an inspired artist could produce.

Planning of Temple

Elaborated rituals brought some changes in temple planning and architecture. Buildings were increased in number within the temple enclosure making it a complex. In addition to main temple in the middle, there are separate shrines, pillared halls, pavilions and other annexes each having its purpose. Pavilion containing groups of columns form the principal part of the temple scheme. An important such building that had taken place here is the Kalyana Mandapa (Marriage hall), a most ornate structure. This is an open pillared pavilion with a raised platform in the centre for the reception of the deity and consort on the annual celebration of their marriage ceremony.

Order of Pillars

The number, intricacy and prominence of pillars and piers produced rich beauty in Vijayanagar temples. They were sculpted into most complicated compositions, strange and manifold. Each pillar is a figurative drama in stone.

A very striking type of pillar design is that in which the shaft becomes merely a central core for the attachment of a group of statuary, often of heroic size, having its most conspicuous element a furiously rearing horse, a rampant Hippogryph or upraised animal of a supernatural kind. A cluster of miniature pillars, which are slender, mystical and dreamy sometimes combined with or encircled the central columns. In some instances the shaft was made of a series of small-scale shrines of the original full size structure and arranged in zones one above the other. (Fig. 10.5)

Capitals

Ornamental brackets are the part of their capital as found in every stage of Dravidian order. Below the bracket is a pendant or Bodegai, which was elaborated into a volute terminating in an inverted lotus bud.

10.3. EXAMPLES

Important structures of this Vijayanagar city are:

1. Virupaksha temple, Vijayanagar, 1510 C.E.
2. Vithala temple, 16th cent.
3. Hazararama temple, 16th cent.
4. Secular structures, 16th cent.

1. Virupaksha temple, Hampi Vijayanagar, 1510 C.E

This is the prime temple at this site dedicated to lord Siva and is now completely intact. This ancient temple exists since 7th century and is enlarged into a temple complex during this period. It has two Prakarams.

Outer prakaram: Outer court is entered through a large Gopuram from east side. This is bounded by a high enclosure wall, the inner side of which has pillared cloisters and also contains small shrines.

Inner court: This contains the main temple and other edifices and is entered through a small gopuram from east side. This is mostly covered by halls, corridors on all sides. Main temple is placed in the center at the extreme western end. (Fig. 10.1, 10.2)

Main temple: Main temple consists of the following compartments.

– Front open large pillared hall also called Rang mandapa

– Anti chambers 3 Nos

– Sanctum sanctorum on west having a processional passage

Pillared hall is the most ornate structure and it is believed that emperor Sri Krishna Devaraya commissioned this in 1510 C.E. Pillars are the main attraction and has rampant lion like mythical creatures (Yalis) standing on aquatic creatures like crocodiles (Makara). The hall has two rows of surrounding pillars leaving a nave in the center. It has three entrances and the main entrance is on east. (Fig. 10.4)

Outside the enclosure and on north side there is a large water tank and number of smaller shrines were built.

2. Vittala temple, Hampi Vijayanagar 16th Cent, C.E

Vithala temple is the most exquisitely ornate temple building in Hampi Vijayanagar. It was begun by the emperor Sri Krishna Devaraya in 1513 C.E, but could not be completed owing to its elaborate character.

Plan

It stands within a rectangular courtyard of 152 metres long by 95 metres wide, which is surrounded by cloisters containing triple row of pillars. Entrance is made through three gopurams, those on east and south being more important. There are six separate structures, mostly in the form of pillared halls. The largest is the main temple occupying the center. The central building is dedicated to Lord Vishnu in the form of Vittala (Panduranga) and is a low structure of one storey averaging 7.5 metres in height and 70 metres in length aligned from east to west.

It consists of the following three compartments.

– Ardha-mandapa or open pillared portico in the front

– Mandapa or closed Assembly hall in the middle

– Garbha-griha or sanctuary in the rear

Ardha-mandapa

The compartment which first attracts is Ardha-mandapa or a columned pavilion measuring 30 metres side with deeply recessed sides. This stands on a moulded plinth, 1.5 metres high with flights of steps elephant guarded on its three free sides. The whole is heavily shadowed by means of an immensely wide eave and above the parapet raises an irregular outline of brickwork turrets.

Order of pillars

The chief feature of this columned hall is its range of pillars, 56 in numbers each 3.6 metres in height. Each pier comprises an entire sculpted group, being fashioned out of one large block of granite. Cluster of delicately shaped columns form the central portion of these broad supports, while interposed between them is the rearing animal motif, half natural half mythical but wholly rhythmic. This cluster design is united with a single capital above and a moulded pedestal or base below. Over these piers are bracket supports of large size combined with profusely carved entablatures and above all a flat ceiling ornamented with sunken lotus flowers. (Fig. 10.5)

Mandapa and Sanctuary

The mandapa and sanctuary combined is a rectangle of 41 metres long and 21 metres wide. This is entered from east. In addition it has two side entrances each having steps and a porch. This is a square hall of 16.80 metres side. It has sixteen pillars in all. At the other end is the Garbhagriha measuring externally 23 metres side. A processional passage in the cella is adjusted during alterations in construction. Due to some reasons this ambulatory was built down to the ground level.

Exterior

The exterior walls of the remainder building were conventionally built with pilaster niche and alcove combination. The Vimana was rather unusual. It has a processional passage down with the level of the courtyard with two flights of steps.

Kalyana Mandapa (Marriage hall)

Out of the remaining structures of the enclosure more ornate is Kalyana Mandapa, placed on southeast side to the temple. It is an open pavilion resembling the Ardha-mandapa. This has a high plinth with deeply recessed sides and flights of steps in the centre of three of them. There are 48 piers all of which were exquisitely carved.

Ratha (Chariot)

Within the main axis of the temple and in front of Ardha-mandapa is a Ratha or a chariot of God built in stone containing wheels and elephant guards at the steps. Every feature is imitated in granite and upper part like Sikhara was in brick and mortar, which is now disappeared. (Fig. 10.6)

3. Hazara Rama temple, Hampi Vijayanagar, 16th Cent. C.E

Within the walled citadel, small but richly ornamental temple is Hazara Rama temple, in which the royal family and members of the court worshipped. A higher wall of 7.30 metres high encloses it. It is believed that Emperor Srikrishna Devaraya began its construction in 1513 C.E.

Plan

The main building is in the centre of a courtyard. It is entered on east through a flat roofed porch and consists of the following compartments.

- An assembly hall with four massive black stone pillars, one at each corner of a central square. Two more entrances are there to this hall through a porch.
- Garbhagriha or sanctuary at the far end with the image of Lord Rama.

Exterior

The Vimana is remarkable with its lower storey of stone and pyramidal Sikhara in brick. It consists of a grouping of replicas of itself in three tiers surmounted by a cupola. The whole height is about 15 metres.

To the side and rear of this temple is the Amman (consort) shrine which is a smaller reproduction of the main structure to which on the Sikhara, a keel roof of Buddhist chaitya hall was added in the place of cupola. Brick and plaster superstructures of these buildings was finished in bright colours. (Fig. 10.9, 1010)

4. Secular structures

Within the walls of the citadel of Vijayanagar, there are the remains of other secular structures that are as follows.

- Palace of Srikrishna Devaraya
- King's Audience hall
- Throne platform (House of Victory).

The Bahmani Sultans devastated this great city after the war at Tallikot in 1565 C.E.

10.4. NAMES OF OTHER STRUCTURES

Srikrishna temple, Vijayanagar, 16th cent.

Narasimha temple, Vijayanagar, 16th cent.

Atchutaraya temple, Vijayanagar, 16th cent.

Lotus mahal, Vijayanagar, 16th cent.

QUESTIONS

1. Describe the architectural characters of Hampi Vijayanagar temples.
2. Describe Virupaksha temple, Vijayanagar in its planning and other architectural features.
3. Explain the planning, architectural features and pillars of Vithala temple of Vijayanagar.
4. Mention any two important temples of Hampi Vijaynagar and explain its architectural features.

Fig. 10.1. Virupaksha temple, Hampi Vijayanagar, 1510 C.E-Arial view

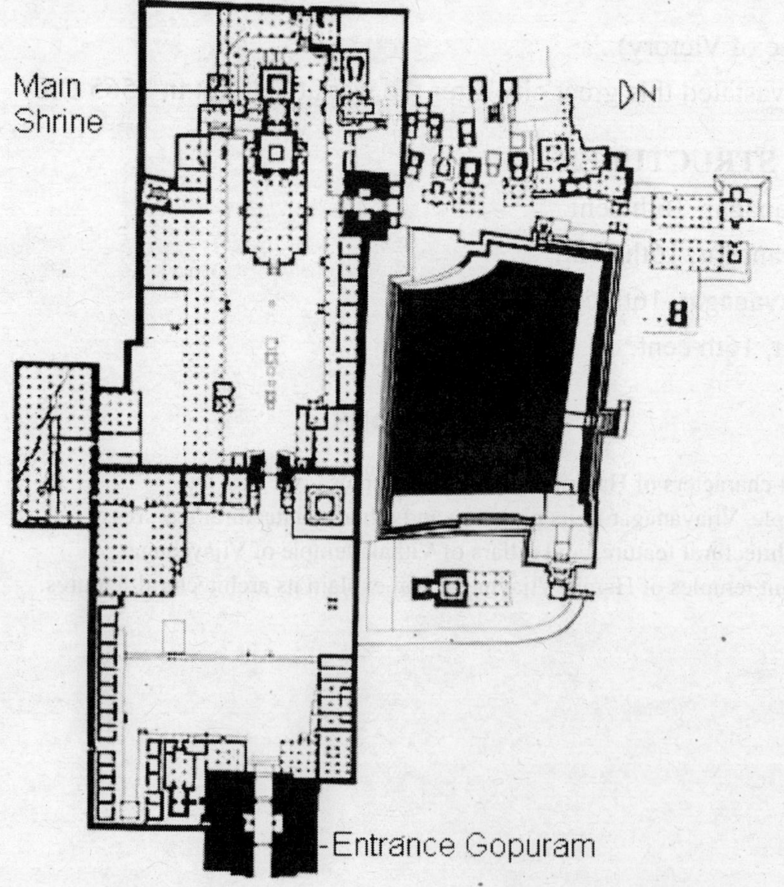

Fig. 10.2. Virupaksha temple-Site plan

Fig. 10.3. Virupaksha temple- Eastern Gopuram

Fig. 10.4. Virupaksha temple-Mandapa pillars

Fig. 10.5. Vittala temple, Hampi Vijayanagar, 16th cent.-Mandapas

Fig. 10.6. Vittala temple-Stone chariot

Fig. 10.7. Vittala temple—Chariot, Marriage hall and Mandapa

Fig. 10.8. Vittala temple-pillar

Fig. 10.9. Hazararama temple-Outer wall

Fig. 10.10. Hazararama temple-view

11

Dravidian Architecture

Under Nayaks, Madurai 1600 C.E)

11.1. INTRODUCTION

After the fall of Vijayanagar empire in 1565 C.E, and owing to the pressure of Islamic aggression, the Hindu elements were forced further to the south to the city of Madurai; as the capital city now in Tamilnadu state. Dravidian style assumed its final form under Nayak dynasty rulers. It was flourished well under the rule of Tirumalai Nayak who reigned from 1623 to 1659 C.E. Earlier this country was ruled by Pandyas.

During this time north India was under the reign of Mughuls and no Hindu temples were under construction since some 400 years except a few examples at Brindavan. Mogul structures under Jahangir, Shahjahan and Aurangzeb were in course of construction. Sultans of Bijapur were contemporaries and Ibrahim Rauza and Golgumbaz were under construction.

11.2. EXPANSION OF TEMPLES

Number of important temples already exist and they require some facilities and additional shrines the existing shrines, the result of which is that a number of ancient temples became expanded into structural complexes of vast size and impressive appearance. The expansion of temples was occasioned by a corresponding expansion of the temple rituals and ceremonies, which naturally reacted on the arrangement of the buildings in which they were celebrated.

The inner portion of the temple was strictly reserved and secluded as the sacred habitation of the god and was not disturbed. The temple may be resolved into two main divisions.

– Inner part, more covered and most sacred part

– Outer part, more open, more public and less sanctified part

The former comprises the inner central portion consisting of the sanctum, the cupolas of which, often richly gilt projecting through the flat roofs, thus denoting the focal centre of the entire scheme. The outer part of the temple is made of a concentric series of open courts called Prakarams.

11.3. PROCESS OF EXPANSION OF TEMPLE

Expansion was proceeded on the following lines. The preliminary step in expansion was to enclose the shrine within a spacious structure. Hence within this there grew up pillared aisles, verandahs, halls and other arrangements of like nature. The entrance to this whole was through a small Gopuram in the front. Increasing temple rituals and ceremonies demanded additional accommodation. Hence outside this enclosure sometime later the structures like granaries, storerooms, pillared halls and other edifices grew up. This has demanded an enclosure for want of inwardness and security. Hence new enclosing walls containing new Gopurams still larger and higher in size than the predecessor came into existence. Like this, the structures of demanding needs and the solution continued. Within these enclosures large and important structures like Hypostyle halls of thousand pillars and water tank lined with steps and surrounded by an arcade were developed.

The temple gradually grew from initial stage of a small village shrine. And in course of time structures were added one by one. The temple complex grew according to the raising needs and followed Mandala plan.

Mandala plan

In south India, temple complexes grew into temple towns. They were planned in Mandala form having prakarams (courts) and surrounding walls. Mandala is an interpretation of cosmological grid diagram. The temple was built like a human body in which there are sheaths from Annamaya Kosha (Biological sheath made of food) to Anandamaya Kosha (Supreme bliss sheath) which is deep internal and most subtle. The temple courts interpret these sheaths. The outer courts are less sanctified and the sanctity increases as it nears the central shrine.

Embryo of the town starts from main sacred shrine in the center and gets concentric rings around it. Each inside area is accessible through gates called Gopurams.

There is yet another Mandala called Navagraha Mandala (Nine planet Mandala) containing nine squares symmetrically placed in three each in rows. This Mandala form is more in use in north India.

Such important towns are:

– Srirangam (Tiruchchirapali)

– Chidambaram

– Madurai

– Kanchipuram

– Tiruvannamalai

Most of the temples in south India were not abandoned after their inception, as the forceful threat from other faiths was less and somehow they were protected. Temples continued to survive by the patronage of rulers and the rituals and ceremonies are being continued. This resulted in construction additional shrines, ponds, enclosing walls, Gopurams making the temples bulged in their size.

The additional accommodation is in the form of halls and corridors and was built with multiple rows of pillars and simple flat roofs, which resulted in fine perspective of exquisitely carved columns and brackets on all sides. Pillars and the Gopurams became the most prominent features of these temples.

Gopurams

Temple complexes needed a proper controlled entry through gateways which were built into monumental structures called Gopurams. The Gopurams and the layout of the temple complex show similarity to the Pylons of Egypt and the Egyptian temple planning. Undoubtedly, Dravidian Gopuram had reached its maturity and majesty and has occupied a most prominent place in Indian Architecture. The Gopuram was embellished with groups of plastic imagery profusely carved from Hindu mythology, often over thousand figures of large-size.

One cannot fail to be impressed by the profound religious atmosphere, emotional and spiritual. Extensive elaborations and additions were made during this time.

Profusely carved pillars

Pillars are the principal part in Dravidian temples and in no other style such profusion is found. The chief features of the pillars are the square moulded rampant dragons, foliated brackets and pendants.

Each pillar had its own unique design. There is continuous change in the design of pillars and brackets.

Geometrical patterns and imagery were multiplied in pillars and brackets. Each artist working for the temple had created innovative own designs (Fig. 11.11, 11.12). In some temples like Rameswaram, the brackets were made heavy with multiple carvings. People visit these temples with equal desire of seeing the deity and the temple architecture.

The temples of Madurai class are nearly thirty in number and the following few important are described here.

11.4. BEST EXAMPLES

1. Meenakshi temple, Madurai, 17th cent
2. Srirangam temple, Srirangam, 13th to 18th cent
3. Rameswaram temple, Rameswaram, 17th cent

1. Meenakshi temple, Madurai (17th Century C.E)

Layout and Planning

One of the larger and greater temple of Dravidian architecture is the Meenakshi temple, Madurai of 17th century mostly built in one time. It is a double temple, as it has two separate sanctuaries, one dedicated to Lord Siva (Sundareswara) and the other to his consort the goddess Meenakshi. These two shrines are temple within a temple. The temple is popularly called Meenakshi temple. It was built is Mandala plan having courts (Prakarams), pillared halls and enclosure walls (Fig. 11.1 to 11.3). As the temple is major and more prominent in Madurai, hence it is also called Madurai temple.

The outer wall of this temple surrounds an area of 259 metres by 221 metres, with four large gateways one each in the centre of four sides. Admission is through the Gopuram on east. This is connected to a fine-pillared avenue of over 61 metres long and about 31 metres wide, which is called Viravasantaraya mandapam in which a Nandi pavilion was placed. This leads to a smaller Gopuram forming the eastern entrance to the second Prakaram. This is a rectangular enclosure of 128 metres by 94 metres also having four gateways (Gopurams) one in the middle of each side but smaller than the preceding.

Most of this second enclosure is covered with a flat roof, but partly open on north side. This enclosure has the nave and transepts with most intricate grouping of pillars. Within this there is again another covered court with only one entrance on east. This is Siva's enclosure.

Siva's enclosure

Inside the last enclosure the sacred shrine is situated. This contains three compartments an assembly hall

– A vestibule and

– A Cella

All the courts, corridors and halls have flat roofs supported on pillars. The pillars are exquisite, beautiful and wondrous in their design. At the other end the Cella was placed. This was surmounted by a small Sikhara, which penetrates through the flat roofs of pillared halls.

Minakshi enclosure

The other temple of this complex is that of the consort or associate deity, Minakshi- the fish-eyed. This enclosure is attached to the south of Siva temple to the rear. This is a half-size production having one compartment within another. It is entered through two Gopurams one on east and the other on west and that on the west is larger. The enclosure is mostly covered with pillared halls and corridors. Rising above the flat roof is the cupola of the shrine.

Pool of Golden Lotuses

Lying towards the front of Minakshi enclosure and in an angle to the south is a large rectangular water pool surrounded by steps and pillared corridors on its four sides. This is the pool of Golden lotuses, an artificial reservoir measuring 50 metres by 36 metres. Its picturesque appearance is enhanced by the great mass of southern Gopuram raised over 46 metres high, the image of which is reflecting in the pool waters. (Fig. 11.4, 11.5)

In the northeast corner of the tank there is a fair-sized Gopuram placed across the line of Minakshi sanctuary. There are 11 Gopurams in total and it counts to 12 if the newly added Gopuram in the extreme eastern wall opposite to Minakshi shrine is added.

Arianayakam Mudali's Hypostyle Hall

In the northeast portion of the outer enclosure, there is a spacious structure containing some thousand pillars added by Arianayakam Mudali, minister and founder of Nayak dynasty. It is entered from south. The interior consists of central passage with a double row of columns on either side leading to a small shrine at its northern end meant for Sabhapati. Behind the colonnades forming the aisle are row upon row of pillars grotesquely carved making the total to 985 in all. The exterior of the hall is merely a low flat roofed structure.

Pudumandapam or Tirumalai Nayak's Choultry

In front of the temple and opposite to eastern gopuram leaving a thoroughfare is a large hall called Pudu Mandapam also known as Tirumala's choultry. It measures 100 metres by 32 metres. It is a reception hall or temporary residence for the deity during the festival season. It is divided into a nave and two aisles by four rows of pillars elaborately carved.

Conclusion

The temple has some more additional edifices, shrines, pillared halls, corridors and open areas built for specific purposes. As a whole the temple is unique standing amidst large number of pillars and flat roofs.

2. Srirangam temple, Tiruchchirapali, 13th to 18th cent C.E

The largest temple of south India dedicated to Lord Sri Ranganatha Swamy is the temple of Srirangam near Tiruchirapalli in Tamilnadu state. Srirangam is an island area surrounded by Kaveri river waters. The temple complex occupies a land of 156 acres of land. Length of seven prakaram walls is 9934 metres nearly 10 kilometres. Exact date of inception of temple is not known, as the temple exists since much long time in some form.

Layout of temple

The temple has only one sanctuary. Its construction extended over a long period of centuries. This temple was a small village shrine consisting of a sanctuary and a Mandapa at the time of its inception during Chola's time. For various reasons it gained much religious popularity. The space between the walled enclosures is not enough for conducting increasing ceremonies and to accommodate the growing pilgrims. The necessary additional structures were built outside the enclosure and these new structures required an enclosure wall to provide safety. In the centre of each enclosure wall a Gopuram was added much bigger and grander than the earlier. All the kings including Cholas, Pandyas, Hoysalas, Nayaks contributed to this temple. Like this the temple acquired several concentric rings of growth over a period of time. Therefore the temple city had acquired its shape out of necessity and followed Mandala plan having courts and concentric square rings. (Fig. 11.6, 11.7)

Mandala is an interpretation of cosmological grid diagram having concentric rings and central shrine in the center. Access to each enclosure inside is obtained through gateway structures called Gopurams.

Unusually this temple is laid out from south to north instead of usual orientation of east to west. It measures a huge size rectangle of 950 metres by 816 metres enclosing an area of 0.77 square kilometer. It is having 21 Gopurams including large, small and unfinished, 13 of which are in axial line. There are six prakarams making in all seven concentric walls, with the shrine in the centre.

The three outer prakarams contain town, streets, houses and shops. From the fourth court the sacred and religious zone starts. This enclosure possesses a Gopuram on the middle of three sides on south, north and east that on the south is the fine and larger. Within this court northeast corner occupies a thousand-pillared hall with flat roof measuring 152 metres by 49 metres built by Cholas. There are over 900 carved granite monolith pillars in this hall. Pillared pavilions of ordinary type covered other areas.

In the third enclosure, there are two Gopurams on south and north and opens into Garuda Mandapam having flat roof. Within this court there are two pools.

Surya Puskarini (pool of Sun)—a covered tank

Chandra pushkarini (pool of Moon)—horseshoe shaped water pool at northern end

The second court is entered through a Gopuram each on south and north sides. Pillared pavilions mostly covered this court. Within this is the first or innermost enclosure having its entrance on south side with a Gopuram. The sanctuary is a square compartment surrounded by flat roof, over which a golden Sikhara rises. The view of the 13 Gopurams in south to north axis is impressive. (Fig. 11.8)

The temple as a whole achieved sacred and profound religious atmosphere.

3. Rameswaram temple, 17th Century, C.E

Dravidian temples have certain common similarities and at the same time some of them possess some special characters to distinguish them from others. Such notable example is the temple of Rameswaram in Tamilnadu state in which distinguishable features are the pillared corridors. Temple enshrines Lord Siva in the form of Sive Lingam.

Plan

This temple consists of double shrines enclosed within three concentric perimeter walls, the outer of which measures 268 metres long and 205 metres wide. The temple was planned and built within one period.

Corridors and Pillars

All the greatness and glory of the temple lies in its long avenue corridors whose length was extended over 914 metres, a few metres less than a kilometer. The width of the fine columned corridors varies from 5 metres to 7.6 metres. The columns rise to 3.6 metres in height from a moulded stylobate of 1.5 metres high. Richly decorated and closely set pillars of good proportions continue along the entire length of corridors in linear and lateral directions. There is a long impressive perspective of columned corridors, those on the north and south side being more effective and they are over 213 metres in length. Each column contains massive, expansive foliated bracket capital. Individually each pillar bracket is impressive and especially when viewed in a perspective, they are utmost pleasing and dramatic. (Fig. 11.10, 11.11)

The roof over the halls and corridors is flat. The corridor ceilings have inlaid painted circular patterns in each bay. There are simply moulded shrines over the sanctuaries. Externally the temple was enclosed all round by a solid plain wall of 6 metres high. The Gopurams are unfinished and show straight and strong lines with no figure work.

11.5. NAMES OF OTHER IMPORTANT TEMPLES

Jambukeswara temple near Trichinapally

Tiruvarur temple

Chidambaram temple

Tirunelvely temple

Tiruvannamalai temple

Srivilliputtur temple

QUESTIONS

1. How Dravidian temples became large complexes. Explain its expansion process.
2. In south India temple complexes developed into temple towns in Mandala plan. Explain briefly its form, contents, shape and mention any two best examples of such towns.
   or
   Describe the Mandala plan of Dravidian temple and mention any two best examples of such temple towns.
3. Describe the layout, internal compartments and Gopurams of Madurai temple.
4. Sketch the plan of Madurai temple and name the halls and parts.
5. Explain the Layout, compartments and Gopurams of Srirangam temple.
6. What are the important features of Rameswaram temple. Briefly explain its planning and architectural characters.
7. Sketch the corridor of Rameswaram temple.

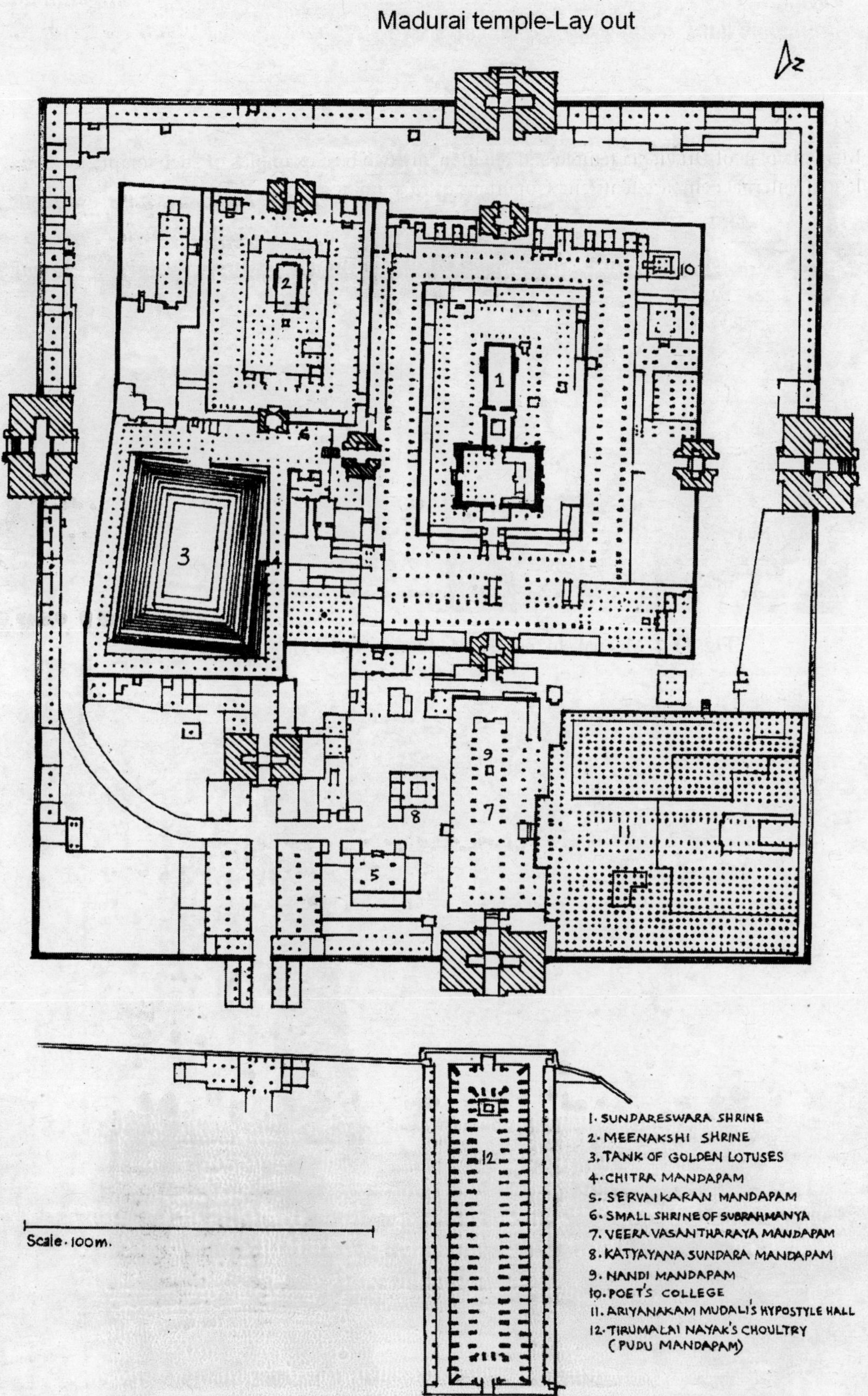

Fig. 11.1. Meenakshi temple, Madurai, 17th cent. C.E—Layout plan

Fig. 11.2. Meenakshi temple, Madurai—Aerial view from West

Fig. 11.3. Meenakshi temple, Madurai—View showing Gopurams and Golden Sikhara

Fig. 11.4. Meenakshi temple—Tank of Lotuses

Fig. 11.5. Meenakshi temple—South gopuram

Fig. 11.6. Srirangam temple, 13 to 18th cent.C.E—Satellite image showing concentric rings

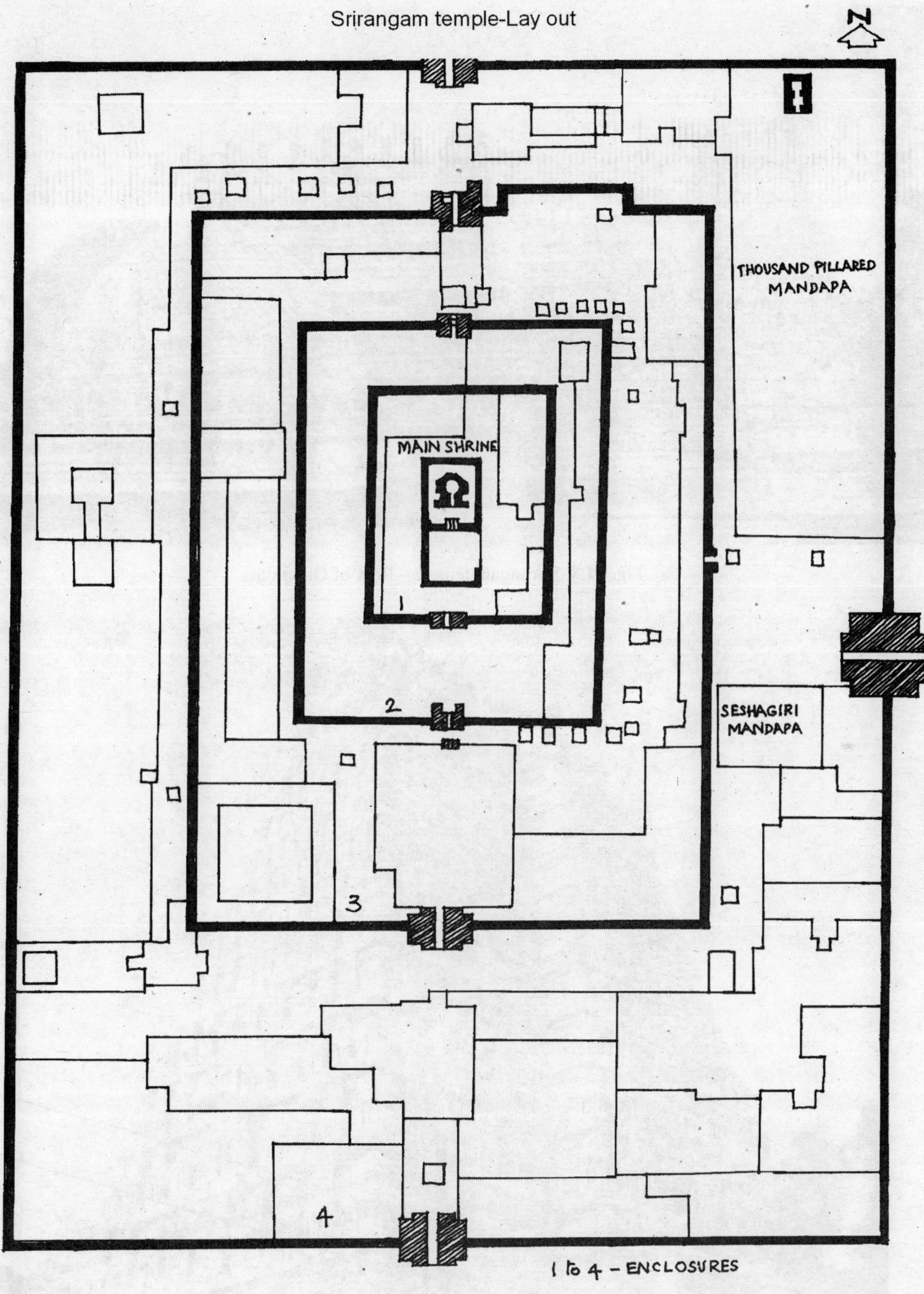

Fig. 11.7. Srirangam temple—Plan

Fig. 11.8. Srirangam temple—Row of Gopurams

Fig. 11.9. Srirangam temple—Gopuram with repeating elements

Fig. 11.10. Rameswaram temple—Corridor showing great pillars and ceiling

Fig. 11.11. Srirangam temple-Pillars with Imagery

Dravidian Brackets

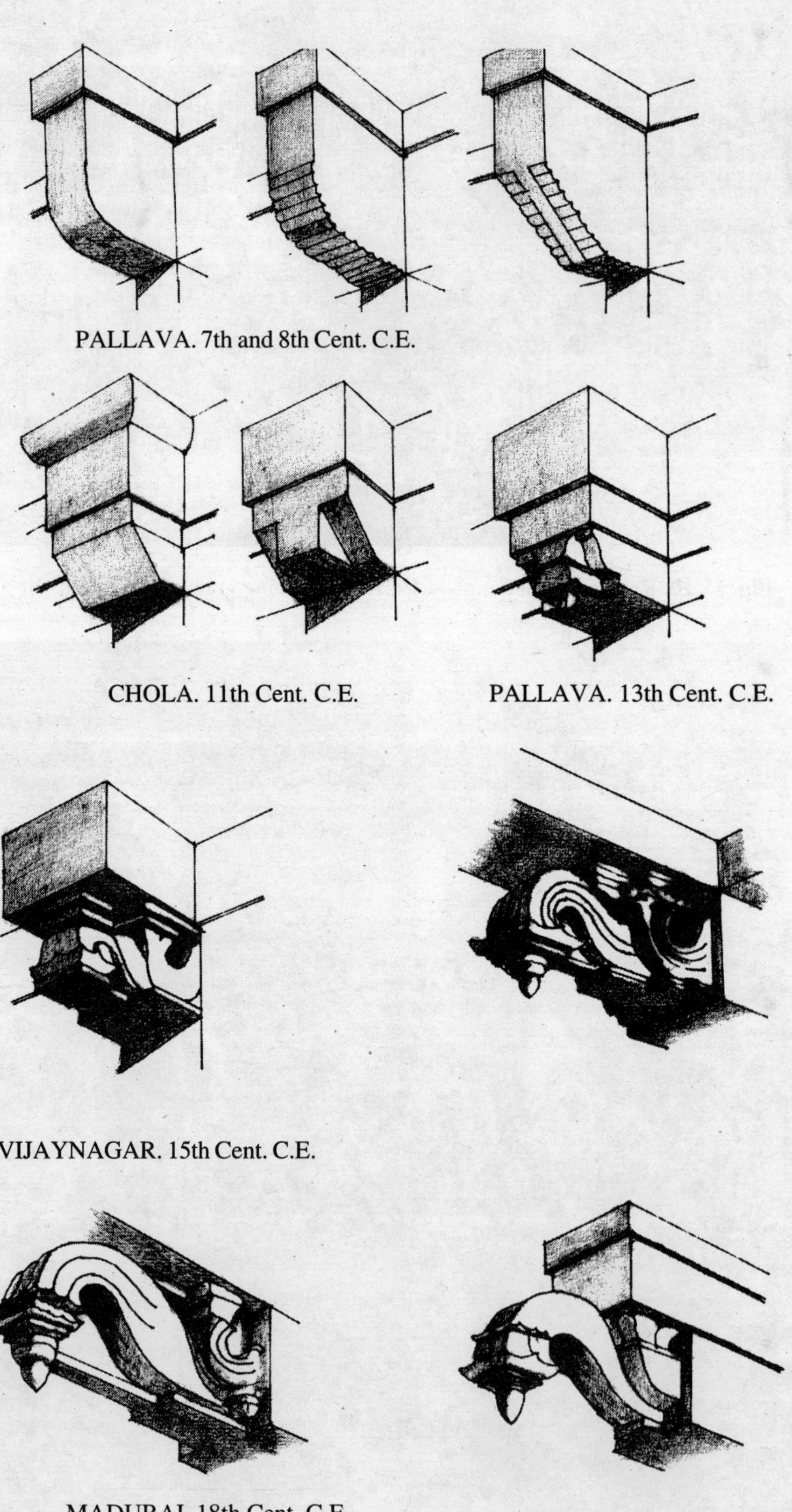

Fig. 11.12. Dravidian temple Brackets

12

Later Chalukyas or Hoysala Architecture

(1050 to 1300 C.E)

12.1. INTRODUCTION

Hoysala empire was prominent in South India in Karnataka state embracing the delta areas of Tamilnadu and south west Andhra Pradesh flourished in between 11th to 14th centuries. Hoysala kings originally hail from Malnad district in Karnataka state. Belur was the initial capital town and later moved to Halebid in Hassan district. Nripa Kama was the founder of Hoysala dynasty. There were active, social, cultural, economic and political activities.

Pandyas in Tamilnadu, Gurjars in Rajputana, Solankis in Gujarat (west), Yadavas in Maharashtra (central and Deccan) and Gangas in Orissa were the contemporaries and construction of temples in these areas were in progress. In 13th century C.E Delhi was under the reign of Sultatans of Slave dynasty and Islam constructions were in progress.

Religious trends influenced vigorous temple building activity in this area. About a hundred temples were now surviving in Malnad district.

The building art was already much nurtured early under Chalukya kings from 5th to 8th centuries. Under the patronage of Hoysala kings richly decorated and unique temples were built. However these temples resemble much like Dravidian temples, as the country is lying in South India, which is Dravidadesha. As the Dravidian temple structures mostly confined to present day Tamilnadu state, likewise the Chalukya Hoysala structures confine to Mysore state.

The temple architecture in this country is too distinctive, original, separate, decorative, creative and unique. The building craftsmen in these temples have created fine, most intrinsic, minute carvings and mouldings. The stone used in these temples was a greenish or bluish-black stone, which is a close textured stone, very tractable under the chisel and specially suitable to make minute carvings.

12.2. ARCHITECTURAL CHARACTERS

The distinct characters of these Hoysala temple structures are described here item wise.

1. Temple plan
2. Wall surfaces
3. Sikhara or tower
4. Order of pillars

1. Temple plan

The temple layout comprises a central structure within an enclosure. The surrounding walls support the pillared cloisters inside the compound.

The typical temple building is not rectangular in plan comprising row of compartments in an axis, which is usual and common in most Indian temples. Some temples have multiple sanctuaries. Hence the shapes of plans are varied much. The temple stands on a high raised terrace called Jagathi 2.7 metres in height. The basement terrace is much wider and spacious all-round the temple useful for processions and circumambulations.

Asthabhadra or stellate

The plan of these temples is distinctive and different. The walls of compartments intensely project or recede. They are elaborated into the shape of a star by means of a series of recesses and offsets. The Asthabhadra or stellate (like a star) plan is made by means of a geometrical combination of equal size squares, each with a common center but their diagonals vary by several degrees.

The main building has three compartments namely:

Mukhamandapa – an open pillared pavilion

Navaranga – pillared hall

Garbhagriha – cella

2. Wall surfaces

The walls are not at all plain. They are fully immersed, soaked and intoxicated in a carving world. It is all an elation, ecstasy and trance.

The horizontal emphasis in the treatment of walls is most striking. The basement terrace wall is not made of solid mouldings, but made up of number of bands containing continuous animated designs. These carved borders contain the following in rank.

– The lowest on the ground, a procession of elephants

– Then a border of Horsemen

– A band of spiral foliage

– Kirtimukh or sun-face (a grotesque mask)

Next in order is the most interesting of all, a continuous row of events selected from great epic stories. It is a picture-gallery in stone executed in great fine details. (Fig. 12.8)

Then above is the border of Yalis, scaly hippopotamic monsters

While at the top is a running pattern of Hamsas, a kind of goose or legendary bird

An Asana or sloping seat back above terminates the basement of the pillared hall. Rising above this are the exterior pillars of the hypostyle hall, the spaces in between the pillars filled by perforated stone screens fixed at a later stage. The Vimana structure has prominent stringcourse, one of the most typical features of the style.

3. Sikhara

The Sikhara is separated from its substructure by a wide projecting cornice or eave. The stellate projections were carried into the Vimana producing fluted effect in the tower. The upward swing is balanced by horizontal mouldings by means of diminishing tiers terminating at the apex in a low parasol-shaped finial. The horizontal and vertical pattern of the Sikhara consist of a complex grouping of miniature shrines and niches, each tier separated by sunk mouldings or ornamental string courses. The shape of the tower is slightly parabolic. It possesses fine beauty and rich sculptured texture.

4. Order of pillars

The order of pillars relates in many respects to Dravidian order. But the pillars took a special form owing to the mechanical process of monolithic long stone blocks by turning them on a large lathe, which has conditioned the design. This practice was most in use in this region. The stone was first roughly shaped to the required size and proportions and then mounted in an upright position on a wheel, on which the block was rotated against a chisel, set as a turning tool. A wondrous baluster like appearance was the result. Hence the pillar shafts are a series of rounded horizontal mouldings. The base and the pedestal are left square. In the capital the strut-like brackets were carved into images, here termed as Madanakai figures elaborately and richly carved. (Fig. 12.3)

12.3. EXAMPLES

The following important temples are selected for description.

1. Chennakesava temple at Belur, 1117 C.E
2. Hoysaleswara temple at Halebid, 1150 C.E
3. Kesava temple at Somanathpur, 1268 C.E

These temples are UNESCO's world heritage structures.

1. Chennakesava temple, Belur, 1117 C.E.

The temple of Belur exhibits unusual artistic merits, the construction of which was commissioned by the king Vishnu Vardhana in 1117 C.E. The temple was dedicated to lord Vishnu. It was built on a high and wide platform measuring 54 metres long by 48 metres wide. It consists of the following compartments.

– A Hypostyle hall called Navaranga having deeply recessed angles

– A stellate Vimana with a small square vestibule connecting the two compartments

Hypostyle hall (Navaranga)

The Hypostyle hall has three entrances, one each on three free sides approached by flight of steps flanked by a pagoda-like shrine. Inside dimensions of Navaranga hall are 28 metres by 24 metres. The main colonnades in the hall made two passages crossing each other in the middle of the hall forming a central nave. The cruciform passages leave spaces in the angles of the hall, in which smaller pillars were placed. The roof of the hall is plain. Wide inclined eaves surround the whole building. (Fig. 12.1, 12.2)

Pillars

The pillars are closely set and every part was overlaid with carving. Each group of four pillars supports beams above and created a sunken-coffered ceiling above, where the sculptors exhibited their great artistic ability. The total number of pillars is forty-six. Each pillar is different in its design. The variety of designs and complexity is astonishing. Each sculptor had created and contributed to the temple a specimen of his own design and handwork. (Fig. 12.3)

Narasimha pillar

One column in the middle of the hall is so unique in character that it was distinguished by the name Narasimha, the sculptor that made the pillar. The sculptor has carved its capital, shaft and base into a repeating pattern in niches in each of which is enshrined an image and has skillfully devised that the whole pillar could be rotated at will.

Sculpted perforated screens

The figure-subjects are elaborated and are made on perforated screens between the exterior pillars of Hypostyle hall. Such elaboration was not found elsewhere. There are 20 such screens, ten of which bear the illustrated stories from the Epics (Puranas) and the rest were carved geometrically treated in common. (Fig. 12.2)

Three elegant exterior shrines were attached to three projecting sides to the Vimana, which were now lost.

2. Hoysaleswara temple, Halebid, 1150 C.E

This is an outstanding temple monument situated within the walls of the ancient city of Darasamudra, which flourished as the capital City of Hoysala empire for about three centuries. It is now declined into a small hamlet called Halebid in Hassan District in Karnataka state, some 75 kilometres northwest of Mysore. The temple was built by king Vishnu Vardhana. (Fig. 12.4)

Plan

In this temple adjacent transepts connect two complete temples. The length of each is 34 metres and width about 30 metres with each a Nandi pavilion in the front. The main temple structure stands on a broad platform having angles corresponding to the buildings. The platform encircles the whole structure useful for processions.

The temple has usual compartments of pillared hall and attached sanctuary. The junction between the sanctuary and assembly hall is well built skillfully by profusely decorated buttresses. The sanctuary is stellate in plan with acute angular projections. The walls of main hall are at right angles.

Interior

The interior is congested and complex owing to closely set pillars. It is a four square group of pillars making nave and aisles by intersection. The shaft of the columns were carved and fluted. The capital supports a heavily figured Madanakai brackets.

Exterior

The entire exterior has continuous mouldings, borders, friezes, cornices and bands of statuary carried round the whole building. The average height of the exterior is only 7.5 metres.

Finest ornamentation

The plinth wall was carved into horizontal bands containing numerous figures like elephants, cavaliers and mystical motifs. Above this on the walls is the remarkable exposition of the whole company of Indra's heaven portrayed one after the other enshrined in niches and canopied by hanging foliage. The divine beings in the centre are framed with rich ornamental borders comprising repeating patterns of natural forms, conventional animals, scenes from myth and legend with infinite details. The central space of the wall is the main sculpture gallery each occupied by a minutely wrought, splendidly appareled, each figure half-life size in height. (Fig. 12.5)

On either side of the main entrance the statues of Dwarpala or doorkeepers in life size were elaborated into extravagantly fanciful creations. There are no words of any language that can describe the beauty and fineness of these intricately and richly decorated carvings of this temple. One must see, enjoy and understand the great designs made by the artisans, who dedicated their lives and left their mighty and tiresome work.

As a whole the temple of Halebid is the supreme climax of Indian temple architecture in its most plastic manifestation.

3. Kesava temple, Somanathpur, 1268 C.E

This is best preserved temple of Hoysala architecture. It was built by Somnatha a general in the army of king Narasimha III.

This is a most complete temple situated about thirty kilometers from Srirangapatnam in Karnataka state. The deity in the temple is lord Vishnu. The main temple placed in the middle of a rectangular courtyard measuring 66 metres by 54 metres surrounded by pillared cloisters containing 64 cells each with pillars in front. The temple is entered through a gateway on eastern side from where the entire temple can be seen at a glance. (Fig. 12.6)

Triple shrine temple

The plan of the temple is stellate shaped having a wide terrace platform serving as an Ambulatory. It contains the following compartments.

– A main pillared hall

– Three shrines on western end, one in axial alignment and the others were placed laterally. This is a triple shrine temple having three Sikharas termed as Trikutachala. (Fig. 12.9)

The pillared hall has two compartments.

– Mukhamandapa or front open pillared hall with 12 pillars

– Navaranga or middle hall with 4 pillars

A doorway in the middle of three sides leads to a vestibule or Sukhanasi each of which leads to the Cella. The pillars are elaborate and lathe-turned.

The temple stands on a high platform with striking horizontal mouldings following the stellate projections. The exterior of the walls and sikhares are embellished and finely proportioned as described earlier. The platform has the figures of elephants guarding the temple. The elephant figures were fully decorated with jewelry with chains and bells. Every part of the central wall space of the temple is inhabited by figures of deities. They appear in all their glory adorned with heavy jewels like bangles on arms, towering crowns and chunky anklets on their feet.

As a whole Hoysala temples are fine, intricate in carvings, highly creative with their richly adorned figures.

12.4. NAMES OF OTHER IMPORTANT TEMPLES

Amruteswara temple, Amruthapura, 1196 C.E

Viranaraya temple, Belavadi, 1200 C.E

Iswara temple, Arasikere, 1220 C.E

Lakshi Narayana temple, Nuggehalli, 1246 C.E

Lakshi Narayana temple, Hosaholalu, 1250 C.E

QUESTIONS

1. Explain brief introduction of Hoysala temple with respect to Geographical, Political and contemporary temples.
2. Describe the architectural characters of Hoysala temples.
3. Explain the planning and great ornamental features of Chenna Kesava temple, Belur.
4. Mention the names of three great temples of Hoysala architecture and describe any one temple.
5. Describe the great architectural characters of Hoysaleswara temple, Halebid.
6. Describe the architectural characters of Kesava temple, Somanathpur.
7. Explain the design and order of pillars of Hoysala temples. Sketch any one pillar.

Fig. 12.1. Chennakeshava Temple, Belur, 12th cent.C.E—Front view

Fig. 12.2. Chennekesava Temple, Belur —Details of Mouldings

Fig. 12.3. Chennakeshava temple, Belur—Ornate Lathe turned pillars

Fig. 12.4. Hoysaleswara Temple, Halebid, 1150 C.E

Fig. 12.5. Hoysaleswara temple—Wall Carvings

Fig. 12.6. Kesava temple, Somanathpur—front, 1268 C.E

Fig. 12.7. Kesava temple, Somanathpur—Stellate projections

Fig. 12.8. Kesava Temple, Somanathapur—Wall decoration

Fig. 12.9. Kesava temple, Somanathapur-Rear side Twin Sikharas

13

Northern or Indo-Aryan Architecture

Orissa (800 to 1250 C.E)

13.0. REGIONAL DIVISIONS

In northern areas of India, there is another movement of great style of architecture. This was designated as Northern or Indo-Aryan architecture. This is also called Nagara style. Unlike Dravidian architecture Indo-Aryan architectural development was not confined to a restricted area, but was spread over to more distant places in North India. Hence this part of architectural development is dealt geographically, which is convenient for division according to regions.

These regional developments may be classified mainly into six following divisions for study purpose.

1. Orissa	: (800 to 1250 C.E)
2. Khajuraho	: (950 to 1050 C.E)
3. Rajasthan	: (8th to 11 th cent. C.E)
4. Gujarat and the West	: (940 to 1310 C.E)
5. Maharashtra (the Deccan)	: (11th to 13th cent. C.E)
6. Gwalior	: (11th Century)
and Brindavan	: (16th century)

The above regional developments are separately described here chapter wise.

INDO ARYAN ARCHITECTURE—ORISSA

(800 TO 1250 C.E)

13.1. INTRODUCTION

Orissa has distinct and definite culture of its own. The other names to Orissa are Kalinga and Odissa. Bhaumakaras and Somavamsis played a major role in cultural development of Orissa upto 11th century. Gangas took over the country after Somavamsis. Gangas had their capital city at Cuttack in 12th century. They followed Vishnu faith. Orissa temples were out of threat from Islam rulers.

Simultaneously at this time, the temple buildings were in course of construction in other parts of north India at Khajuraho, Rajasthan, Gujarat and Maharashtra and in south temple constructions under Cholas and Pandyas in Tamilnadu and Hoysala temples in Karnataka were in progress.

Orissa had developed a separate architectural movement with defined characters. The main group of temples is concentrated in the city of Bhuvaneswar, the present capital city of Orissa state, where there are over thirty temples.

At some distance away from this city, are the most important and large temples namely Jagannath temple at Puri and the remains of the temple of Sun at Konark. The temple building activity persisted for about 4 ½ centuries from 9th century to 13th century C.E.

They were built in sandstone around an inner core of laterite. Sandstone was quarried in nearby Udaigiri and Khandagiri hills.

13.2. ARCHITECTURAL CHARACTERS

Orissa temple architecture was largely of an independent nature and the building art has separate and distinct nomenclature of its own. All the structures were built in stone. The temples are moderate in size except a few.

Plan

The temples are rectangular consisting of row of compartments standing in an axis with their sides parallel. The temple mainly consists of the following two compartments.

– Mandapa or Jagamohan – a square assembly hall in the front called Pida Deul

– Garbhagriha or Deul on the rear side, which is the sanctuary called Rekha Deul

The word Deul is employed to the shrine over Garbhagriha. These two edifices constitute the essentials of Orissa temples. As the style progressed and as the temple rituals were increasing, hence additional accommodation was found necessary and was added to the front of the assembly hall. These additional structures are:

– Natmandir or Natya mandir – Dancing hall or a festival hall

– Bhogmandir or Bhog mandapa – A hall of offerings

Examples: Names of few important temples which have the four compartments are:

Lingaraja temple, Bhuvaneswar

Jagannath temple, Puri

Externally the walls of these temples are made projected and recessed into offsets symmetrically. These offsets are carried from ground to the top in elevation as vertical segments. Inside the hall, the walls are plain. Each vertical segment is named as follows.

Rahapaga – The main middle or central projection

Anardhapaga – The projection adjacent to Rahapaga

Konakapaga – Corner projection

These segments are repeated symmetrically on the external sides of compartments and are skillfully adjusted at the juncture of compartments by adding a vestibule, so that the beauty, composition and symmetry are not disturbed. (Fig. 13.1)

Exterior

These structures were of one storey only and contain the following divisions from ground to the top. Jagamohan contains:

– Pista—the lower portion or basement or plinth

– Bada—the cubical vertical portion above Pista

– Pida—the pyramidal portion or the roof above Bada

Natya mandapa and Bhog mandapa also followed the same divisions.

In the same way, the Deul or Rekha Nagara tower contains – Pista and Bada and in addition it contains the following in its Sikhara.

– Chhapra—the middle paraboloidal portion

– Amla—the flat fluted solid disc at the summit

– Kalasha—the finial over Amla.

The Sikhara is made of cluster of vertical bands that bend inward making a tapering curve. It has the vertical panels of recessed offsets and was decorated by means of horizontal moulds and deep grooves. (Fig. 13.2)

Interior

A most remarkable characteristic feature of Orissa temple is the plain and unadorned interior walls contrasting with profusely ornamented walls of exterior. This difference can only be accounted for by the existence of some doctrine tradition, which the builders either followed or were compelled strictly to observe.

Pillars

Pillars are being notable by their absence. However some such structural support is necessary to sustain the heavy load of the pyramidal roof. Hence accordingly a group of four solid piers making a square in the hall and roof beams were laid.

13.3. EXAMPLES

Major numbers of temples of Orissa were grouped in the city of Bhuvaneswar, out of which the following important temples are selected for description here.

1. Parasrameswara temple, Bhuvaneswar, 8th cent. C.E
2. Vaital Deul, Bhuvaneswar, 850 C.E
3. Mukteswara temple, Bhuvaneswar, 975 C.E
4. Lingaraja temple, Bhuvaneswar, 1000 C.E
5. Rajarani temple, Bhuvaneswar, 13th cent, C.E
6. Jagannath temple, Puri, 1100 C.E
7. Sun temple, Konark, 1250 C.E

1. Parasrameswara temple, Bhuvaneswar, 8th cent. C.E

The oldest building of the entire series is the temple of Parasrameswara a small structure, built in 8th century C.E at Bhuvaneswar. The entire length is only 15 metres and it consists of:

– Jagamohan or Pillared hall on west also called Mukhasala

– Deul or Sanctuary on east

Entrance to the temple is on west side through Jagamohan. It is a low rectangular structure comprising the hall of the temple. This has a double roof and plain massive eaves. There is a doorway in each of its three sides and four perforated stone windows. Sanctuary walls are recessed and projected. (Fig. 13.3)

Interior

In the interior of Jagamohan there are two rows of pillars three in each row. The pillars have plain square shafts, volute bracket capitals and no bases. They supported a massive architrave raising the ceiling of the central nave higher than the aisles, thus forming a clerestory. The walls are perfectly plain with no carvings. The pilasters show vase and foliage decorative order, an ornamentation associated with Gupta's period. The cella is a dark square room.

Perforated stone windows

The two stone window grills on each side of the west door are of exceptional merit. They represent figures of young dancers and musicians with trumpet, flute and other instruments so grouped as to form a perforated stone window.

Exterior

The Sikhara over the Deul 13 metres high is rudimentary in its design containing a fluted Amlasila on its top. The walls on the exterior are richly decorated by means of horizontal moulds and deep grooves. The junction between pillared hall and the sanctuary shows that the two structures were built at different times. (Fig. 13.4, 13.5)

2. Vaital Deul, Bhuvaneswar, 850 C.E

The Vaital Deul temple was built around 850 C.E. The temple is dedicated to goddess Chamundi also named Mahishasura Mardini. It is a small building measuring 5.50 metres by 7.60 metres in plan and is strongly fine and beautiful. As usual it consists of two conventional compartments of Jagamohan and Deul. (Fig. 13.6)

Jagamohan

The Jagamohan is a rectangular structure in the front on eastern side. And embedded in each angle is a small supplementary shrine, making it a Panchayatana or five shrined temple. These small shrines are the replicas of main Vimana of the temple in mini size. The roof of Jagamohan is in two levels leaving clerestory ventilators.

Deul

The design of Deul tower is different and is not in Nagara style. This is more allied to southern style as exemplified in Dravidian Gopurams. A wide body pyramidal structure rises over the rectangular cella. Its elongated vaulted roof in two storeys with its ridge finials and Chaitya arch gable ends are expressive elements of Buddhist style. The proportions of the tower, balanced arrangement of its parts, architectural decoration are most satisfying and denote a highly trained aesthetic experience. This specially applies to plain shallow buttresses placed around the vertical (Bada) portion. Such similar wide body Sikhara is found in the temple of Teli ka Mandir built at Gwalior in 11th century C.E.

Foliated gable

In the front face of the Deul tower, there is an elegant foliated gable, in the form of Buddhist Chaitya arch containing Tandava (dancing) Siva motif within a circular panel in place of sun window. This is a decorative element of fine mastery.

3. Mukteswara temple, Bhuvaneswar, c.975 C.E

This small temple was situated with number of others on the outskirts of the city of Bhuveneswar. The temple was probably built about 975 C.E. This is a richly finished structure ornamented with fascinating carvings. The elements of this temple are a considerable advance over Parasrameswara temple and Vaital Deul. (Fig. 13.8)

Plan

The temple consists of a sanctuary or Deul on east side and an assembly hall or Jagamohan attached to the Deul with one entrance on west side. The temple is 13.7 metres long, 7.6 metres wide and its tower is hardly 10.7 metres high. It is also exceptionally well proportioned and its parts are skillfully adjusted and it readily attracts the viewers. No pillars are there in Jagamohan. The solid walls of the Jagamohan are carrying the entire load of the pyramidal roof.

Exterior

The roof of Jagamohan is a low stepped pyramidal roof. This was elegantly proportioned and made. The Deul is the usual design of Orissa sikhara with its projecting and recessed vertical panels decorated with horizontal moulds and deep grooves and surmounted by Amlasila and Kalasa. (Fig. 13.9, 13.10)

Torana

An exceptional structure in this temple is the Torana in front of the temple. This detached portal has two solid piers supporting a semicircular arch the whole very gracefully proportioned with exquisite carvings. Such similar Torana is seen in Sun temple at Modhera, Gujarat state built in 11th century C.E. (Fig. 13.11)

An artificial water tank is lying behind the temple. It has paved steps on all sides. The temple is a rare example of Orissa group, which has sculptured decoration in its interior.

4. Lingaraja temple, Bhuvaneswar, 1000 C.E

The largest temple of Bhuvaneswar city is the Lingaraja temple dedicated to lord Siva. It ranks as one of the foremost architectural productions of the country. The temple was built in 11th century C.E by the king Jagati (Yayati) Kesari who shifted the capital from Jaipur (Jeypore) to Bhuvaneswar. It was built near vast Bindu Sagar Lake.

The temple occupies the centre of a large quadrangular enclosure measuring 160 metres long and 142 metres wide contained within a high and solid wall of some 2.30 metres thick on the inner face of which is a platform. With in the enclosure around 150 subsidiary chapels and shrines have been grouped around the main temple. The temple was built in laterite stone.

Plan

The main temple building consists of four structures which comprises a fully developed temple from front namely:

1. Bhogmandapa — Hall of offerings
2. Natyamandapa — Dancing hall or Festival hall
3. Jagamohan — Hall for assembly of people
4. Deul or Srimandir — Main shrine

These compartments are placed in the same axis, which extends from west to east with Bhogmandapa on east and Srimandir on west. The temple originally had only two compartments containing Jagamohan and Srimandir. The two other halls were added probably a century or more later. (Fig. 13.12)

Jagamohan

The Jagamohan is an oblong structure measuring 22metres long and 17 metres wide. Four large piers are placed inside to carry the heavy load of the pyramidal roof. There are four doors each in the center of four sides. Externally its lower storey or Bada is 10.4 metres high over which raises the substantial roof in the shape of a stepped pyramid. The lower part of the pyramid are square and stepped, the upper part round and fluted, the whole attaining the height of 30.5 metres from the ground.

Srimandir

The most impressive and dominating part of this temple is the great tower of Srimandir. It measures 17 metres square at its base and rises to a height of 55 metres. Its elevation contains the following from bottom to top.

– Vertical portion consisting of Pista (plinth) and Bada (the cubical portion) which is approximately 1/3 of the height of the tower
– Inward curved cube namely the Chhapra, whose treatment is distinguished from the lower cubical portion
– Fluted Amlasila
– Whole being crowned by a vase shaped finial or Kalasha bearing the Trisula- the trident of Lord Siva

The tower has clusters of vertical bands that bend inward to make a tapering. It is richly decorated by means of horizontal moulds and deep groves. A prominent projection on each side of the tower is the figure of a Lion crushing down an elephant. With in the tower is the Cella 5.8 metres square. (Fig. 13.13)

Additional halls

The additional halls of Natmandapa and Bhogmandapa although belonging to the later date are much in the same style as the Jagamohan. These compartments were added in front of Jagamohan within the axis. Each hall has a group of four massive piers inside to support the solid mass of the roof. (Fig. 13.14, 13.15)

There are small window openings in the massive walls containing row of uprights at close intervals. These uprights carry a luxurious female figure on its shaft.

The exterior of these structures is too richly decorated but at the same time, the interior is entirely devoid of ornamentation. The outer walls have the figures of birds, animals, floral motifs, human figures, gods and goddesses.

The great Lingaraja temple is still standing gracefully in its sobriety and dignity exhibiting the greatness of the patrons, designers and the workers who built it.

5. Rajarani temple, Bhuvaneswar, 13th cent. C.E

One of the graceful and elegant Orissa temples is the Rajarani temple built in 13th century C.E. Rajarani name was arrived from a local red gold coloured stone called Rajramiya, which was used in construction of this temple. There is no deity in the sanctuary. It is believed that the temple was built to Lord Siva. But some believe that it was built to Lord Brahma. The design of temple is a departure from other temples of Orissa group. It comprises the Deul (Sanctuary) and Jagamohan (Assembly hall).

Diagonal plan

The plan of the Deul is not parallel to the rest of the building, but was placed diagonally. Such an arrangement is an exception in the temples of Orissa, where the sides of all compartments are in the same alignment. The walls are projected and recessed both outside and inside creating vertical bands. (Fig. 13.16)

Similar to Khajuraho temples

A close similarity is found in the Sikhara to the temples of Khajuraho of Central India containing attached shrine bands (Urusringas). The Deul is practically complete and displays a refinement in its curves and contours denoting a change in building art. There are no pillars inside. Roof of Jagamohan is a low pyramidal type. (Fig. 13.17, 13.18)

6. Jagannath temple, Puri, 1100 C.E

This is the famous, notable and an appreciably larger building than the Lingaraja temple of Bhuvaneswar constructed in 1100 C.E at Puri, a seacoast town on Bay of Bengal sea in Orissa state. Choda Gangadeva built this temple at Puri. Built on the same principle of Lingaraja and consists of four edifices in one alignment. (Fig. 13.19)

Plan

The temple stands with in a spacious courtyard surrounded by a high wall forming a rectangle 134 metres long 107 metres wide. The main building is in the centre and distributed over the remaining area are some 30 or 40 edifices of various shapes and sizes. Originally the temple comprises only the Sanctuary and an Assembly hall. Later the Natmandir and Bhogmandir were added in 14th or 15th centuries. The entire length of these four buildings in a line is 94 metres with a width of 24 metres, while the tower is nearly 61 metres in height.

Exterior

The tower is a massive structure with its impressive proportions and profuse ornamentation. Puri temple tower is the replica of its predecessor Lingaraja temple. From this it is understood that Orissa architecture continued to be a moving and living art. The tower is some 61 metres in height, which is the highest tower in entire India. Other such higher tower examples are

- Brihadeswara temple, Tanjore, 60 metres in height built in 1010 C.E
- Gol Gumbaz, Bijapur, 61 metres high built around 1660 C.E

The profuse ornamentation to Natmandir and Bhogmandir is stiff and stylized. During renovations and restorations, cement was applied to the stone surfaces. This made the structure heavy and stiff and the beauty of original stone work is concealed. The Natmandir a large building of some 24 metres side has its ceiling supported on 16 pillars in 4 rows of 4 each.

The outer compound walls were added later around the whole of the temple with entrance gateways in the center of each side having pyramidal roofs.

7. Sun temple, Konark, 1250 C.E

The Sun temple is dedicated to Surya, the Sun god built at Konark on the Bay of Bengal seacoast some 30 kilometres away from Puri in Orissa state. This was built in the reign of king Narasimha Deva of Ganga dynasty around 1250 C.E. This is now UNESCO's world heritage site.

The site measures 264 metres long by 165 metres wide, having a compound wall containing entrance gateways on three sides except on west. The temple was built like a huge Ratha or a giant chariot being drawn by seven horses on twelve pairs of exquisitely carved giant wheels. The base of the structure is an immense terrace with 12 giant wheels on each side, each nearly 3 metres high. In the front is wide flight of steps, the sides of which were richly carved with the figures of horses. (Fig. 13.20, 13.24)

The main temple building consists of two compartments.

- Jagamohan
- Deul

Jagamohan

The Jagamohan is a large hall of 30 metres side and 30 metres high. It is a square hall having four solid piers inside. The ceiling of the hall is remarkable as it was corbelled out by means over sailing courses of masonry each course projecting beyond the one below thus enabling the sides to converge gradually towards the crown. Many precautions were taken to sustain the heavy load of pyramidal roof. They are:

- Stone lintels were introduced tying the piers
- Each Laterite stone lintel was reinforced by number of wrought iron beams

In spite of these precautions, the structure was slowly crumbling due to the heavy load of the pyramidal roof. Hence the hall was made inaccessible and filled with rubble inside at a later stage to prevent the corbelled roof from collapsing down to save the magnificent monument.

Blocks of Laterite stone were used in construction. The courses of Laterite are not bonded with mortar but they are held together mainly by a system of counter balancing the weight. (Fig. 13.21)

Exterior of Jagamohan

Externally it consists of two main elements, a Bada or cubical portion and a pyramidal superstructure. Proportions are well balanced in this structure. The width of the Bada is twice to its own height and the entire width is equal to its height.

Its great appearance lies in the treatment of pyramidal roof. The pyramidal roof consists of three tiers diminishing as they ascend. The wide spaces between each stage opens into platforms to accommodate number of boldly sculptured groups of statuary of heroic size. Each of these tiers are stepped, the two lower with six and upper most with five string courses producing a pattern of horizontality of utmost architectural value. Above this, the apex is a massive circular finial moulded and fluted a contrast to the square portion below. (Fig. 13.22, 13.23)

Exterior was too richly decorated to all the above buildings but at the same time the interiors are left completely plain. Out of many figures the erotic Mithuna art figures were also presented on the walls. Similar voluptuous figures are seen in Khajuraho temples also.

Deul

On the western side is the great sanctuary tower over the cella believed to have been built to a great height of some 68 metres high from the ground which is 4 metres less than Qutb minar, Delhi. But this great tower has disappeared. The vertical portion (Bada) is remaining now. It was probably an advance over the Lingaraja tower. At the base of the Deul three subsidiary shrines were attached with the statue of the deity. The massive tower could not be completed owing to its huge size, which started sinking and was crumbled. Hence the temple was abandoned. Some believe that Islam rulers desecrated the Sikhara. Had the tower completed and exists now, it would be the highest temple Sikhara in whole of India.

Natmandir

The other most important building is the Natmandir confronting the main entrance to the temple but separated from it by an interval of 9 meteres. The Natmandir resembles the same design like Jagamohan with its Bada and pyramidal portion, but the roof is now disappeared. (Fig. 13.20)

Figure Carving

Every part of the temple was intricately decorated in sculptures of unsurpasing beauty and grace ranging from miniature to monumental. The carved images include the deities, celestials, human musicians, dancers, lovers, scenes of courtly life like hunts, military battles, pleasures, birds, animals, lively elephants, mythological creatures, intricate botanical and geometrical decorative designs. Myriad figures of humans, animals and divine personages are exhibited engaged in full festivity.

The great writer Sri Rabindranath Tagore remarked on this temple- 'Here the language of stone surpasses the language of man'.

Miscellaneous Structures

There are the remains of an incomplete temple which is also a Sun temple built in southwest corner within the compound.

13.4. NAMES OF OTHER IMPORTANT TEMPLES:

- Ananta Vasudeva temple, Bhuvaveswar, 1278 C.E
- Maitreswara temple, Bhuvaveswar
- Makareswara temple, Bhuvaveswar
- Paramguru temple, Bhuvaveswar
- Papanasini temple, Bhuvaveswar
- Siddheswara temple, Bhuvaveswar
- Sisireswara temple, Bhuvaveswar

QUESTIONS

1. **Describe architectural characters along with nomenclature used in Orissa temples. Sketch plan and elevation of a typical Orissa temple and name the parts.**
2. **Explain Parasrameswara temple, Bhuvaneswar with respect to its planning and architectural characters.**
3. **What are the special features of Vaital Deul, Bhuvaneswar. Explain its plan and elevation features.**
4. **Describe the specific architectural features of Mukteswara temple, Bhuvaneswar.**
5. **Name the largest temple of Bhuvaneswar city and explain its plan and architectural features. Sketch its plan and side elevation.**
6. **Which temple in Bhuvaneswar had a diagonally attached Sanctuary. Describe its plan and Sikhara.**
7. **What is the name of the famous temple of Puri. Describe its planning and architectural features.**
8. **Name the great temple of Konark, Orissa. Describe its plan, elevation and ornamental features in detail. Sketch the Jagamohan elevation.**

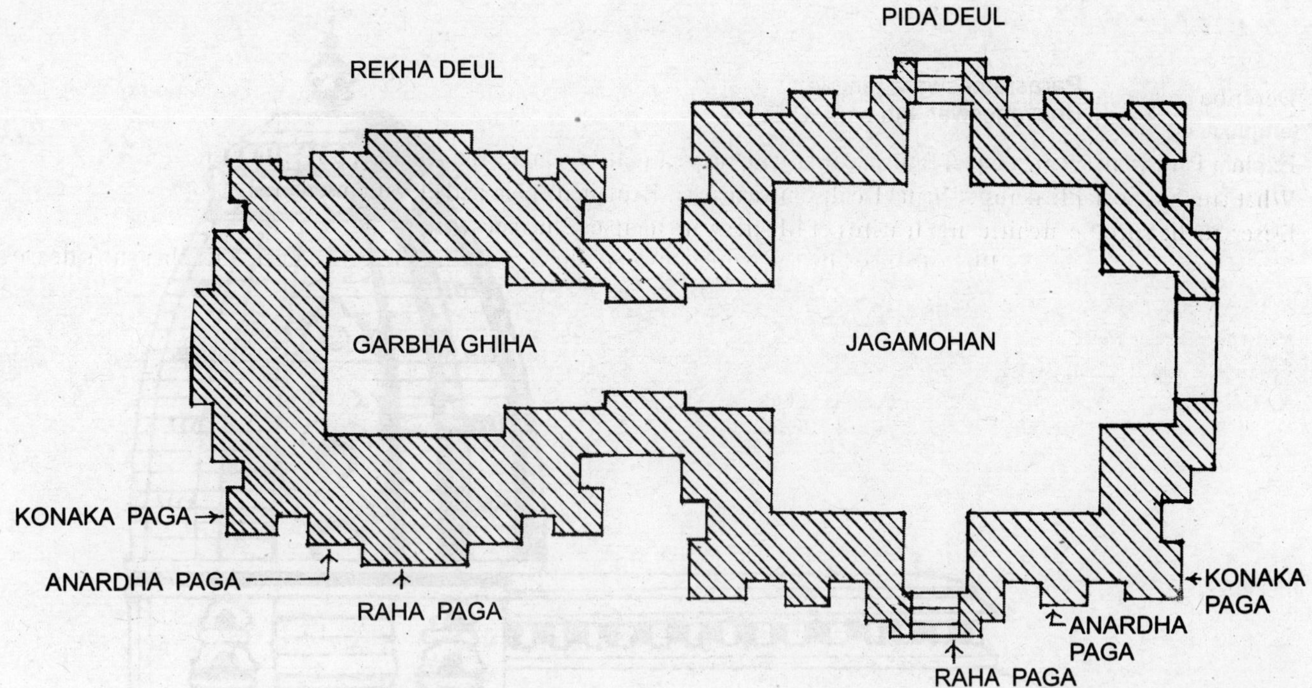

Fig. 13.1. Orissa temple—Typical Plan

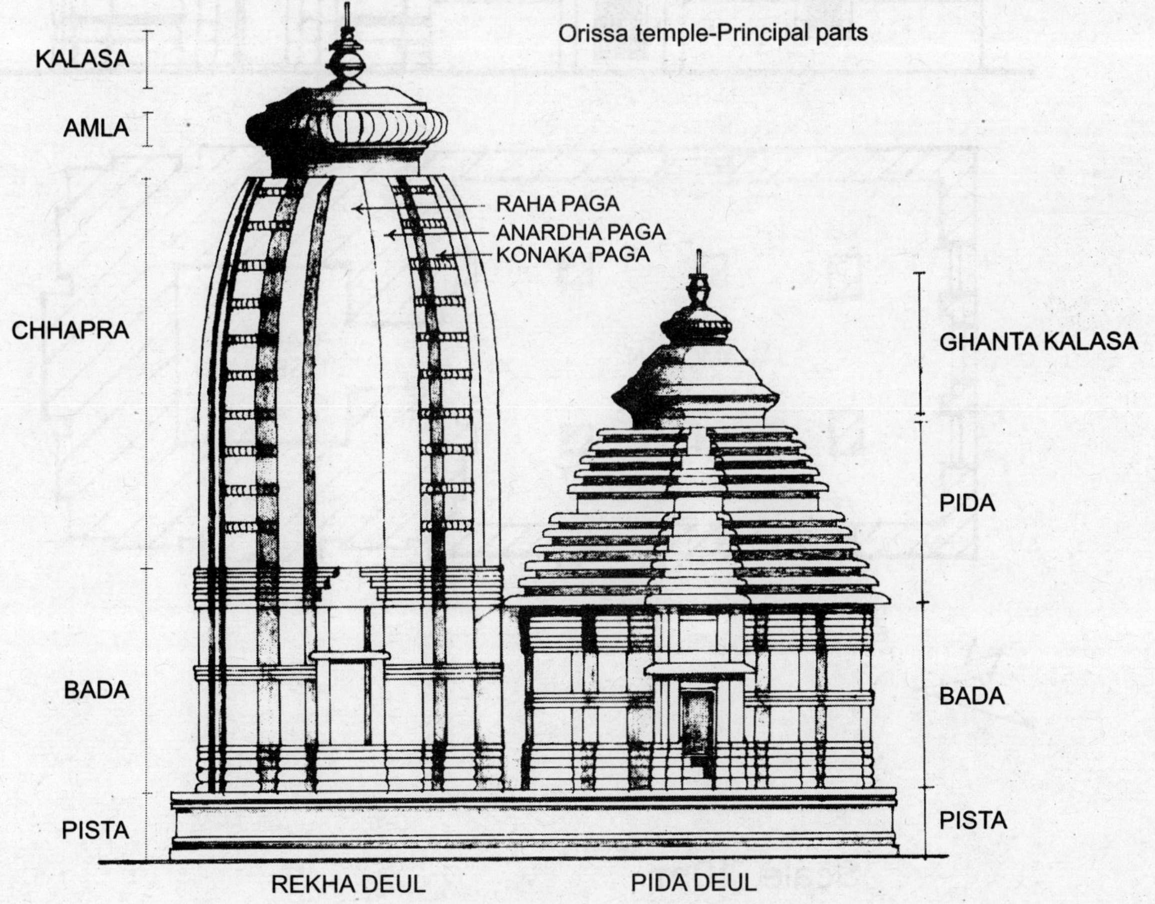

Fig. 13.2. Orissa temple, Typical side elevation

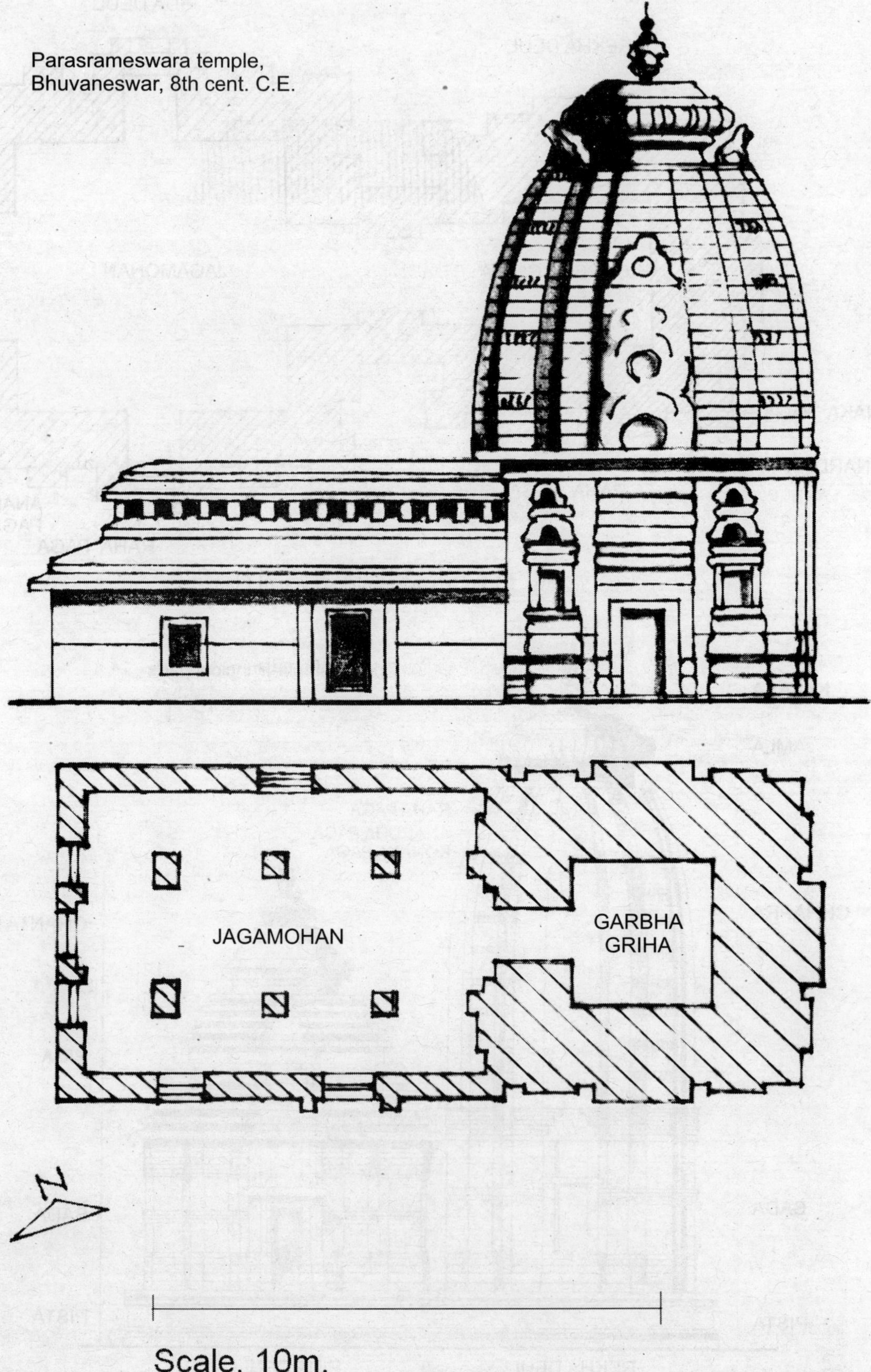

Fig. 13.3. Parasrameswara temple, Bhuvaneswar—Plan and Side elevation

Fig. 13.4. Parasrameswara temple, Bhuvaneswar—view, 8th cent.C.E

Fig. 13.5. Parasrameswara temple—Wall carvings

Fig. 13.6. Vaital Deul, Bhuvaneswar, 850C.E

Fig. 13.7. Vaital Deul, Bhuvaneswar—Side

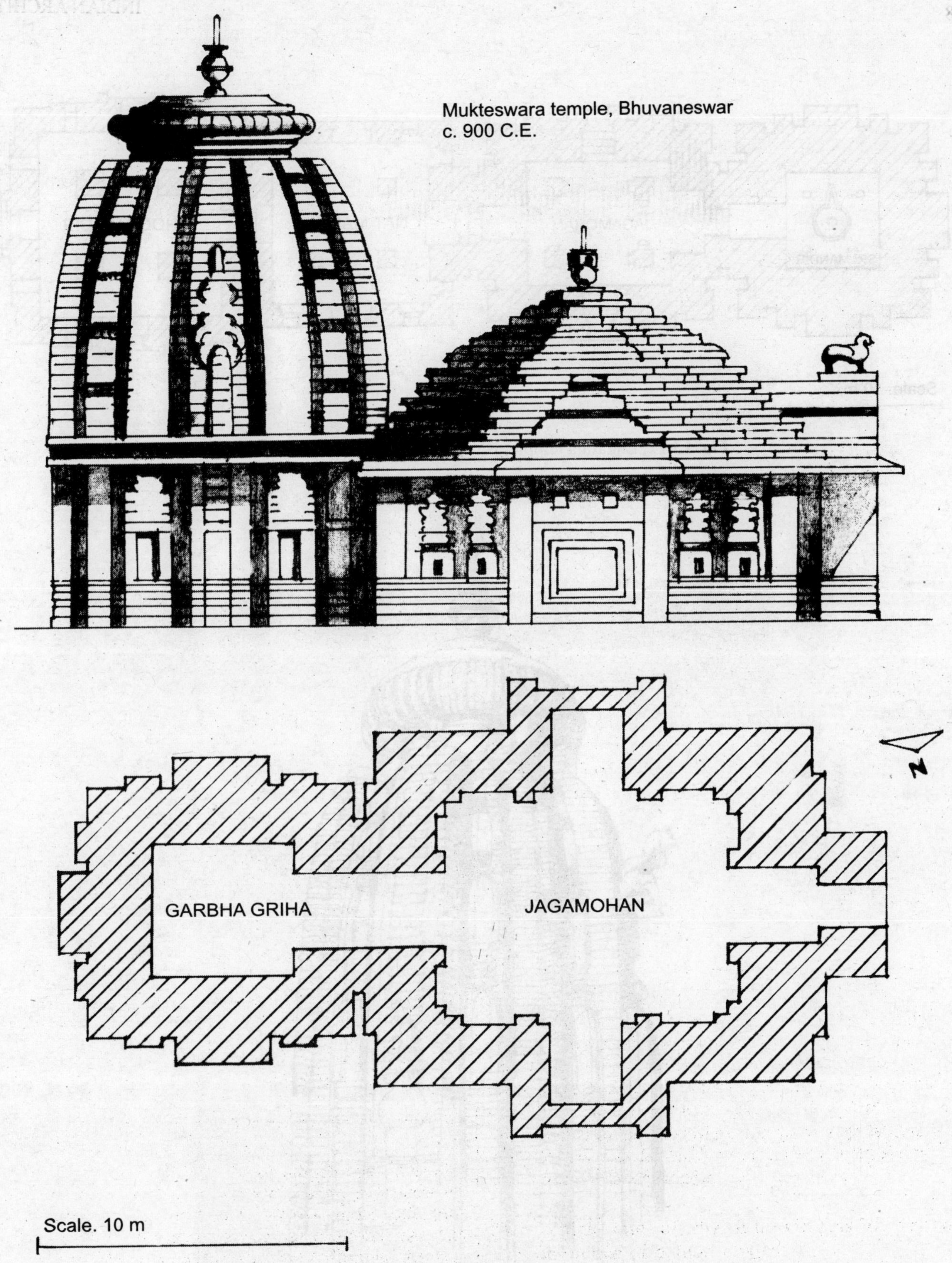

Fig. 13.8. Mukteswara temple, Bhuvaneswar, C.900C.E—Plan and Side elevation

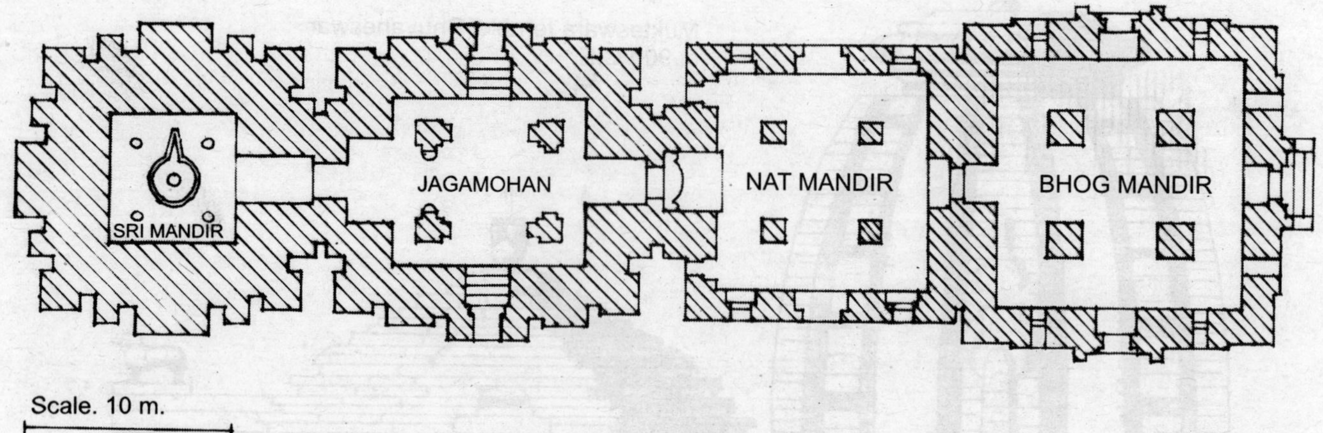

Fig. 13.12. Lngaraja temple, Bhuvaneswar C. 1000 C.E.—Plan

Fig. 13.13. Lingaraja temple—Sikhara

Fig. 13.9. Mukteswara temple, Bhuvaneswar

Fig. 13.10. Mukteswara temple, Bhuvaneswar—View from lake

Fig. 13.11. Mukteswara temple—Torana

Fig. 13.14. Lingaraja temple, Bhubaneswar—View from North-east, 1000 C.E

Fig. 13.15. Lingraja temple, Bhuvaneswar—Main temple and other subsidiary shrines

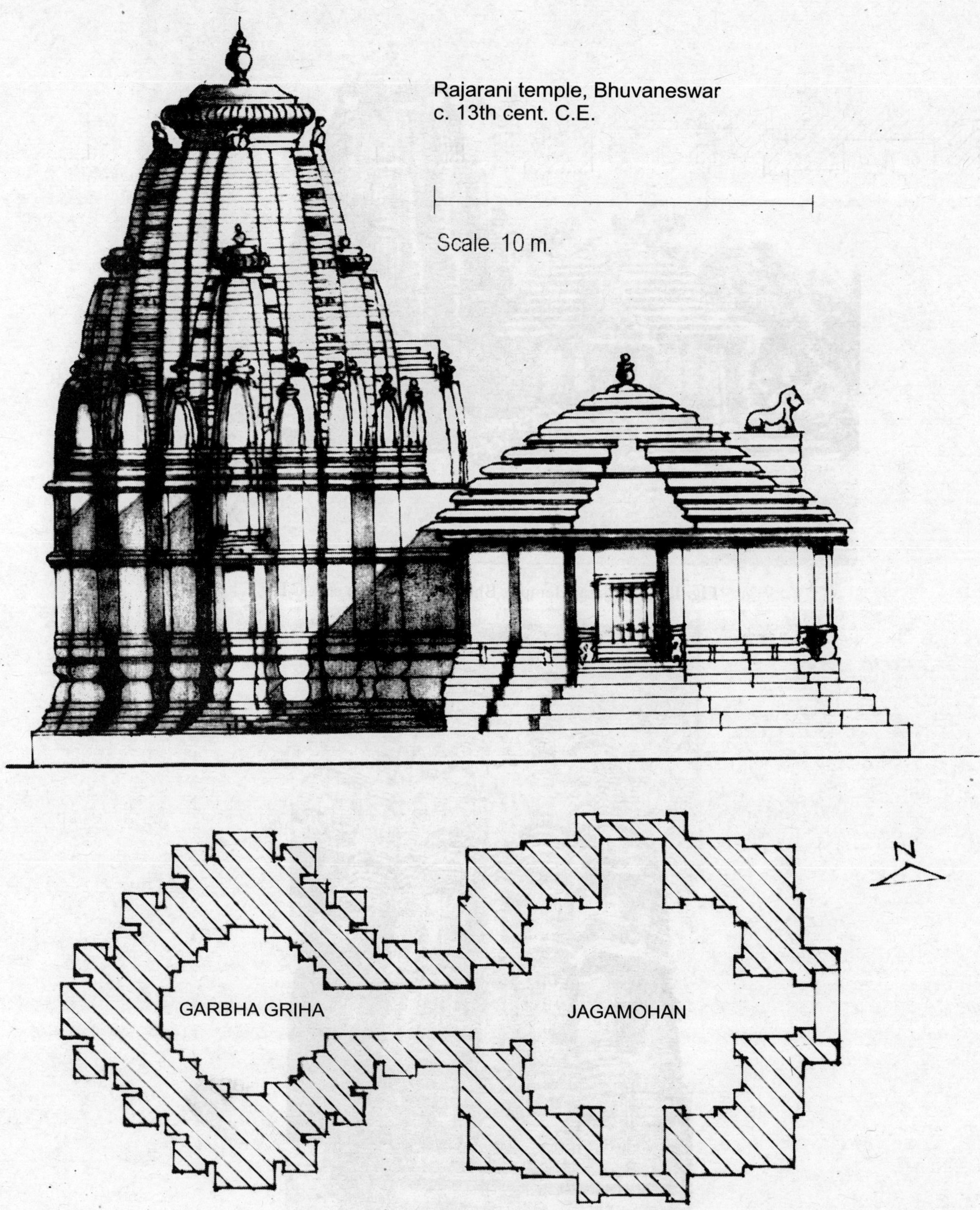

Fig. 13.16. Rajarani temple, Bhuvaneswar—Plan and Side elevation

Fig. 13.17. Rajarani temple, Bhuvaneswar, 13th cent.C.E

Fig. 13.18. Rajarani temple—view of sikhara

Fig. 13.19. Jagannath temple, Puri—view, 1100C.E

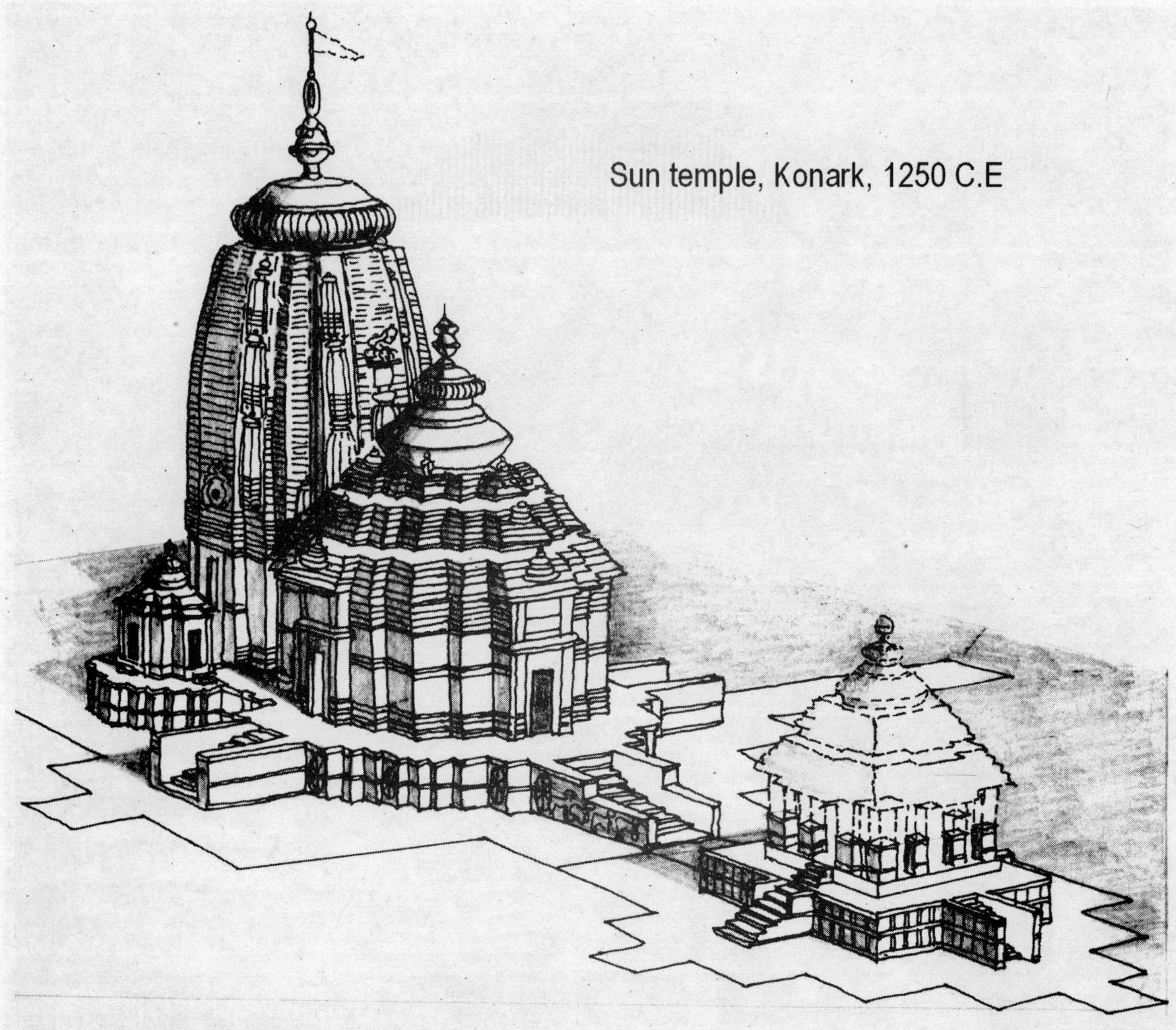

Fig. 13.20. Sun temple, Konark—Sketch view

Fig. 13.21. Sun temple, Konark, Jagamohan—front

Fig. 13.22. Sun temple, Jagamohan—Pyramidal roof

Fig. 13.23. Sun temple, Konark—Jagamohan view

Fig. 13.24. Sun temple, Konark—Wheel

14

Indo-Aryan Architecture

Khajuraho (950 to 1050 C.E)

14.1. INTRODUCTION

The most refined, elegant and excellent style of Indo-Aryan architecture is found in a group of temples at Khajuraho situated in Chatarpur district of Madhya Pradesh state in central India. Khajuraho is situated some 150 kilometres southeast of Jhansi. Actual name of Khajuraho is Khajur vahaka. Khajur means date palm.

These temples have with stood the effects of climate, threat from Mohammedan rulers and neglect for about thousand years. Even then they are standing in solitude in good condition. Important temples are spread within an area measuring around one and half kilometers. They were built within 100 years from 950 to 1050 C.E during the supremacy of Chandela Rajaputs, a dynasty notable for its structural productions. Chandelas' capital city was Kalinjar and later moved to Mahoba. There is no regular worshipping in most of these temples except a few. The temples are standing mute to the regular international visitors. Out of a total of 80 temples some 22 temples remained now.

The temples are the pinnacle of Hindu art and sculpture. They inspire the emotions of awe and wonder. Every surface is sculpted and ornamented. The figures on the walls are sinuous, twisting, voluptuous, human and divine, hunt, feast, dance and love without any false modesty. There are some erotic figures to which various theories have been explained. One such theory is to show the dispassion, detachment and emptiness of human desire.

The contemporary temples under construction were in Tamilnadu, Orissa, Rajaputana, Gujarat, Maharastra and Gwalior.

Khajuraho is now an important UNESCO's world heritage site.

14.2. ARCHITECTURAL CHARACTERS

The temples of Khajuraho show definite individual architectural characters different from that in any part of the country. Instead of being contained with in a customary enclosure wall, each temple stands on a high solid masonry terrace. There were no enclosure walls. None of the temple is of any great size. The largest is only slightly over 31 metres in length. The temples are like solid sculptural showcase pieces carved in fine details.

Plan

On the ground, the compartments were built in an axis from east to west, the sole entrance being on east and the temple looking towards east in most cases. But some temples have entrance on west. The temple has three main compartments from front to rear. (Fig. 14.7)

1. Portico or Artha Mandapa
2. Assembly hall or Mandapa

3. Cella or Garbha Griha

The temple has only one entrance approached by a single tall flight of steps raising steeply owing to the excessive height of the plinth but increasing its dignity. Through the door way one entrance porch expands into a rectangular portico (Artha Mandapa) the whole with open sides. The roof was carried on pillars. It contains sloping seat backs (Asana). Next one is Mandapa a square compartment with four pillars in the center connected with balcony windows opening outside. Next is the vestibule or Antarala leads to the Cella door. The more developed temples have the transepts or Mahamandapa together with a processional passage surrounding the Cella.

Exterior

The intention of the builders is to raise the building to a more height. The building resolves vertically into the following three main parts.

1. High solid Basement
2. The dark intermediate portion
3. Grouping of roofs

The high solid basement contains continuous horizontal moulded layers projected or recessed following the offsets of the basement. Over this basement at a higher level the intermediate portion consists of a range of horizontal window openings. These are bringing in light and air making a vivid band of dark shadow around the whole temple. Above these openings a wide eave or chajja overhangs the whole. The intermediate dark and void portion has been striking in between the solid top and bottom portions. Interior as well as exterior was too richly decorated with statuary moulds in dimensions rather less than half life-size. In Kandariya Mahadev temple there are some 650 statues.

Roofs

A separate roof distinguishes each compartment. The smallest and the lowest is the portico. Next in height came the central hall. Next one is the tallest Sikhara in a raising line. Unlike the Orissa roof which is pyramidal, these roofs are domical in contour. (Fig. 14.1)

Urusringas

The Sikhara has projections and recesses called Urusringas (Miniature Sikharas or Sikhara stripes) added to the main shrine, which are the principal elements of beauty to the shrine. Urusringas are the decorative vertical offset bands attached to the main central body of the Sikhara each crowned by Amalasila ans Kalasha. They act as buttresses supporting the Sikhara. (Fig. 14.8, 14.9)

Best example:

Kandaria Mahadev temple

14.3. EXAMPLES

Kandaria Mahadev temple, Khajuraho, 1000 C.E

The largest and finest temple of Khajuraho group is Kandaria Mahadev temple, a Siva temple standing in a row on western line with entrance on east side.

Plan

The temple measures 33 metres long, 20 metres wide externally at its floor. It has the compartments namely the portico, main hall, transepts, vestibule, sanctum and ambulatory. (Fig. 14.7)

Exterior

The structure stands on a high broad terrace with space all round which is approached by single tall flight of steps rising steeply. The base of the temple is 3.9 metres high rose upwards steeply in slope and was terminated by a parapet. On the inner side of the parapet are the inclined seat backs (Asana). Above this there are horizontal window openings presenting a dark void portion in the solid mass of the temple. A wide eave or chajja projects above these openinigs overhanging the whole. The gable roofs rise over these eaves. A separate roof distinguishes each compartment raising in a row upto the Sikhara. The lowest is over the portico and the highest is over the Sikhara rising to a height of 36 metres above the ground. Some of the turrets that rise from the base are carried up to the roof. There are two transepts projected in the form of balconies to the ambulatory. (Fig. 14.1)

The arrangement of compartments affected the shape and appearance of the exterior, which is an effective combination of lines, masses, bold projections and recedings.

The walls are too richly decorated and immersed in statuary moulds less than half size. There are over 650 statues in this temple. The combinations of horizontal and vertical elements, the dark intermediate portion, the projecting eaves and the turrets (Urusringas) are all superbly combined. (Fig. 14.1, 14.2)

Sikhara

Sikhara is unique in its design raising high from the body of the temple. It is Nagara type having curved surfaces added with Urushringas making it excellent in beauty. Above the Sikhara at the apex are Amalaka and Kalasha making an end. (Fig. 14.1, 14.8)

14.4. OTHER IMPORTANT EXAMPLES

The following temples were built in two lines both Vaishnavite and Sivite shrines standing side by side.

1. *Viswanath temple*: Measuring on the ground 27 metres by 14 metres having double transepts and has small supplementary shrines at each of four corners making it Panchayatana or five-shrines type of temple.
2. *Chaturbhuji temple*: Measuring 26 metres by 13 metres built in 1080 AD. And has small supplementary shrines at each corner of the platform, making it an example of Panchayatana or five-shrived type of temple.
3. *Devi Jagadambi temple*: Measuring 23 metres by 15 metres has only one pair of transepts and has four compartments, the Ardha-mandapa or portico consisting of only one chamber and there is no processional passage round the cella. (Fig. 14.4)
4. *Chatr-ko-patr*: Dedicated to Surya, the Sun god measuring 27 metres by 18 metres, has only one pair of transepts.
5. Lakshman temple: Built on a terrace and having shrines at four corners. (Fig. 14.5)
6. *Jain temples*: They were grouped together and they are six in number. These temples are usual type and are standing on plinth of normal height and has enclosure wall. They do not have the intermediate void portion.

QUESTIONS

1. Describe the location, political position and brief note on Khajuraho temples.
2. Explain the planning and architectural characters of Khajuraho temples.
3. Name the great temple of Khajuraho and explain its architectural features.
4. Sketch the plan and side elevation of Kandaria Mahadev temple of Khajuraho.
5. Sketch the Sikhara of Khajuraho temple.

Fig. 14.1. Kandariya Mahadev temple, Khajuraho—view, 1000 C.E

Fig. 14.2. Kandaria Mahadev temple —Endless figure carvings

Fig. 14.3. Khajuraho temple— Figure carvings

Fig. 14.4. Devi Jagadamba temple, Khajuraho, 11th cent. C.E

Fig. 14.5. Lakshmana temple, Khajuraho, 11th cent. C.E—Panchayatana class

Fig. 14.6. Adinath temple, Khajuraho

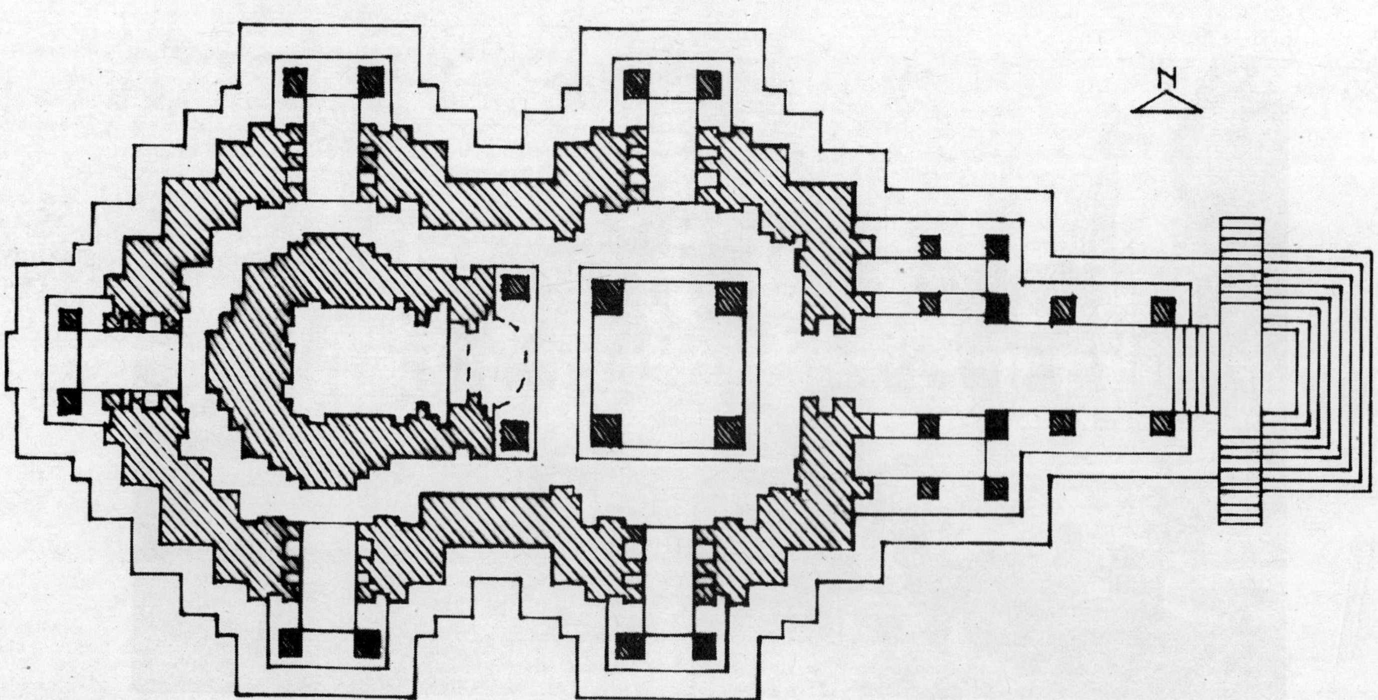

Fig. 14.7. Kandaria Mahadev temple, Khajuraho, C. 1000 C.E.—Plan

Fig. 14.8. Kanadaria Mahadev temple, Khajuraho, 1000C.E—Sikhara Sketch

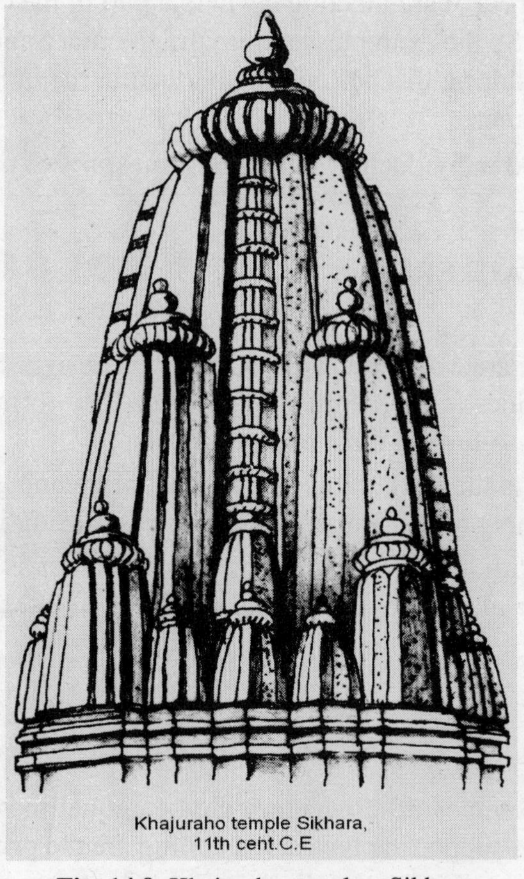

Khajuraho temple Sikhara,
11th cent.C.E

Fig. 14.9. Khajuraho temple—Sikhara

15

Indo-Aryan Architecture

Rajaputana (8th to 13th Cent. C.E)

15.1. INTRODUCTION

A development of great beauty in the art of temple building expressed in parts of Rajaputna and central India from 8th to 11th century C.E at Osia. Osia is situated some 60 kilometres northwest of Jodhpur city in Rajasthan state. It was a major religious center during Gurjara Pratihara dynasty. During this time other contemporary temples in south and north India were in course of construction.

Unfortunately much of the fine form of architecture lay in that part of the country which suffered most from the earlier invasions of Mohammedans. So the examples are rare, fragmentary and destroyed. Fine quality of carvings and pillars produced in the temples during this period may be seen in the buildings of Qutb Mosque at Delhi and Arhai-din ka Jhompra mosque at Ajmer.

The temples show originality and individuality in their design, spirit of progressiveness and innovation. They were built in locally available stone.

15.2. ARCHITECTURAL CHARACTERS

Plan

The temples of this region are moderate in size and pleasing in their design. Some temples are of the Panchayatana class containing four additional shrines at each corner. With these they formed a very attractive composition. In general these temples consist of the following three compartments.

1. Nal Mandapa. Nal Mandapa is the portico built over the Nal meaning stairs leading into Mandapa of the temple. Two pillars support this portico. Entrance is from east through this pillared portico.
2. Assembly hall or Mandapa with low pyramidal roof. The Mandapa is an open pillared hall with the lower part of the pillars supporting a characteristic sloping seat back or Asana.
3. Cella with its shrine

Eg: Sun temple at Osia

Interior

The Mandapas of some of the temples of 8th century are octagonal in plan with their eight pillars elegantly carved. The pillars with their capitals supporting the carved ceiling are the principal architectural features. In some of the temples of Osia, the distinctive motif vase and foliage order of Gupta period attained its supreme form. However in the later temples of 10th and 11th century, the vase and foliage capitals are rare and the shafts of the pillars are not fluted but octagonal in section.

In Qutb mosque at Delhi the temple pillars appear to have been mainly those of 8th and 9th centuries. The beauty of some of the capitals is highly remarkable indicating that they were excellent examples of post Guptas' architecture. A great rhythm and harmony is seen in the structures.

Shrine doorways

Reference to the shrine doorways is a must in these temples. It was here that the artist had put his entire imagination. Figures of Navagrahas (nine planets), coils of the snake (Sesha) the river goddesses of Ganga and Yamuna at the base of the jamb were moulded and decorated on the shrine doorways. (Fig. 15.8)

Exterior

The shrine of the temple is in Nagara style having strong horizontal groove gaps catching dark shade. Mandapa has simple flat roof supported on pillars. (Fig. 15.1, 15.2)

15.3. TEMPLES OF OSIA—EARLY EXAMPLES

The village of Osia accommodates some 16 temples of Hindus and Jains mostly in neglected condition. Three early temples are located within the village of Osia probably built in 8th century and dedicated to god Harihara are small but particularly pleasing in their design. Two are of Panchayatana class having four subsidiary shrines built at four corners so that the temple would be an attractive combination. The temples were raised on high plinths and their Sikharas resemble the early Orissan type. The Mandapa is an open pillared hall with the lower part of the pillars adjoining the characteristic sloping seat back (Asana). Fine plastic decoration and carvings are seen in pillars, capitals and ceilings.

15.4. LATER EXAMPLES

The later group of temples belongs to 10th and 11th centuries located on a hill overlooking the village of Osia.

1. Sun Temple at Osia, 10th cent. C.E

This is the temple dedicated to Surya- the Sun god probably a later temple of Osia group and in some respects the most graceful of the entire group. These temples also consist of same compartments as the early examples have. They are:

– Portico or Nal mandapa

– Open assembly hall or Mandapa

– Cella with its shrine

Entrance is from east through Nal mandapa which contains two tall fluted pillars. The temple is of Panchayatana class. Its four subsidiary shrines are connected by a cloister, which not only provide shelter to visiting devotees, but also serves as an enclosure wall. The pillars of the portico has the Base, Capital, Vase and foliage order together with a band breaking the slender lines of the shaft, which were the matured work of an experienced hand.

The shape of Sikhara and its proportions as a whole are remarkable. The temple is a fine illustration in Art and Architecture. (Fig. 15.1, 15.2)

2. Jain temple of Mahavira, Osia, 10th cent. C.E

The most complete example of Osia group is the Jain temple dedicated to Mahavira. It consists of the following usual compartments.

– An open porch (Nal mandapa)

– A Mandapa

– A Sanctuary which is a closed cell

Immediately in front of the porch is an ornate Torana or archway. It appears to have first built at the end of 8th century and then repaired and added in 10th century. This shows a record of development of two periods. This is seen by the changes in the design of pillars of Mandapa belonging to the earlier original structure and the pillars of the porch added later. Nal mandapa is so called because it was built over the Nal (stairs) giving access into the building. The Torana or entrance arch appears to be even still later addition, probably of 11th century. (Fig. 15.3, 15.4)

The outstanding features are the pillars of the porch as they present post-Gupta order in its ripest state.

3. Vimala temple, Mount Abu, 11th Cent C.E

Abu is a hill station situated at a height of 1200 metres in thick green trees in Sirohi district in south Rajasthan very close to north Gujarat border. It was the custom of Jains to build their temple buildings on the summit of mountains, as higher places and mountains are regarded as sacred. Very nearer to Abu, Dilwara temple complex consists of five temples devoted to Jain Tirthankars (saints). These temples are famous and popular for their marvelous marble stone carvings.

One such important temple is Vimala temple built by Vimal Shah the minister in the court of the king Bhimdev I of Solanki dynasty in 1021 C.E. The temple enshrines gold-brass alloy idol of Adinath, also called Rishabdev the first Jain Tirthankar. There are some 57 subordinate cells containing small deities. The temple is also called Vimal Shah or Vimal Vasahi. It was built entirely of white marble.

Plan

A high enclosure wall surrounded the main building of the temple, on the inner side of which is a corridor. The temple building covers an area of 43 metres long and 27 metres wide. Entrance to the temple is through a domed porch on east entering into the cloistered courtyard. The temple resolves mainly into the following.

Rang mandapa – Front open columned hall
Navchowki – Mandapa
Gudha mandapa – A vestibule
Garba Griha – Sanctuary

Rang mandapa

It is the front open columned hall containing richly decorated twelve pillars supporting the dome. It measures 7.5 metres in diameter. The architrave is 3.6 metres from the floor and the apex of the dome was less than 9 metres high. The dome is supported on an attic system of dwarf pillars with volute braces in between. The capitals are of four-branched bracket order. The pillars are circular in section richly carved and embellished. (Fig. 15.5, 15.6)

Domical ceiling

Supreme beauty and fineness was found in the treatment of volute ceiling of the nave including the pillars. The dome has eleven concentric rings, five of which are interposed at regular intervals with patterns of figures and animals. They contain the figures of elephants, horsemen, ducks, swans, ornamental pendants and dancing figures. At the apex they form a grouping of pendants suspended from the centre of the dome. Marvelous minute carvings are filled over on pillars, Ceilings, doorways and panels.

The pillars have carved figures playing instruments and 16 Vidyadevis the goddesses of wisdom.

The columned hall is open to criticism as the remarkable dome is clearly too heavy in appearance to rest on slender pillars. The columns seem to serve only ornamental purpose. But surprisingly the hall stood firmly for some ten centuries. (Fig. 15.7)

Navchoki

Navchoki is a mandapa containing nine bays. The pillars and the ceilings are too richly and intricately decorated with carvings.

At the far end of this and slightly at a higher level is the vestibule having two rows of pillars. And at the end of this a doorway opens into the shrine. (Fig. 15.8)

The exterior of the temple has no special architectural characters. It is simple and plain. Hasthi shala (Elephant hall) was an addition made later containing rows of elephant figures.

Nonetheless the Vimala temple is a notable production. Its fame is not resting much on architecture but on the infinite sculptural decoration, which is notable for its intrinsic delicacy and plasticity.

15.5. NAMES OF OTHER TEMPLES

Sachiya Mata temple, Osia, 9th cent. C.E

Group of temples at Kiradu in Mewar, 11th cent. C.E

Tejapala at Mount Abu in Rajputana, 13th cent. C.E

QUESTIONS

1. Describe the specific architectural characters of Rajaputana temples.
2. Briefly explain the features of temples of Osia.
3. Name the great temple of Mount Abu. Describe its plan, compartments and other decorative features.
4. Sketch the typical sikhara of a temple of Osia, Rajputana.

Fig 15.1. Osia temple, 10th Cent.C.E

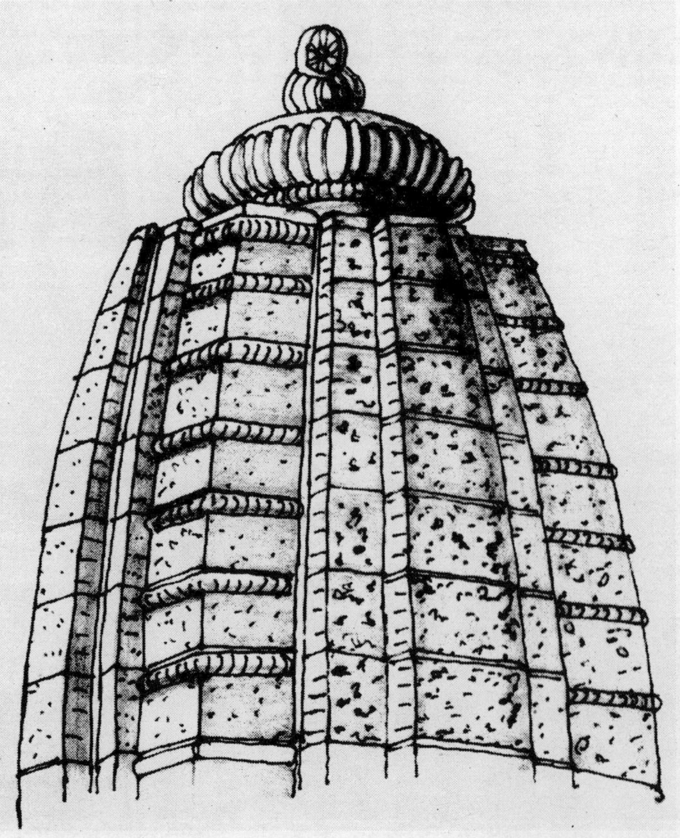

Fig 15.2. Osia temple c. 9th cent. C.E.—Typical Sikhara

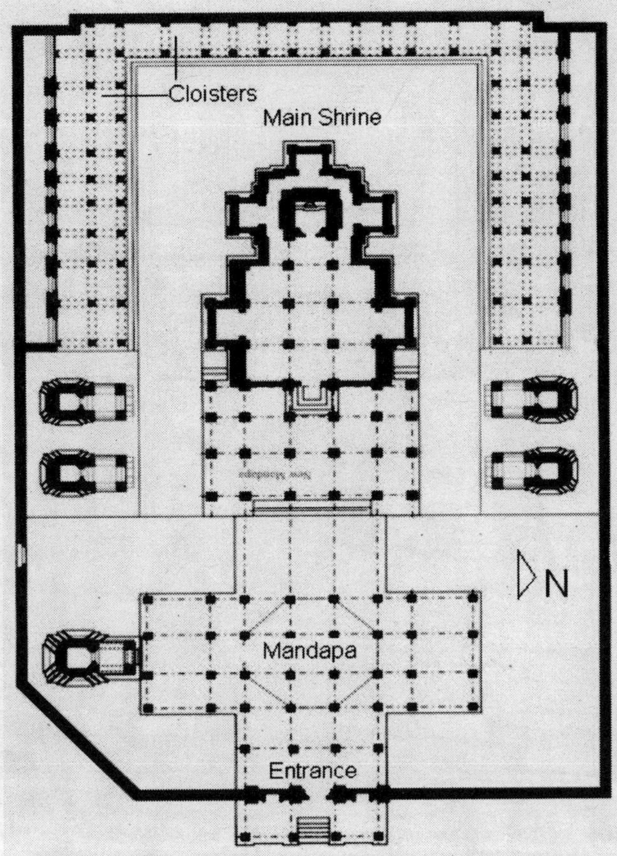

Fig 15.3. Jain temple of Mahavira, Osia—Plan

Fig 15.4. Jain temple of Mahavira, Osia, 10th cent.C.E—View

Fig 15.5. Vimala temple, Mount Abu—Interior front hall carvings, 11th cent. C.E

Fig 15.6. Vimala temple, Mount Abu—Interior

Fig 15.7. Vimala temple, Mount Abu—Ceiling details

Fig 15.8. Vimala temple, Mount Abu—Door details

16

Indo-Aryan Architecture

Gujarat (940 to 1300)

16.1. INTRODUCTION

One of the most refined and prolific developments of Indo-Aryan architecture are that which prevailed in western India built during early centuries of 2nd millennium. Solanki rulers a Saivite sect were the patrons who undertook many of the building undertakings, whose power extended over a large area centering on Gujarat, Kathiawar and much of Rajaputana.

Solankis were Hindu Agnivamsh Rajputs. They were the descendents of Gurjars. Solankis ruled western and central India from 10th to 13th century C.E. The capital city was Anhilwara, which is now the modern town of Siddhapur Patan in Gujarat state. Gujarat was a major center for overseas trade. They faced severe fights and threats from Mahmud of Ghazni around 1026 C.E. The city of Karnavati was built by king Karandev on the banks of Sabarmathi river. It is now the modern Ahmedabad.

Simultaneously the temples under Cholas and Pandyas in Tamilnadu, Hoysala temples in Karnataka in south and temples in Orissa, Khajuraho, Rajputana, Maharastra and Gwalior were under progress.

Gujarat temples are similar to Hoysala temples in their intricate and plastic embellishment in basement and main wall decoration.

16.2. ARCHITECTURAL CHARACTERS

Plan

The general layout of the temples of this western group consists of the same system of compartments as in most of the Indian temples namely the shrine with its Cella and a pillared hall (Mandapa). The plans of these temples may be divided broadly into two kinds.

Parallel type

In this case the two compartments are joined so as to unite the entire building within a parallelogram.

Eg: Sun temple at Modhera, 11th cent.

Diagonal type

In this case the two compartments are attached diagonally in which each compartment forms a separate rectangle.

Eg: Somanath temple, Kathiawar, 12th cent.

In all the above instances the walls have their sides interrupted at intervals by projected or recessed chases making angles. These were carried up into the elevation. This has produced a strong vertical effect of light and shade. These angles are of two kinds. In one class of building they are straight sided and in other class they are rounded and foliated. Some of the larger temples appear to have been in two or three storeys.

Interior

The interior of these temples display several notable characters. The columns are placed geometrically making an octagonal nave in the centre of the main hall and leaving surrounding space into aisles. The shaft of the pillars is divided horizontally into decorative zones diminishing by stages to finish in a bracket capital. The central pillars carry the architrave above raising the height of the nave. They support the central dome, which consists of a shallow shaped ceiling formed by a succession of overlapping courses.

Shrine doorway

The significant feature of the temple interior is the shrine doorway designed so that its decorative scheme matches with that of the pillars. It consists of horizontal bands of figures and foliage.

Exterior

The building elevation may be divided horizontally from bottom to top into three main sections. They are:

– Pitha – the Basement

– Mandovara – the wall face up to the entablature

– Sikhara – the superstructure

Pitha

The Pitha contains a series of carved mouldings and stringcourses. The respective mouldings from bottom to top are shown below.

Garaspatti : A row of horned heads (Rakshas)

Gajapathi : A row of elephant fronts

Aswathara : A row of horses

Narathara : A row of human beings

Such series of figure carvings on basement walls are also found in Hoysala temples in Karnataka.

Mandovara

Above the basement is the second or middle portion called Mandovara, the most significant portion of the entire elevation of the building. It is the main vertical wall face reserved for figure sculpture. The images of deities and saints were carved in niches on these walls. The Chalukyan and Hoysala temples also had such figure carvings exhibited on main walls. (Fig. 16.1)

Sikhara

And however the Sikhara (spire) is no longer one single member but formed into a group of members surrounded by turrets or Urushringas arranged symmetrically, each a replica in miniature of the large central structure.

The roof of the assembly hall is a low pyramid composed of horizontal courses diminishing as they rise and terminating in a usual vase-shape finial. (Fig. 16.7)

16.3. EXAMPLES

Sun temple at Modhera, (11th cent. C.E)

The Sun temple at Modhera in Gujarat was built during the reign of the king Bhimdev I of Solanki dynasty. This was built in an arrangement of rectangular platforms and terraces on the western side of an ornamental tank.

Plan

The temple is resolved into two separate structures connected by a narrow passage. It consists of - Sabha mandapa or an open pillared hall in the front

– The main enclosed temple building consisting of Mandapa and Garbhagriha

Sabha mandapa

On plan the front structure Sabha mandapa is a square compartment of nearly 15 metres wide placed diagonally within the axial line. Its sides are interrupted at regular intervals by recessed chases. There are pillared entrances with an archway at each of the four corners and two small pillars at recessed angles. The dwarf wall was richly paneled with figure subjects and has a leaning seat back inside. The interior of the hall has two rows of pillars crossing each other at right angles. The central pillars at the junction of the passages were omitted to make an octagonal nave in the center. Over this nave rises a domed ceiling elevated higher than the aisles by means of attic pillars. (Fig. 16.2, 16.3)

Main temple building

This is more a closed rectangular structure consisting of the following two compartments.

– Mandapa (Assembly hall)

– Garbha Griha (Cella)

The main temple building is on the rear side to Sabha mandapa and measures externally 24 metres in length and 15 metres in width. It is having its long sides not diagonal as in the case of Sabha mandapa but parallel to the axis of the whole. The main entrance is on eastern side through a pillared portico where it connects to the western doorway of Sabha mandapa. The walls of this mandapa were also interrupted at regular intervals by recessed chases.

Interior

The interior of the Mandapa contains eight columns around a central octagonal nave, above which rises a highly ornamental ceiling. However the interior is plain except the images of Sun god in every bay.

A four-pillared vestibule connects the square cell with a processional passage around it. The shrine doorway has its jambs and lintel divided into sections each crowded by figures. (Fig. 16.4)

Exterior

The building was elevated on a high plinth. Elevation consists of the following three main sections from bottom to top. (Fig. 16.1)

– Pitha (Basement) consisting of range of carved mouldings and string courses

– Spacious Mandovara richly carved with figure subjects

– Superstructure or the roofs

The roof of Mandapa is a traditional arrangement of a low pyramidal roof and a tall turreted Sikhara built over the cella. In both these structures the recessed chases were carried upward into the Sikhara giving a striking vertical effect in its elevation.

Torana

An exquisitely carved and fluted archway or Torana was built to the main entrance of temple. From this wide flight of steps ascends to the temple. But the arch Torana was now disappeared and only the two fine pillars are remaining. (Fig. 16.2, 16.3)

Ornamental tank

The colossal tank in front of the temple is called Suryakund. It has a series of carved steps reaching down to the water. Mini shrines adorn the steps of the tank. It is the general practice in Gujarat to build such tanks and wavs with decorated carved steps which are superior in design and beauty. (Fig. 16.5)

Common and similar features are found in Mukteswara temple in Bhuvaneswar city of Orissan Indo Aryan architecture. Both these temples have in common an ornamental tank and a Torana. But the Torana of Mukteswara temple is too solid and is still remaining.

In view of aesthetics, elegance and proportions as a whole the Sun temple at Modhera is fine and superb.

16.4. NAMES OF OTHER TEMPLES

10th cent – Temples at Sunak, Konoda, Delmel and Kasara in Gujarat

11th cent – Navalakaha temples at Ghumli and Sejakpur in Kathiwar

12th cent – Rudramala at Siddhapur in Gujarat

Somanath temple at Kathiawar

16.5. STRUCTURES OF SEMI-RELIGIOUS OR CIVIC CHARACTER

There are other structures of semi-religious or civic character and they are:

- Kirthi Sthambas (Fig. 16.6)
- Temple archways
- City gateways,
- Tanks,
- Wavs or public wells

QUESTIONS

1. Gujarat temples have specific architectural characters and nomenclature. Explain them in detail.
2. Name the great temple of Modhera. Describe its plan, compartments, elevation and other features.

Fig. 16.1. Sun Temple, Modhera-Main temple, 11th cent.C.E

Fig. 16.2. SunTemple, Modhera—Sabha mandapa

Fig. 16.3. Sun Temple, Modhera—Close view of pillars, brackets, shades and carvings

Fig. 16.4. SunTemple, Modhera—Sabha mandapa interior and ceiling

Fig. 16.5. Sun temple, Modhera—Surya Kund

Fig. 16.6. Kirti stambha in front of a temple

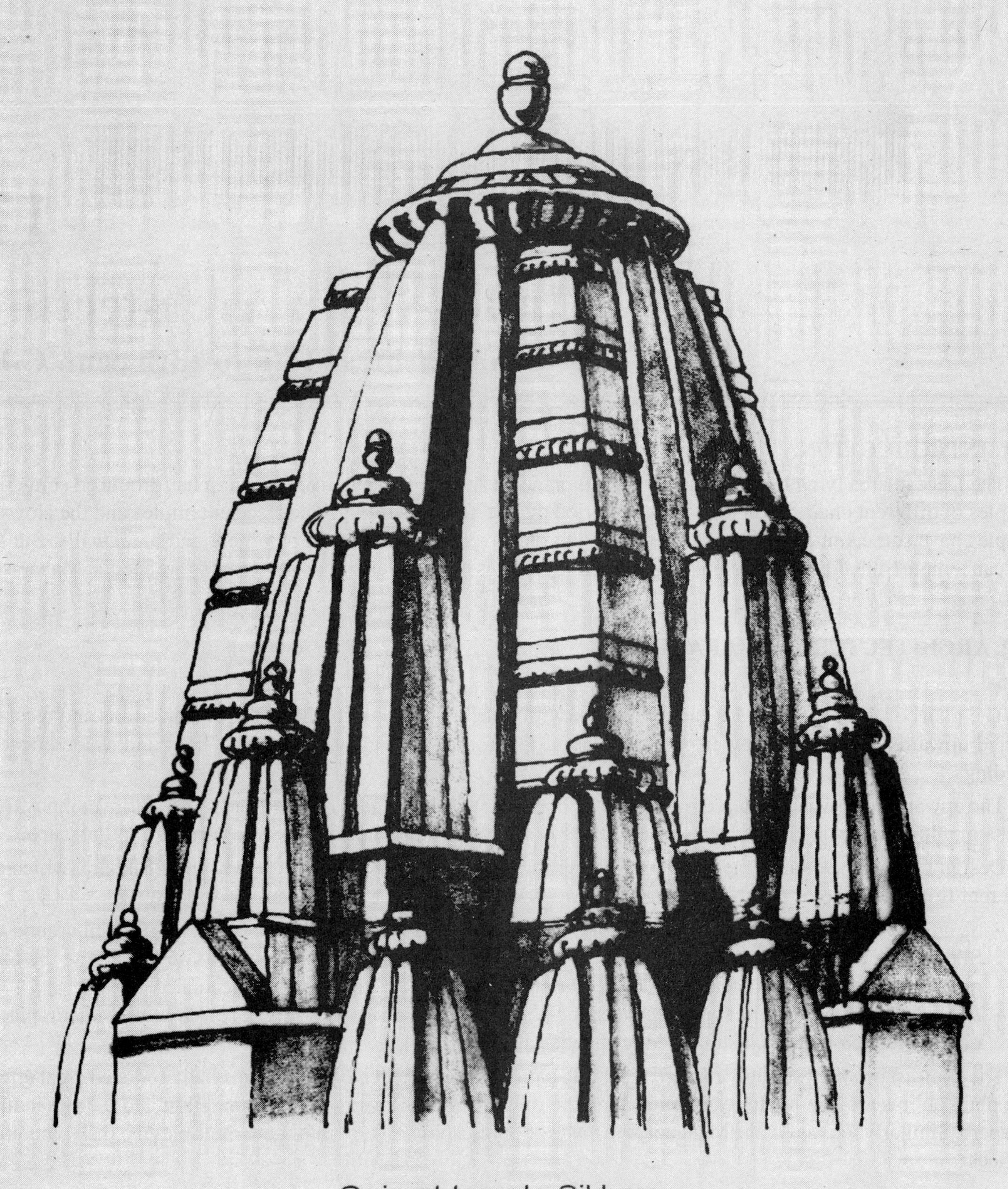

Fig. 16.7. Guarat temple Sikhara

17

Indo-Aryan Architecture

Maharashtra (11th to 13th cent. C.E)

17.1. INTRODUCTION

The Deccan area lying between the river Tapti on north and the Krishna river on south has produced some fine temples of different character in the medieval period during Yadava's ruling. The Deccan temples and the Hoysala temples have some similar features in their fine and plastic embellishments in basement and main walls. But the Deccan temple Sikharas had different and distinctive features. Some such important temples are seen in Maharastra state.

17.2. ARCHITECTURAL CHARACTERS

Plans

The plans of these temples are laid diagonally within the axis. The walls have sharp projections and recesses carried upwards to the top. They catch the light and retain the shade creating a strong light and shade effect in buildings.

The upward trend was countered by closely set horizontal grooves (gaps) carried across the entire composition. These mouldings have a knife edged section called Kani. These Kani mouldings were carried in pillars also.

Design of Roofs: Some of the distinctive and prominent features are seen in the design of Sikhara, which are different from the temples of other regions. The two distinctive features of Deccan Sikhara are:

- *Strong vertical bands like a spine or quoin*: The turrets or Urusringas instead of being grouped around the Sikhara the Deccan Sikhara has strong vertical bands carried upwards at each of its angles taking the form of a spine or quoin. This feature extends from the lower cornice right up to the finial.
- *Row of mini Sikharas*: The spaces between these quoins are filled in by a vertical row of mini Sikharas placed one above the other, each supported on a pedestal. (Fig. 17.4)

The contrast between strongly marked repeating pattern and the delicate plain quoins had produced great effect. The plain quoins are like photo frame enframing the rows of mini Sikharas. The combination and their execution is superb. Similarly the roof of the Mandapa was made of diminishing rows of miniature multiples of small pyramidal edifices.

Pillars

The pillars have decisive features apart from use of Kani moulding. Struts or brackets were not used in the capitals. A scroll or volute support was used in the uppermost mouldings. The vase and foliage motif is absent but occasionally visible. The pillar shaft was richly moulded but the lower third part is left plain as a square block. In some examples the lower part of pillar was profusely carved with figures. Similar designs were carried in the jambs of the shrine doorways in the form of pilasters.

Unit of Measurement

A unit determined the proportions of the building. This unit is the height of the monolithic shaft of the pillar, which in turn depended on larger length of stone economically possible to extract from the quarry. The pillar shaft served as a standard of measurement. Entire design was carried to that scale. All the parts of the temple were proportioned according to the unit, each member being in a fixed ratio to the other.

17.3. EXAMPLES

Deccan temples are smaller in size. The spacious temple at Sinnar measures 24 metres in length. The following are important selected examples.

1. Temple of Ambarnatha, Thana District, 11th cent.
2. Gondeswara temple at Sinnar, Nasik District, 12th cent.

1. Temple of Ambarnatha, Thana district, 11th cent. C.E

One of the earliest and finest is the temple of Ambarnatha at Akoli in Thana District near Mumbai on Mumbai Pune route in Maharastra state built in 1060 C.E during Solanki dynasty king Mahamandaleswar. Temple was built in black stone and lime in Hemadpanti style. The temple is dedicated to lord Siva and is now under the control Archiological Survey of India.

The temple has two essential compartments aligned diagonally joining them at their inner angles. The building is measuring 23 metres long and 7 metres in width. Cut corner domes, close fitting, mortar less stone joints, bands of mini figures are the main features of these temples. A long deep pool situated by the side of this temple.

INTERIOR

The temple is entered through three doorways of the assembly hall. Inside, there are attached pillars at each of eight angles and a group of four pillars formed a square nave in the centre. There is excellent carving in the ceiling panels and shallow domes. The pillars of the hall are too intricately carved with both conventional designs and figure subjects from base to capital. The most richly finished are the central four pillars carved with images of gods in niches and figures in friezes. The design of pillars recalls the marble columns of Vimala temple of Abu.

Exterior

The walls of this temple are made close by a series of vertical projections and recesses, which are fully and richly decorated. These projections and recesses catch light and create shadows of striking beauty. The other decorative treatment comprises mainly the horizontal mouldings of the Kani or knife-edge type. The quoins of the Sikhara and the multiplication of mini ornamental Sikharas in between the plain quoins are excellent. (Fig. 17.1, 17.2)

2. Gondeswara temple at Sinnar, Nasik district, 12th cent, C.E

Actual name of the temple is Govindeswara. This is the most complete and best-preserved temple of Deccan series constructed during the first half of twelfth century at Sinnar, Maharastra state. The temple has a wide platform measuring 38 metres by 29 metres with four small supplementary shrines at each corner making the temple a Panchayathana class.

Plan

The main building occupying the center of a large terrace is elegantly proportioned. It contains a Nandi pavilion, an assembly hall and a sanctuary. The three entrances to the Assembly hall has columned porticos which added grace and dignity to the structure.

The Nandi-pavilion was placed in front of the main building facing east.

Exterior

The temple stands on a moulded and stepped platform. The roofs of these two structures were made of miniature models of their own body structure. Those on the Sabha-mandapa are short, while on the Vimana they are taller forms. A cornice carried round the whole structure binds the Sabha-mandapa with the vimana behind. The quoins altered by vertical mini sikharas were the main features of Sikhara. Though the general proportions of this temple are good but the sculptures adorning the walls are low in quality. (Fig. 17.3)

17.4. NAMES OF OTHER EXAMPLES

Elephanta caves near Mumbai, 5th to 8th cent. C.E

Jagadambadevi at Kokamthan

QUESTIONS

1. Describe the architectural characters of medieval Maharastra temples.
2. Explain the temple of Ambarnatha with respect to its compartments, interior and exterior features.
3. Describe the plan, elevation of Gondeswara temple, Nasik of 12th century C.E.
4. Sketch the typical sikhara of Deccan Maharashtra temple of medieval time.

Fig. 17.1. Temple of Ambernatha, Thana—Entrance porch, 11th cent.C.E

Fig. 17.2. Temple of Ambarnatha, Thana—Closer view

Fig. 17.3. Gondeswara temple, Sinnar, Nasik, 12th cent.C.E

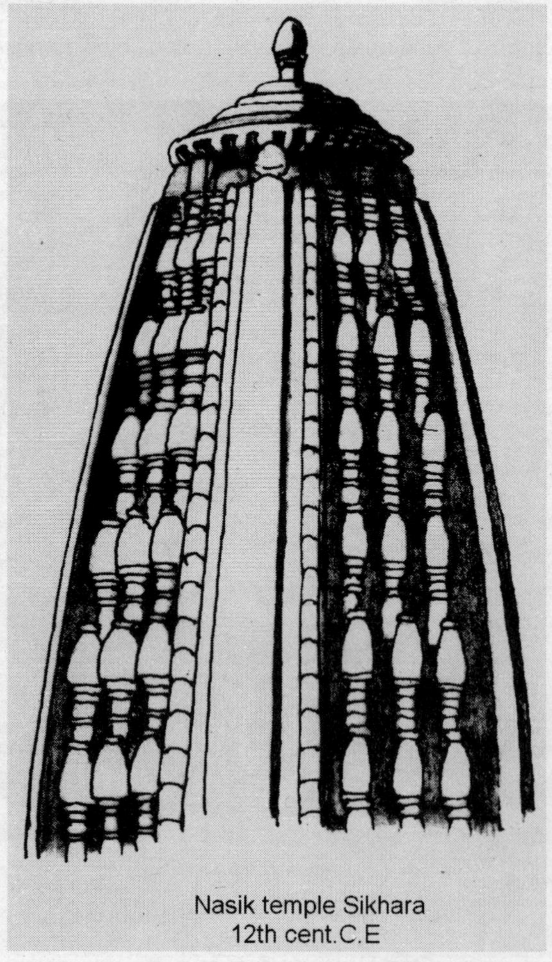

Fig. 17.4. Nasik temple Sikhara

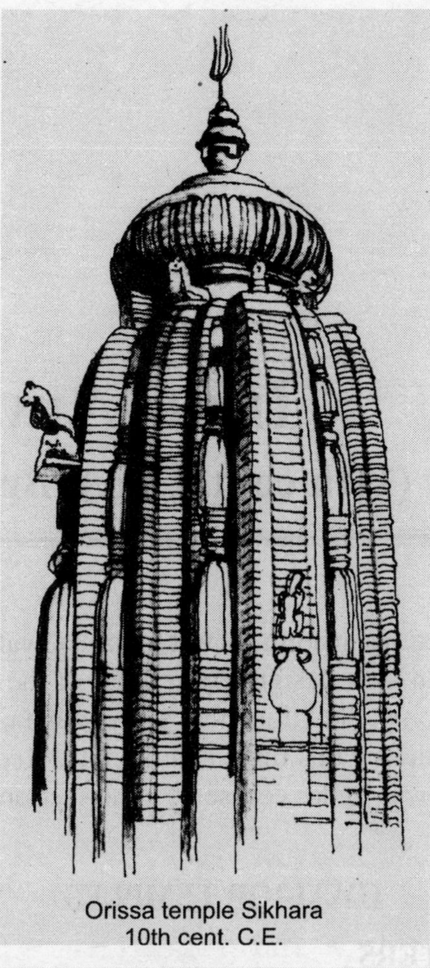

Orissa temple Sikhara
10th cent. C.E.

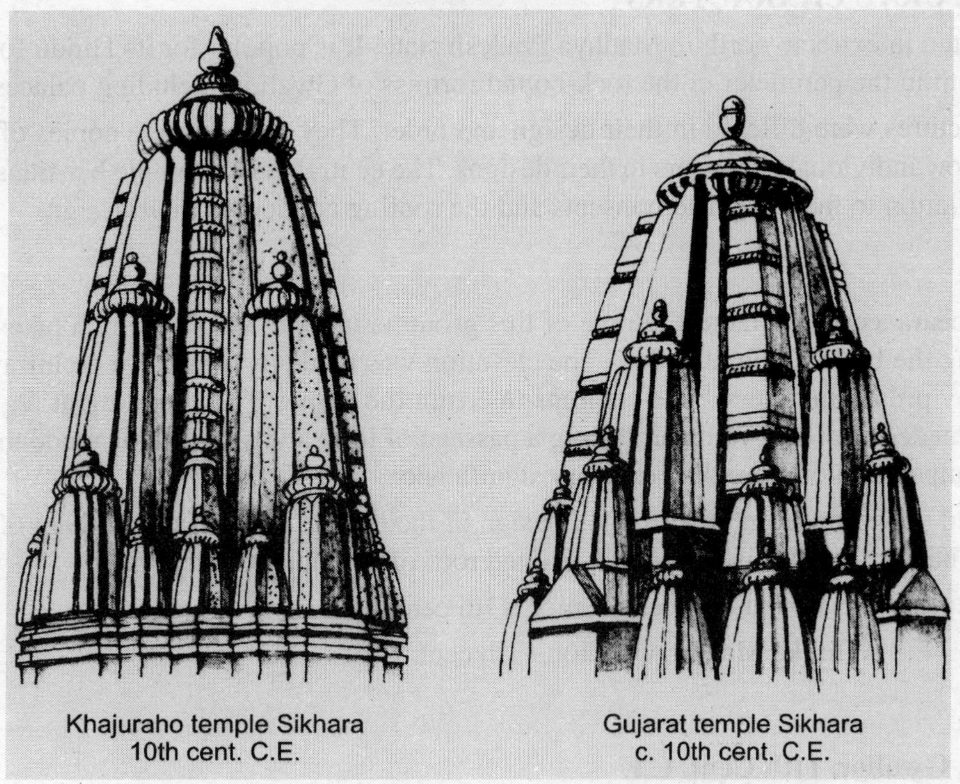

Khajuraho temple Sikhara
10th cent. C.E.

Gujarat temple Sikhara
c. 10th cent. C.E.

Fig. 17.5. Indo Aryan temple Sikharas

18

Indo-Aryan Architecture

Gwalior (11th cent. C.E.), Brindavan (16th cent. C.E)

18.1. INTRODUCTION

There are two groups of building structures in north central India at Gwalior and Brindavan. The temple buildings within the fort of Gwalior are different in their designs from those of the surrounding country. Another group of temples is at Brindavan near Mathura, some 150 kilometres away to the north built several centuries later.

There is no temple building activity during this time in entire north India, as the country was under the rule of Islams. In south India, Madurai temple was under course of construction and Madurai class of temples were in extension process.

GWALIOR TEMPLES

18.2. ARCHITECTURAL CHARACTERS

Gwalior is situated in extreme north in Madhya Pradesh state. It is popular for its Hindu fort. There are some eleven structures with in the perimeter of the rock-bound fortress of Gwalior, including palaces and temples.

The temple structures were differed in their design and order. They are not mere copies of other Indo-Aryan temples, but they show individual characters in their designs. The central hall of temple has transepts on either side which provide ventilation to the nave. The transepts and the roofing are new in their design.

Exterior

The exterior appearance of the largest temple of this group is in three stories, which takes the form of open galleries surrounding the building on all sides. The elevation was made by a massive architrave with the spaces between occupied by pillars and piers. The columns interrupt the planes by alternating at regular intervals with openings. This has made solids and voids producing a passage of light and shade. This made the exterior from all points of view, a composition of more than ordinary significance.

The most marked departure from the orthodox design of the temple tower is the Sikhara of Teli ka mandir or Oilman's temple. The Sikhara of this temple is a vaulted roof of Buddhist Chaitya hall.

Important Examples: 1. Sasbahu temple, Gwalior, 11th cent. C.E.

2. Telika Mandir, Gwalior, 11th cent. C.E.

18.3. EXAMPLES

1. Sasbahu temple, Gwalior, 11th Cent. C.E

There are two temples with the same name in Gwalior fort with variation in size. According to inscription the largest was completed in 1093 C.E. The temple was dedicated to lord Vishnu built by king Mahipala.

Believes as to the name of the temple are- Lord Vishnu is called Sahasra Bahu means One with 1000 hands. It gradually changed to Sasbahu and is not dedicated to Sas (Mother in law) or Bahu (Daughter in law).

Only the main hall or Mandapa remains. The vimana over the sanctuary was probably 46 metres in height was disappeared. The entire length is 30 metres and the width across the transepts is 19 metres. The building has projected transepts.

Interior

The interior of this hall is artistically ingenious. The exterior looks in three storeys. And this does not apply to the interior, which is one large central hall, around which project the loggias, one above the other comprising triple storeys. The central hall has transepts on either side to allow ventilation inside. The Mandapa hall is a new conception in temple architecture in India.

Exterior

Externally the Maha mandapa is in three storeys, which take the form of open galleries surrounding the building on all sides. Each storey is defined by a massive architrave with the spaces between occupied by pillars and piers. The roof was partly fallen. It was an arrangement in diminishing tiers. Ornamental masonry is rising up into a low pyramidal roof. The planes interrupted by columns alternating at regular intervals with openings produced a good effect of solids and voids making the exterior clear and strong in appearance. The transepts, loggias, pillars, projections, recesses and their adjustment all were the innovative features in this temple. (Fig. 18.1, 18.2)

Names of other temples:

Swarn Jain mandir, 1761 C.E

2. Teli ka Mandir, Gwalior, 11th Cent. C.E

This was built in 11th century within the perimeter of the rock-bound fortress of Gwalior in Uttar Pradesh state. This is a tall commanding structure raised to about 24 metres in height and is distinctly unusual in appearance. It is believed to be the oldest temple in Gwalior fort.

Regarding the name of the temple, there are different versions like this:

– Supervising of religious ceremonies was entrusted to Telang Brahmins

– Temple was built by Teli caste men (Oil merchants)

Plan

It consists of sanctuary only comprising a tower together with a substantial porch and a doorway giving access into the cella. There is no assembly hall or Mandapa. The sanctuary is not a square hall but is an oblong measuring externally 18 metres by 14 metres.

Exterior

The most marked departure from the orthodox design of the temple tower is in the composition of the summit of roof. Owing to the oblong form the Sikhara was built into a vaulted roof similar to Buddhisht Chaitya hall roof. It also contains sun-window motif and a keeled ridge surmounted by finials. The front porch also similarly carried up almost to the height of the Sikhara roof. The temple had fine and elegant projections richly decorated making it marvelous. (Fig. 18.3, 18.4)

The Sikhara of this temple is a rare type in its design. The only other example in Indo-Aryan architecture with a Sikhara of this order is the Vaital Deul at Bhubaneswar, a temple of Orissan group.

BRINDAVAN TEMPLES

18.4. ARCHITECTURAL CHARACTERS.

Brindavan is an important town near Mathura in Uttar Pradesh state. This is associated with Lord Krishna and is a most sacred place to Hindus.

The temples of Brindavan built in 16th century consist of specially localized order. All were built in red sandstone and in a style of architecture different from any others of their kind. A change had taken place in this part of the country owing to the condition brought by Islamic domination. By this time, Islamic architecture had already established a strong hold and the buildings were confined to that creed. But however owing to Akbar's religious tolerence, a few temples were allowed to be built at Brindavan.

The typical temple consists of only two compartments- Assembly hall and a Cella. A noticeable fact in this temple is entire absence of figure carving and sculptures.

The Gobind Devi temple consists of balconies, loggias, bracketed archways, moulded buttresses, wide eaves and ornamental parapets, all carefully disposed so as to be in perfect accord with one another. There is at the same time absence of quality and fineness. The roofing shows the influence of contemporary construction of Mughals. The temples lacked full fervour, zeal, religious emotion, faith and freedom as proper patronage and encouragement was missing.

18.5. EXAMPLES

1. Gobind Dev temple, Brindavan, 16th Cent. C.E

The temple is the largest and most important of the temples of Brindavan built in 1590 C.E, the sanctuary of which was completely dismantled in the reign of Aurangzeb. What remains therefore is the assembly hall, which is a spacious structure. Originally the building has transepts projections. There are no figure carvings or niches in this temple.

Exterior

The temple contains balconies, loggias, bracketed arches, moulded buttresses, wide eaves, ornamental parapets.

It is a combination of horizontal and vertical lines covering the whole surface. Wide eaves and ornamental parapets, all carefully disposed so as to be in perfect accord with one another.

The roof is a vaulted dome of intersecting arches. The temple lacks the full spirit of orthodox temple as the rulers of this period were of different faith and full patronage and help was not available. (Fig. 18.5)

2. Jugal Kishore temple, Brindavan, 16th Cent. C.E

This is another prominent temple in Brindavan built in 16th century C.E. It contains a rectangular Mandapa and an octagonal shrine. Though the mandapa is rectangular, but it contains a square hall inside. The shrine is 11 metres in diameter and the cella in its interior is a square of only 5.2 metres side. Hence a great thickness of wall was left around both compartments. In Mandapa within the mass of masonry small chambers have been introduced.

Exterior

The shape of the Sikhara is unique, as it bears no resemblance to any other kind of Indian temple spire. It rises from an octagonal plan and taper into a tall conical tower with vertical band of mouldings outlining each angle. At intervals throughout their height are similar bands of mouldings placed transversely. Over-hanging the whole at the apex is a ponderous finial or Amlasila. It is a flat circular disc, the outer edge of which is ornamented with a border of massive knob-like petals or flutes. The main entrance has a noticeable Islamic flavour with its pointed arch motif.

The whole treatment is very simple with out any embellishments.

18.6. NAMES OF OTHER TEMPLES

– Radha Vallabh, Brindavan, 16th cent

– Gopinath, Brindavan, 16th cent

– Madanmohan, Brindavan, 16th cent

QUESTIONS

1. Explain the Architectural characters of Gwalior temples.
2. Describe the architecture of Sasbahu temple of Gwalior.
3. Teli ka mandir, Gwalior is different in its plan and elevation. Explain it.
4. State the elements of Brindavan temples of 16th century.
5. Briefly explain the following temples.
   (*i*) Govind Devi temple, Brindavan
   (*ii*) Jugal Kishore temple, Brindavan

Fig. 18.1. Sasbahu temple, Gwalior—Side

Fig. 18.2. Sasbahu temple, Gwalior, 11th cent. C.E

Fig. 18.3. Teli ka Mandir, Gwalior—Side view

Fig. 18.4. Teli ka Mandir, Gwalior, 11th cent. C.E

Fig. 18.5. Govind Dev temple—Brindavan, 16th cent. C.E

Inter Chapter Questions

1. Sketch and explain the features of the following.
   – Sikhara
   – Gopuram
   – Mention any two best examples to each.
2. Compare and contrast features of Dravidian, Sikhara and Gopuram. Sketch their exterior appearence.
3. What is temple Torana? Explain its features. Mention the two best examples of such Toranas built. Sketch any one such Torana.
4. Sketch the Orissa and Khajuraho temple SIkharas and explain their features.
5. Which is the great Rock-cut temple in India? Describe its planning and external features.
6. Early Chalukya temples at Pattadkal developed two types of Sikharas. Explain their features in detail. Mention one name of temple to each type.
7. Explain the contrasting features of Madurai and Khajuraho temples.
8. Name the two temples which has highest Sikharas one each from Dravidian and Indo Aryan temples. Explain the construction of these temples.
9. Compare and contrast the features of Indo Aryan and Dravidian temple Sikharas.
10. What are Urusringas and where they are found? Explain and sketch their features.
11. Compare and contrast the plans of the following temples:
    (*i*) Madurai phase
    (*ii*) Hoysala
    (*iii*) Khajuraho
12. Sketch the Indo Aryan temple Sikhara and Dravidian temple Sikhara.

PART—II

Islam

(1200-1750 C.E.)

1

Islamic Architecture in India—Introduction
(12th cent.)

1.1. ADVENT OF ISLAMS IN INDIA

A new era began towards 12th century C.E with the advent of Islams. These people have forced themselves on the ancient and firmly established social and religious structure in India. They brought with them their native practices, conceptions and beliefs. The political position prevailing is briefly explained separately in each chapter.

1.2. INDO-ISLAMIC ARCHITECTURE

This part of the study is concerned with different kind of building art developed in India from 12th century C.E. These new buildings were in marked contrast with that prevailing in India. New building practices have come into existence by now. Hence the architecture flourished during this period was a blend of local and exotic designs. It was a blend of Indian, Islamic and Persian styles. Thus, the Islamic architecture developed in India may be termed as Indo-Islamic architecture.

Indo-Islamic architecture is the impact of Islamic ideas and techniques on the established civilization of Hindu kingdoms in India. It is a synthesis between two divergent building systems that of Hindus and Muslims. Indian craftsmen blended to sculptural traditions of Hindu architecture and structurally advanced techniques of Islam architecture to produce a unique Indo-Islamic style. It is a Hindu-Muslim joint venture.

1.3. TYPE OF STRUCTURES BUILT

The architecture of native Hindus is mostly confined to temples. Where as, the Mohammedan architecture in India had presented many different types. This may be classified into two of the following.

1. Religious structures. These are the Mosques and Tombs.
2. Secular structures. These structures are mainly the forts, palaces, pavilions, town-gates and gardens.

1. Religious structures

Comparison of Hindu and Islam worshipping structures

There is a great contrast in the two religions of Hindu and Islam in respect of worshipping structures, the temple and the mosque.

Planning and focal point

The temple is an abode of the deity to which it is consecrated and contains massive walls, long corridors, compartments and high embellishments. The sacred part of a temple is the Sanctum sanctorum (Garbha griha) often deep inside the temple complex. The focal point is the idol of the deity.

Where as the mosque is open in its design. It has no need of a central shrine or image of deity. It is enough for the devotee to turn to the direction of Mecca, the holy place of Islam. Sanctuary is the sacred part of the mosque and the focal point is the Mihrab in the sanctuary.

The similar elements in an Indian temple and mosque are:

– Surrounding cloisters

– Sanctuary on west. But some temples are exceptional to this.

In a mosque the central court is totally open. But in a temple the main temple occupies the area of the court.

Walls and surfaces

The walls of the temples expand and vibrate with imagery. The temple was given the texture of stone and the natural tint.

Where as, the presentation of human figures, sculptures, imagery are prohibited in Islam structures. The walls of a mosque are decorated in geometrical patterns in different coloured marbles, plaster, stucco, paints and glazed tiles.

Trabeate and Arcuate

There are different construction techniques in buildings, one being Trabeate and the other Arcuate. The indigenous architecture of India was of Trabeate order, in which the void spaces in the walls were spanned by means of horizontal lintels or beams. Required lengths of stones are necessary to make such beams to place them over the openings. Where as, the Arch technique is different used by Mohammedan builders. An arch can be made up of bricks or pieces of stones. Arch transmits the super loads safely to the ground and does not fail.

Roofs

The roofs of Hindu structures are mostly flat. Temples have pyramidal roofs or Sikharas. With the advent of Mohammedans, an entirely new element, the dome came into existence.

There were differences and inconsistencies persisting at this time. In spite of this, in course of time a method of design approach had arrived and a common ground to both religious communities was gradually evolved.

Factors responsible for production of great Islam buildings

India produced most notable Islam monuments than other countries that came under the influence of Islam. There are two factors responsible for the great exposition of architecture in India.

1. First is its relatively late development. The construction had already passed through its experimental stages in other countries. Many of the structural difficulties and problems had been solved and a solution had arrived to a fair level.
2. Secondly it is due to the remarkable genius of Indian craftsmen. The Indian craftsmen have the living knowledge in construction and the required skill to work in stone, in which they were excelled and unequalled.

THE MOSQUE (MASJID)

The mosque or masjid is the worshipping place of Islams. It is open in its design. It contains the following main elements.

– Sanctuary on west side

– Mihrab - a sacred focal point in the Sanctuary

– Mimber - a pulpit in the Sanctuary

– Surrounding cloisters called Liwans

– An open courtyard called Sahn

Sanctuary

The planning of a mosque starts with a sanctuary which is the essential and sacred part of a mosque. Sanctuary is a pillared hall opening itself on east into the courtyard. The hall is used for religious congregations and prayers called Namaz. A portion of the sanctuary is screened off into a compartment for women (Zenana) in some mosques. The sanctuary has a central nave and side aisles. The nave is often spacious and raised higher in roof than the aisles. Some mosques have only sanctuary and they had no central open court and cloisters. The façade of sanctuary was monumentally built in some mosques. There is continuous change, innovation and development in the design of pillars, arches, mihrab, parapets, kiosks and turrets.

Mihrab

A religious structure however needs a focal point. To meet this, a recess or an alcove called Mihrab is placed in the center of western wall in the nave of sanctuary indicating the Qibla or direction of prayer. Mihrab is a prayer niche. This is the most sacred and significant portion of a mosque. It takes the form of an alcove in arch shape. In some examples it was formed into multiple alcoves within each other containing a half dome over it decorated with ornamental geometrical forms.

Mimber

This is a raised platform with steps for the preacher to deliver the sermon. This is placed to the north of Mihrab in the sanctuary. Number of steps and its design and decoration varies from one to other.

Open courtyard and cloisters

In front of sanctuary an open place takes place without roof called Sahn. The other three sides are covered by pillared cloisters called Liwans. By this the mosque is totally enclosed and secured. It is entered usually through three gates each on east, south and north except on west. Main entrance mostly takes place on east. A water tank is placed in the center of open court for ablutions. Occasionally a fountain also takes place in this tank. (Fig. 1.1)

Screen of arches and dome

While constructing the historical earlier mosques at the end of 12th century at Delhi and Ajmer, the pillars and the stones brought from the dismantled temples were utilized. Hence the mosque sanctuary appeared like a temple pillared hall (Mandapa). Therefore to impose the appearance of a mosque, a separate screen of arches of huge size was added across the front of the sanctuary. Arch became a symbol of Islam structures. But the added screen of arches is obstructing the view of the dome of the sanctuary from the front, though this combination is pleasing from the sides or back of the building.

Such examples are:

– Qutb mosque, Delhi (Fig. 1.2)

– Arhai-din-ka Jhompra mosque, Ajmer (Fig. 1.3)

Later in some mosque buildings, the dome was raised to more height than the screen, thus giving a pleasing look from the front.

Eg: Jami Masjid at Ahmedabad
Jami Masjid at Champanir

In the mosques of south India built in provinces in Malwa, Bijapur and Deccan, the sanctuary façade is not separately built or added. The façade was the outcome of united design with its interior.

Designs of mosques

There are large number of varieties of mosques built in India Layout of these mosques is same in all mosques having sanctuary on west side and cloisters on other sides. Entrances, facades, arches and domes are varied in their mass and design. Row of arches became the prominent feature. Sanctuary facades varied much in their designs like simple, ornamental, artistic, monumental, fine and royal. Feature wise examples are mentioned here.

– Sanctuary nave is spacious and pillars less in some mosques.

Eg: Adina masjid, Pandua
Jaunpur mosques

– Classical decorated pillars are made in the nave making a Rotunda extended in tiers above.

Eg: Jami masjid, Ahmadabad. (Fig. 8.2 to 8.4)

– Sanctuary and cloister entrances are much elaborated, projected and high lighted.

Eg: Jaunpur mosques and Jami masjid, Ahmadabad

– Central arch of Sanctuary façade is made different by means of foliated arch.

Eg: Jami masjid, Bijapur (Fig. 11.1)

– One and only example of Mosque which has no open central court is:

Jami masjid, Gulbarga (Fig. 10.1)

– Worshiping hall for Royals (Chapel) and Zenana were added in first floor in a grand scale.

Eg: Adina masjid, Pandua and Jaunpur mosques (Fig. 6.3, 6.4, 7.4)

– Royal and palace type mosques are:

Jami masjid, Fatehpur Sikri, Agra and Jami masjid, Delhi (Fig. 15.16, 15.17, 1.5)

– Simple design mosques are:

Jami masjid, Mandu and Bijapur (Fig. 9.1, 11.1)

THE TOMB

The other class of building of religious order was the tomb building, introduced into India as an entirely new kind of structure. It is not the custom of Indians to raise a structure to mark the resting place of the dead. The custom of Hindus is to cremate the dead body. With the advent of Mohammedans, these new tomb structures were raised in due course into Indian landscape. Islams bury the body and build a structure over it in memory of the dead. Tomb is the everlasting abode for the dead. Finest Indo-Islamic architecture was developed in these structures.

The tomb building usually consists of a single compartment or a chamber known as 'Huzrah' or 'Estanah'. The cenotaph or Zarih is in the center. The whole structure is roofed over by a dome. The mortuary chamber called the 'Maqbarah' takes place in the ground underneath with the grave or Qabr in the middle. Mihrab is placed in the western wall. A separate mosque building is added in some of the larger mausoleums, the whole being contained within an enclosure called 'Rauza. Important tombs are designated as 'Dargahs' a Persian word signifying a court or palace.

Designs of Tombs

Tomb building designs vary from one to other and that of Sultans mainly Tughlaqs, Sayyids and Lodis are either Square or Octagonal in plans built at Delhi. Square tombs are taller and Octagonal tombs are wider in general. These structures had battering walls, sphere head fringes in arches, merlon parapets, central dome and kiosks.

Designs of Mogul tombs are further improved and are more refined. They are large, spacious, fine, rich and monumental in appearance consisting of surrounding garden, enclosure walls and gateways. They are square in plan having chamfered corners. Domes, kiosks and slender turrets sky-lined on these tomb structures. Fine Ashlar masonry and close inlaid patterns are seen in Mogul tomb structures.

Tomb structures of Bijapur, Bidar, Golconda and Malwa provinces were plaster finished. Some distinguished examples are mentioned here.

Examples: Earlier tomb - Tomb of Shams-ud-din Altumush, Delhi (Fig. 1.4)
Beautiful tomb - Taj Mahal, Agra (Fig. 17.23)
Large tomb - Golgumbaz, Bijapur (Fig. 11.4)
Fine and Variety tomb - Itmad ud Daula, Agra (Fig. 16.5)
Later tomb - Mausoleum of Safdar Jung, Delhi (Fig. 1.6)

2. Secular structures

These structures are dealt separately chapter wise.

1.4. MAIN DIVISIONS OF ISLAMIC ARCHITECTURE

Delhi was the capital city and the centre of Imperial power. Islamic architecture developed in various parts of India was much associated, connected and influenced mainly with the ruler at Delhi. For the purpose of study, these structures may be resolved into three main divisions.

1. **The Delhi or Imperial style (1200 to 1526 C.E):** Imperial style of architecture was developed and continued at Delhi and its surroundings for nearly four centuries beginning at the close of 12th century up to the middle of 16th century, when it was succeeded by Moguls.
2. **Architecture of provinces (1150 to 1687 C.E):** The second of these styles, the provincial refers to the building art developed in the self-contained Provinces away from Delhi and their governors under the obeisance to Delhi Sultans.
3. **Mogul period (1526 to 1707 C.E):** In the second quarter of 16th century, Moguls raised and brought whole of India under their control. Mogul architecture was the latest and ripest form of Indo-Islamic architecture continued to flourish till 18th century.

QUESTIONS

1. Compare and contrast the planning and construction features of Hindu and Islam religious structures.
2. Explain the general planning, contents and elevation elements of an Indian mosque. Mention any three names of great mosques of India.
3. Explain the spaces and building elements of a tomb. State the names of its parts. Mention any three names of great tombs built in India.
4. Sketch the layout of a general Indian mosque and name its parts.

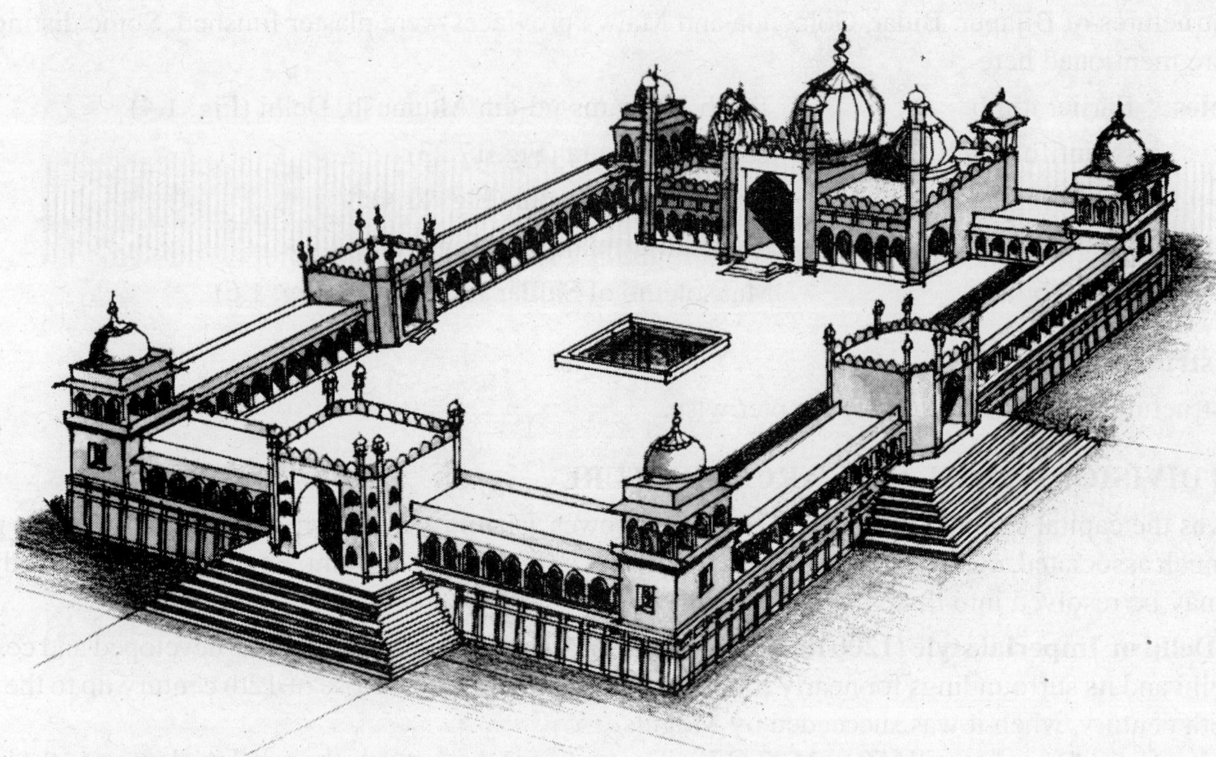

Fig. 1.1. Indian Mosque view

Fig. 1.2. Qutb mosque, Delhi 1195 C.E.—First mosque of India

Fig. 1.3. Ajmer mosque, 1205 C.E

Fig. 1.4. Altumush tomb, Qutb mosque complex, Delhi, 1235 C.E

Fig. 1.5. Jami masjid, Delhi courtyard, 1658 C.E

Fig. 1.6. Safdarjung Mausoleum, Delhi—Last Important tomb, 1750 C.E

2

Delhi or Imperial Style

Under Slaves (1191 to 1246 C.E)

2.0. DYNASTICAL DIVISION

Construction of Islam structures continued for over three and quarter centuries in Delhi and its surroundings which were built for emperors and by emperors of sultanate, hence it is called Imperial style or Delhi style. Beginning in the last years of 12th century, five Mohammedan Sultan dynasties have ruled northwestern region of India with the city of Delhi as capital city. Indo-Islamic architecture at Delhi illustrates every stage of development of the style from the conversion of temples and its materials to build mosques and tombs in initial stages to the vast structures of Mogul emperors.

The imperial architecture may be divided dynastically into five divisions corresponding to five Mohammedan Sultan dynasties who ruled from 12th to 16th centuries.

Names of Dynasties

Slave dynasty (1191 -1246 C.E)
Khalji dynasty (1290 – 1320 C.E)
Tughlaq dynasty (1320 – 1413 C.E)
Sayyid dynasty (1414 – 1451 C.E)
Lodi dynasty (1451 – 1526 C.E)

IMPERIAL STYLE- UNDER SLAVES
(1191 to 1246 C.E)

2.1. INTRODUCTION

The name of slave here means, its members do not belong to royal community. They were slaves who can be bought or sold. Slave system is an accepted practice with the majority of Mohammedans of high rank. Eastern Persian king Mohammed Ghuri appointed his slave Qutd-ud-din Aibak as governor to take care of his possessions around Delhi in 1191 C.E. Aibak belonged to a Turk family from central Asia. He was sold two times in his childhood and second time to Mahmud Ghuri.

Hindu Chauhan dynasty kings were ruling the kingdom of Delhi. Later after the death of Mohammed Ghuri, Qutb-ud-din Aibak played active political role and captured the Hindu stronghold of Qila-i-Rai pithaura in Delhi. He established his prominence in Delhi, Punjab and Rajasthan and became the first Muslim ruler at Delhi. Qutb-ud-din and his son-in-law Shams-ud-din Altumush were the active patrons of building art.

During this period Pandyas were ruling south India.

2.2. EARLY STRUCTURES

The following are the important buildings built during this period.

1. Qutb mosque, Delhi, 1195 C.E
2. Qutb minar, Delhi, 1200 C.E
3. Arhai-din-ka Jhompra mosque, Ajmer, 1205 C.E

1. QUTB MOSQUE, DELHI, 1195 C.E

Mosque on a temple basement

This is the first mosque building on the soil of India at Delhi built by Qutd-ud-din Aibak. The mosque is also called Kuwwat-ul-Islam (The power of Islam). This was commenced in 1195 C.E. The large temple within the fort of Qila-i-pithaura, Delhi was dismantled. The stone basement of the temple was retained and enlarged to large size to accommodate the mosque. This covered an area of 65 metres long by 46 metres wide, the whole being enclosed by a wall and cloisters on all sides. To provide ready dressed stone to this mosque, as many as 27 temples nearby were dismantled and the material thus obtained was used to build the mosque. The existing temples have become the quarries for the emerging new Islam structures. (Fig. 2.1)

Main features

The mosque consisted of a courtyard of some 43 metres by 32 metres surrounded by pillared cloisters three aisles deep. The arrangement of pillars on west or Mecca side of the court was more elaborated into a series of bays with shallow domed ceilings to form the sanctuary. The short pillars of the temples are placed one above the other to secure necessary height. These pillars are beautiful in their details and show the carvings in most perfect Hindu style (Fig. 2.3). And in front of the sanctuary in the courtyard the famous iron pillar brought from its original place near Mathura was stand erected. (Fig. 2.2)

Screen of arches

Later after some years, an expansive screen of arches was added across the entire front of the sanctuary to give mosque appearance. This formed into a great wall of masonry over 15 metres in height at the centre, its width 33 metres and thickness of 2.6 metres. This has five arched openings consisting of larger one in the centre and two lesser arches on either side. Small arched openings were placed one each over the side arches giving an appearance of clerestory. But these had no any specific purpose. They are only for void mass and beauty. (Fig. 2.2)

As a whole this screen of arches of red sandstone is by itself a noble conception. The pointed arches with their fine curves produced an effect of lightness in such a massive volume. By turning the curve of the arch upwards a slight ogee curve was made at the apex of the arch. The entire surface is covered with rich pattern of carving. But the upper parts of this screen of arches had fallen and some fragments remain now.

Now this Qutb mosque complex is UNESCO's world heritage site.

2. QUTB MINAR, DELHI, 1200 C.E

Qutb-Minar is a victory tower and is a part of Kuwwat-ul-Islam mosque built at Delhi. After inspired by the minaret of Jam in Afghanistan, Qutb-ud-din wanted to build a mighty memorial tower to show his growing power. Accordingly foundation was laid in the last year of 12th century for an immense and lofty tower Qutb-Minar, named after him. It became one of the most remarkable architectural monuments in India. This is still standing in its gracefulness. (Fig. 2.4)

The tower was placed in southeast place of Qutb mosque. This is the world's tallest brick tower. Only the base of the tower could be completed during Aibak's period. Altumush added three more storeys. Firuzshah Tughlaq completed the tower in 1386 C.E. Qutb-Minar suffered some damages by earthquakes. Repairs were undertaken during the course of time.

Cross-sections

The tower is circular in plan. The base is 14 metres in diameter and it tapers to a width of 3 metres at the summit. This originally was raised to some 72.5 metres in height. On the north side it was entered through a doorway within which a stairway spirals its way to each balcony. The tower consisted of four storeys diminishing in size as they ascend. A projecting balcony divides each stage.

Each of its four stages is a different pattern in section.

– Lowest stage has wedge shaped flanges alternating with rounded flutes

– Second stage has circular projections

– Third is star shaped with wedge-shaped projections

– Fourth is simply round and plain

Over the fourth tower a circular kiosk takes place with window openings. A domical cupola covers the kiosk.

Balconies

The most artistic and elegant features of the monument are the balconies and the method of supporting them. The balconies are supported by means of cluster of miniature arches or small alcoves with brackets in between. The balustrade around the balconies took the form of stepped battlements or Merlons called Kanjuaras.

Decorative elements

The chief beauty of this structure lies in the strong colour of its red sandstone and its changing texture. Further the following features have added great beauty to this structure. (Fig. 2.5)

– Inscriptional bands

– Alternating surfaces of plain masonry and rich carvings

– Fine and intricate design of balconies and their shadows

As a whole Qutb minar is a most impressive production still standing gracefully in its solemnity.

3. AJMER MOSQUE (ARHAI-DIN-KA-JHOMPRA), AJMER, 1205 C.E

Another important structure attributed to Qutb-ud-din is the mosque at Ajmer situated in Rajasthan state. In Hindi language Arhai din ka Jhompra means Hut of 2 ½ days. It is believed to have been built in 2 ½ days. The edifice was originally a Sanskrit college once. The construction of this mosque began in 1200 C.E. The same course of action, which was taken in Delhi for constructing Qutb mosque, was followed here by dismantling some temples in the surroundings and rebuilding them to make the mosque. This is a very large mosque occupying twice the area occupied by Qutb mosque. It is designed on the same principle of having a central open courtyard surrounded by pillared cloisters. Three of the Hindu temple pillars were placed one above the other to get the desired height of 6 metres from the pavement. Roof is plain. Pillars show fine ornamentation of Hindu and Jain temple pillars. The sanctuary hall gives the appearance of a Hindu temple mandapa with decorated pillars. (Fig. 2.7)

Screen of arches

As was done at Kuwwat-ul-Islam mosque at Delhi, here also an arched wall screen was added across the front of the sanctuary. Shams-ud-din Altmush, the son in law of Qutb-ud-din added this wall screen. This is a fine work of art with seven arches extending over a width of 61 metres. The central arch was raised more higher than the side arches, thus making an emphasizing central rectangle. It rises to some 17 metres high and its thickness is 3.6 metres. There are no upper storey arches. Above the parapet over the central archway are fluted minarets one on each side. The lines of the main arch are gentle and less curved and the four side arches are of multifold pointed variety, first ever produced in India. The surface of the wall is decorated with patterns of stylized and mechanical order. The small rectangular panels and solid circular projections in the spandrels are giving relief and beauty to the arches. As a whole the arched screen is a work of great elegance and dignity. (Fig. 2.6)

2.3. SHAMS-UD-DIN ALTUMUSH'S BUILDINGS

Shams-ud-din Altmush the son-in-law of Qutb-ud-din ruled from 1211 to 1236 C.E has succeeded after Qutb-ud-din. The important building works commissioned during this period were

1. Addition of arched screen to Ajmer mosque (Already described earlier)
2. Extension to Qutb mosque, Delhi 1229 C.E
3. Shams-ud-din Altumush's tomb, 1235 C.E

Extention to Qutb Mosque, Delhi, 1229 C.E

The cloisters and the sanctuary of Qutb mosque were extended on both sides along with screen of arches doubling the entire complex. Here the cloisters are simply a plain copy and replica of the previous one. The screen also simply duplicates the existing range of arches only to a larger scale. The change in the shape of the arches is that the ogee curve gave place to a simple arc and the curves are firmer and more divided than those of the earlier type. With this extension, the Qutb Minar, which was lying outside Qutb mosque enclosure, now has been brought inside the extended mosque.

Shams-Ud-Din Altumush's Tomb, Delhi, 1235 C.E

A new structure first of its kind in India is the tomb of Shams-ud-din Altumush situated outside Qutb mosque, Delhi at northwest corner. Almost this is the first tomb structure built in India sometime around 1235 C.E.

Features

This is square in plan of 13 metres side with an entrance doorway in the centre of each side except on west, where three mihrabs inside were accommodated. The exterior surfaces are simple and plain. The interior cubical hall of 9 metres side is very elaborately carved and decorated with patterns and inscriptions of extracts from Quran with insertions in white marble. The cenotaph and the Mihrab were in marble. (Fig. 2.8)

Squinch arch system

The method of supporting the dome and its base in this tomb is the earliest and first attempt in India. The building is square and a domical roof is to be built over it. This requires a supporting system that converts the square to a circle. This was done by means of projecting an arch (squinch arch) at the angle of the square hall, thus making the square shape into an octagon. Here the Squinch takes the shape of a vault or half dome with an arch on its outer face. Octagon was made into sixteen sided figure by means of brackets and then a circular base was built. The dome was built on the circular frame thus obtained. But the dome of this tomb was collapsed and probably it may be a shallow dome. (Fig. 2.9)

No prominent buildings were built after this for some time.

QUESTIONS

1. Describe Quwat ul Islam mosque of Delhi with respect to its planning and other architectural contents.
   Alternatively: Which is the first mosque built in India. Explain its planning and other architectural features.
2. What is Qutb Minar and where it lies? Describe its construction features.
3. What is the alternate name to Ajmer mosque of 13th century? Who built it? Explain its planning and construction features.
4. Describe briefly the important features of Shams ud din Altumush's tomb.

Fig. 2.1. Qutb mosque, Delhi—Birds'eye view

Fig. 2.2. Qutb mosque, Delhi—Arched screen and **Iron** pillar

Fig. 2.3. Qutb Mosque, Delhi—showing beautiful carvings of Hindu temple pillars

Fig. 2.4. Qutb Minar, Delhi

Fig. 2.5. Qutb-minar, Delhi—Carvings and Inscriptions

Fig. 2.6. Ajmer mosque—Screen of Arches

Fig. 2.7. Ajmer mosque interior—Resembling a temple Mandapa

Fig. 2.8. Altumush tomb, Delhi, 1235 C.E—showing Squinch arch and Cenotaph

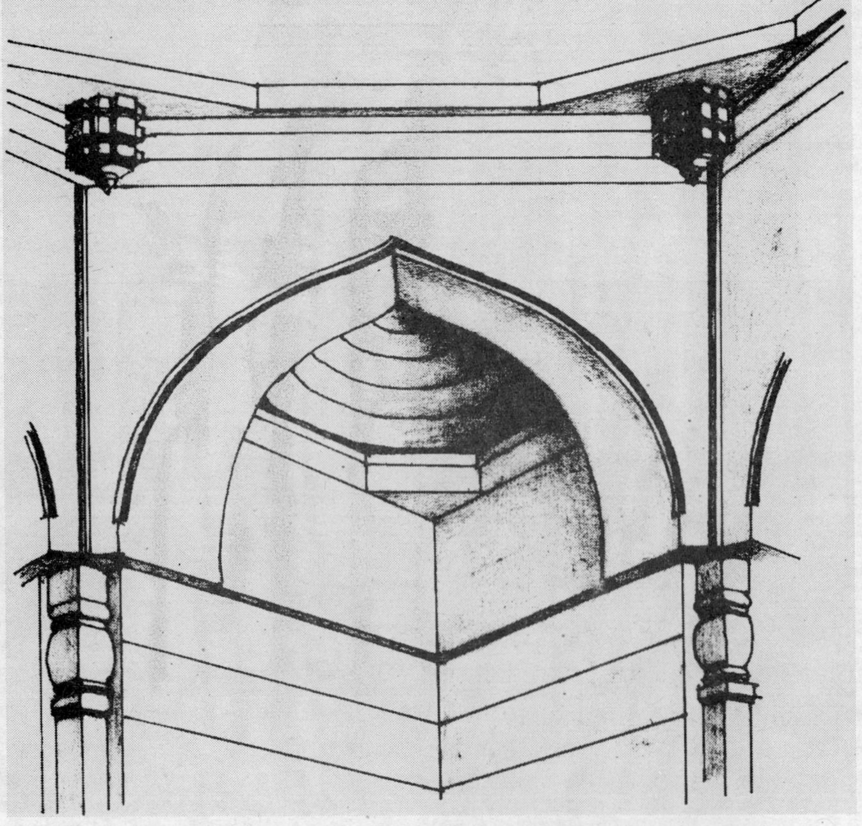

Fig. 2.9. Squinch arch in Shams ud din Altumush's tomb—Sketch

3

Delhi or Imperial Style

Under Khaljis (1290 to 1320 C.E)

3.1. INTRODUCTION

After the death of Shams-ud-din Altumush of Slave dynasty in 1236 C.E, there were no prominent kings and no buildings were undertaken for about three quarters of a century. There was a gap in between the dynasties as there was no proper political leadership for some time. Jalal-ud-din Khalji was governing the kingdom at Delhi. He was assisted by Alla-ud-din Khalji who hails from a village near Ghazni in Afganisthan. Alla-ud-din killed Jalal-ud-din and became independent king and ascended the throne in 1296 C.E.

3.2. IMPORTANT EXAMPLES

1. ALLA-UD-DIN KHALJI'S EXTENSION TO QUTB MOSQUE, DELHI: 1300 C.E Alla-ud-din further extended Qutb mosque already built earlier. The sanctuary of the mosque was extended on north and the cloisters were extended on north and east sides. By this the mosque became large in size.

Within the mosque in the spacious northern courtyard, a colossal Minar with its proportions double to that of Qutb minar was commissioned. Construction of such a grand and huge Minar could not be completed by the death of Alla-ud-din in 1316 C.E. This Minar was named as Alai minar after the name of Alla-ud-din. It rose up to nearly one storey where the work was stopped. The tower now remains solid as blunt tree trunk. (Fig. 3.5)

2. ALAI DARWAJA, DELHI, 1305 C.E: A small building having been completely finished is the southern entrance structure to Alai mosque at Delhi. Extension done by Alla-ud-din to Qutb mosque here is named as Alai mosque. Darwaja means door in Hindi language. Alai Darwaja is a self-contained Gateway built about the year 1305 C.E. This is one of the four entrances to Alai mosque, two of which to be on the long eastern side and one each on north and south sides. This is a cubical structure of 17 metres side in plan with a total height of over 18 metres up to the top of its domical finial. Though this is a small building, but the design is new and original. (Fig. 3.1)

Inspired by this, Ghiyas ud din Tughlaq's tomb was built after some 20 years having similar features.

Interior

It consists of a square hall inside having a dome roof. Its circular rim was supported on Squinch arches built at each of four corners following the method of radiating Voussoirs, thus converting the square base into an octagon. The Squinch arch has taken the shape of a semi-vault made with mini semi-vaults in rows. (Fig. 3.4)

Exterior

In their design the three outer faces of Alai Darwaja are much alike. Each contains a tall archway over a flight of steps leading to the interior. Below is a plinth elegantly carved in varied bands. The wall surface above the plinth is divided into two storeys. The two lower were built into arched recesses filled with perforated stone grilles. Above this the upper was carved into rectangular panels. All this was well executed in a combination of red sandstone and white marble. The borders were finely decorated with arabesques and inlaid geometrical patterns. A shallow white marble dome rises above as a roof. (Fig. 3.2)

Central arch

The outstanding gracefulness of the facades lies in the shape of central arches. The arch is pointed horseshoe type. Around its outlines is a band of fine inscription carved in white marble. On its underside or intrados of the arch there are fringe of sphere heads. On either side of the arch two slender ornamental pillars took place, which have some fine carving on its shaft. The whole of this arch with its pillars was fitted in a rectangular frame bordered with repeating patterns and inscriptions in white marble. (Fig. 3.3)

Conclusion

The various qualities of Alai Darwaja are remarkable, particularly in the shape of arches, the method of walling, the system of support to the dome, the surface decoration, coloured texture and fringe of sphere heads in arches. All these were well executed in a combination of dressed sandstone and white marble.

3.3. OTHER STRUCTURES

The other structures, which were built during this period are here listed which are now crumbled and broken pieces.

- City of Siri, second of the seven cities of Delhi
- Alla-ud-din Khalji's tomb
- Madarassa
- Jamaat khana masjid

QUESTIONS

1. Explain the plan, elevation and other decorative elements of Alai Darwaja, Delhi.
2. Sketch the view or elevation of Alai Darwaja, Delhi.

Fig. 3.1. Alai Darwaja in Qutb mosque, Delhi also showing Qutb Minar

Fig. 3.2. Alai Darwaza, Delhi, 1305 C.E

Fig. 3.3. Alai Darwaza, Qutb mosque complex, Delhi—Central arch and Close inscriptions

Fig. 3.4. Squinch arch in Alai Darwaja, Delhi

Fig. 3.5. Alai minar, Qutb Complex, Delhi

4

Delhi of Imperial Style

Under Tughlaqs (1320 to 1413 C.E)

4.1. INTRODUCTION

Out of many rulers of Tughlaq dynasty at Delhi, only three appear to have influenced the art of building. These were:

– The founder of the dynasty, Ghiyas-ud-din Tughlaq (1320 – 1325 C.E)

– His son Mohammed Bin Tughlaq (1325 – 1351 C.E)

– Firuz shah Tughlaq (1351 – 1388 C.E)

Besides other important architectural undertakings, each added his own capital city to the two already existing at Delhi.

4.2. ARCHITECTURAL CHARACTERS

Buildings of Tughlaqs developed strong building forms and elements and had influenced further future buildings. The striking elements here are:

- Battering walls
- Simple straight line arches
- Sphere heads in intrados of arches
- Projection of middle portion of wall on each face
- Lintel and Arch combination
- Buildings of Sayyids, Lodis, Jaunpur and Malwa province structures built in 15th century showed the influence of Tughlaq dynasty architecture.
- irst of the dynasty Ghiyas-ud-din Tughlaq an elder man and a soldier came to the throne and reigned for barely five years. Important buildings built during this period are described here under.

4.3. GHIYAS-UD-DIN TUGHLAQ'S BUILDINGS

1. Tughlaqabad

This took the form of a third city at Delhi known as Tughlaqabad. Standing on a highest point, this city is now totally in ruins, wild, lifeless and desolate. It is now huge masses of broken masonry.

2. GHIYAS-UD-DIN TUGHLAQ'S TOMB, DELHI, 1325 C.E

In contrast to the ruins of Tughlaqabad, the tomb of Ghiyas-ud-din is surprisingly in perfect condition. This is standing within an artificial lake by the side of Tughlaqabad connected by an elevated causeway. This is a self-contained mini size fortress in the form of an irregular pentagon with a spreading bastion at each angle with a greatest length of 91 metres. The unusual shape is conditioned by the contours of the rocky land on which it was built. It contains a high terrace on which the tomb building was placed in the center.

Tomb building

The tomb building was placed at widest part in the courtyard in orientation with Mecca. Its square base is 19 metres and the height of the structure including the finial is over 24 metres. In the centre of each side, a tall pointed archway is recessed. Three of which contain doorways while the fourth or western side is closed to accommodate the mihrab in its interior.

Interior and dome

It is a single chamber of 9 metres square inside, to which the source of light is only the three arched openings over the entrances. The dome was supported on four squinch arches in the same manner as that of Alai Darwaja. Three projecting stone brackets filled the angles between the octagon and sixteen-sided figure. The dome is a tartar dome having single shell and is crowned by a finial resembling the Kalasa and Amla (Vase and Melon motif).

Exterior

The exterior design is similar to Alai Darwaja built by Alla-ud-din Khalji earlier at Delhi. The pointed arches have a row of fine sphere-heads in its intrados. The striking part of this tomb is the slope of the outer walls inclined at an angle of 75 degrees. A notable element in the arch is the imposition of a lintel across the base of the arch, thus combining the arch and the beam. The tomb building is of red sandstone with certain portions including the dome in white marble. The total structure is outlined with merloned parapets. (Fig. 4.1, 4.2)

Other Features

Surrounding the terrace are the cloisters and on western side it was built into a mosque containing a mihrab. Within the courtyard there are several solidly built underground vaulted strong rooms to keep wealth. Some records reveal that a great treasure was laid here and molten gold poured into a cistern to make a mass of solid gold.

As a whole the structure reveals the appearance of strength, solidity and powerful expression.

4.4. MOHAMMED BIN TUGHLAQ'S CITY (1325 – 1351 C.E)

Mohammed Bin Tughlaq built the fourth city at Delhi enclosing the space between the first and second cities by means of fortified walls of prodigious thickness. Very little of this city and the walls remain now and it is all in ruins.

4.5. FIRUZ SHAH TUGHLAQ'S BUILDINGS (1351 – 1388 C.E)

Firuz shah has passionately devoted to building art. He built structures by using inexpensive materials and restored and repaired predecessors' old monuments and replaced top floors of Qutb Minar in white marble damaged by lightening. The following few structures are selected for description.

1. Firuzabad (the fortress of Firuz shah), Delhi, 1354 C.E:
2. Tomb of Khan-i-jahan Tilangani, Firuzabad, Delhi, 1370 C.E:
3. Tomb of Firuz shah Tughlaq, Delhi, 1388 C.E

1. FIRUZABAD, DELHI, 1354 C.E

Firuz shah Tughlaq constructed a new palace fort at Delhi which is the fifth successive fort built at Delhi. Now it is called Kotla Firuz Shah. The remains of this city now show the amenities, necessities and fully equipped royal residences. It is adjacent to Yamuna river. The fort is a rectangle of less than ¾ kilometre long by 1/3 kilometre broad. Its longer axis is running north south surrounded by high battlemented walls with tall spreading bastions at intervals. The main entrance is on western side consisting of a strongly fortified gateway. The fort consists of the following structures.

Palaces

On opposite side to the main gate across the width overlooking the river were the palaces, royal and private residences receiving pleasant air carried across the river water. The other area of the fort is divided into rectangular courts.

Diwan-i-Am

One of the large structures was the Diwan-i-Am or Hall of public audience with a spacious open quadrangle surrounded by pillared verandahs for transactions of official and court affairs.

Jami masjid

Towards the centre and against the river was the Jami masjid, a large structure to accommodate ten thousand persons.

Arcaded terraces

Another large structure occupying a prominent position is series of square arcaded terraces diminishing as they ascend to produce a kind of stepped pyramid, on the summit of which one of the Asoka's famous pillar brought from Ambala was placed. The remainder was pavilions, grape and water gardens, baths, tanks, barracks, armoury and servants' quarters all conveniently disposed.

Firuzabad is the most pulsating example. Similar fortresses were built by Moguls later inspired by this fort, especially the Red fort, Delhi.

2. KHIRKI MASJID, DELHI, 1380 C.E

This was built by Prime Minister Khan i Jahan Tilangani during the reign of Firuz shah Tughlaq in 1380 C.E. The word Khirki means window in Urdu language. The mosque has perforated stone windows and hence named as Khirki masjid.

The mosque is unusual in its design and was built in two storeys like a fort and the upper floor is the mosque. It measures 52 metres square in plan and raised on a high plinth of 3 metres in which some cells were made on outer ring. It is a blend of Hindu and Islam architectural features and the central court was covered by crossing corridors making the court divided into four courts each measuring 9.4 metres square. Inside it was encircled by arcades and has 180 square columns and 60 pilasters. (Fig. 4.4)

Outside there are bastion towers at corners and three protruding gateways having two tapering turrets one on each side. It was built in red sandstone rubble masonry and was plaster finished. Square plan was divided into 25 bays and 9 bays have 9 small domes in each. Main gate on east leads to central Mihrab. Mosque appears like fort by the bastion towers. (Fig. 4.3)

Some part of the roof was collapsed and was in neglected condition.

3. TOMB OF KHAN-I-JAHAN TILANGANI, DELHI, 1370 C.E

Khan-i-jahan Tilangani was the prime minister in the court of Firuz shah. He was also called Malik Maqbul. His tomb building is remarkable because it illustrates new kind of a tomb. This is the first octagonal tomb building built in India. Its design has strongly influenced other tomb buildings in the successive future.

Interior

The plan of the building is an octagon instead of usual square plan. For placing the dome over a square building it requires a device to convert the square shape into an octagon and then to a circular shape. But here the building itself was planned in an octagon. Hence the need of corner Squinch arches ceased. The main chamber was roofed by a low dome and surrounded by verandahs.

Exterior

Each side of the octagonal verandah has three Tudor arches. Over these arches a chajja (an eave) projects. A range of eight cupolas one over each of octagonal side was imposed on the roof of the verandah. As this type of structure is a first attempt, hence the proportions are not much satisfying. But the octagonal shape, enclosing corridors and the cupolas over verandah roof are totally a new conception. But the structure is much ruined.

From the design of this small earlier building, those large and stately octagonal mausoleums emerged. But the earliest octagonal tomb built in India was of the famous saint Shah Rukn-i-Alam at Multan in Punjab state of Pakistan, built some fifty year ago. But it had no surrounding verandah.

4. TOMB OF FIRUZ SHAH TUGHLAQ, DELHI, 1388 C.E

This tomb now known as Hauz-i-khas is one among other ruined structures at Kotla Firuz Shah, Delhi. The other is identified as Madarassa (college) all situated beside an ornamental lake. This is square in plan of some 14 metres side.

Inerior

The interior is a square chamber with squinch arches above (Fig. 4.6), at each angle of the square compartment to support the dome roof. An arched mihrab is sunk in the western wall.

Exterior

Externally the building has plain plastered walls sloping gently. The middle portion of the wall on each side was projected which enhanced the beauty of the facade. Within this, an arched door was fitted with a lintel on its top. Two sides have arched openings and the one on south is the entrance. The arched opening above the lintel is filled with a stone grill. The walls are crowned by ornamental merlon parapet. Above this rises an octagonal drum supporting a shallow dome. In front of entrance a low platform is extended surrounded by a stone railing made of uprights and two horizontal bars. As a whole the structure is graceful in its proportions with its gently sloping, plain, unadorned wall surfaces. (Fig. 4.5)

Attached to this building by the side is identified as Madarassa.

QUESTIONS

1. Describe plan, interior and exterior features of Ghiyas ud din Tughlaq's tomb, Delhi.
2. State the name of the fort built by Firuz Shah Tughlaq at Delhi and explain the layout and structures of the fort.
3. Describe the planning and elements of Khirki Masjid, Delhi.
4. Explain the plan and other elements of Khan i Jahan Tilangani's tomb at Delhi.
5. Describe the interior and exterior features of Firuz Shah Tughlaz's tomb, Delhi.
6. Sketch the elevation or the view of Ghiyas ud din Tughlaq's tomb, Delhi.

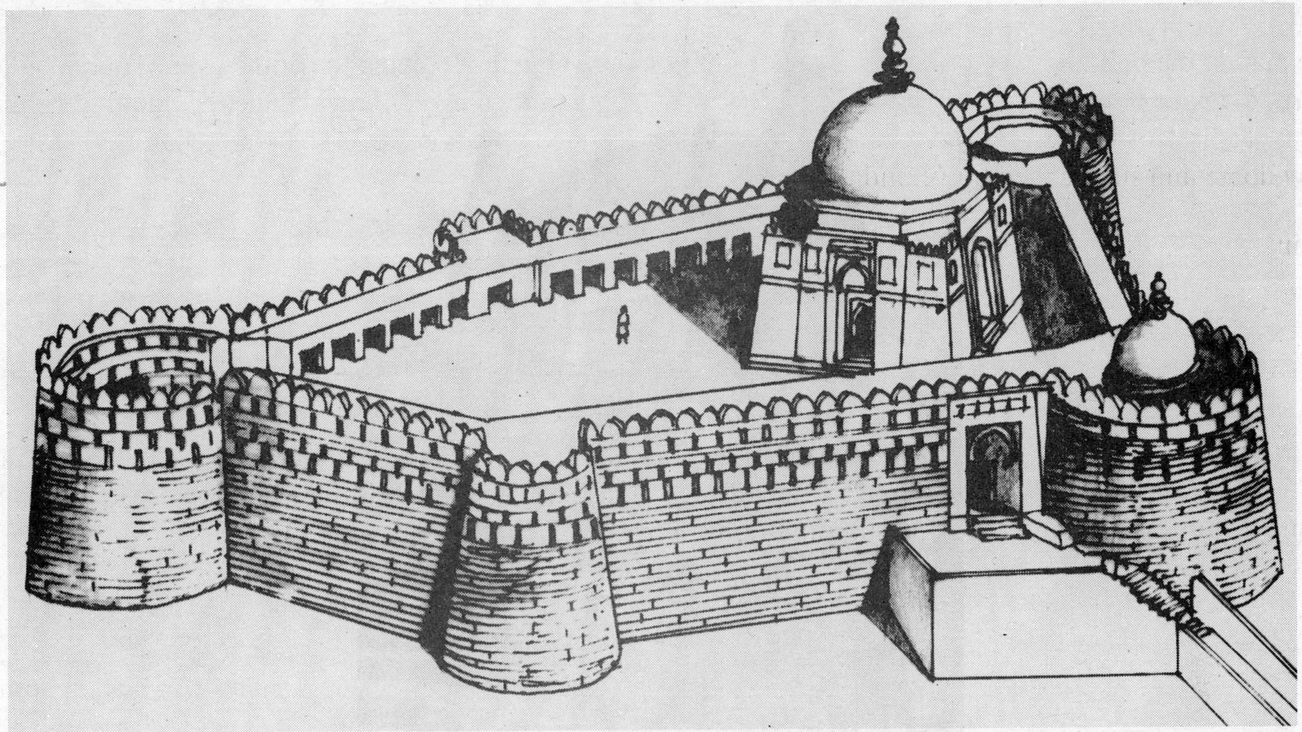

Fig. 4.1. Ghiyas ud din Tughlaq's tomb, Delhi

Fig. 4.2. Ghiyas ud din tughluq's tomb, Delhi, 1325 C.E

Fig. 4.3. Khirki Masjid—Main south entrance

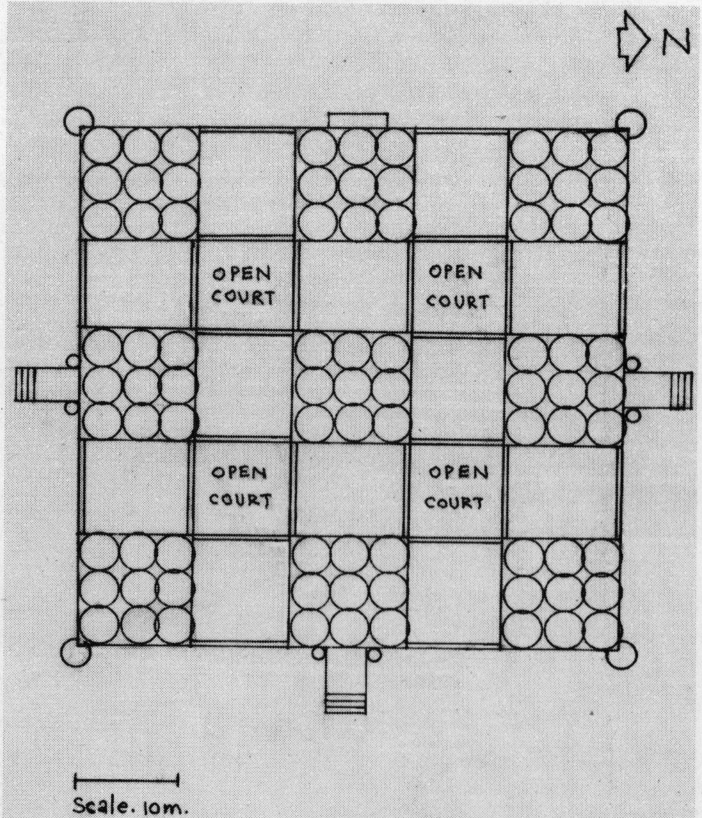

Fig. 4.4. Khirki Masjid, Delhi—Plan

Fig. 4.5. Tomb of Firuz shah Tughlaq, Delhi adjoining Madarasa, 1388 C.E

Fig. 4.6. Squinch arch in Ghiyas ud din Tughlaq's tomb, C.1325C.E

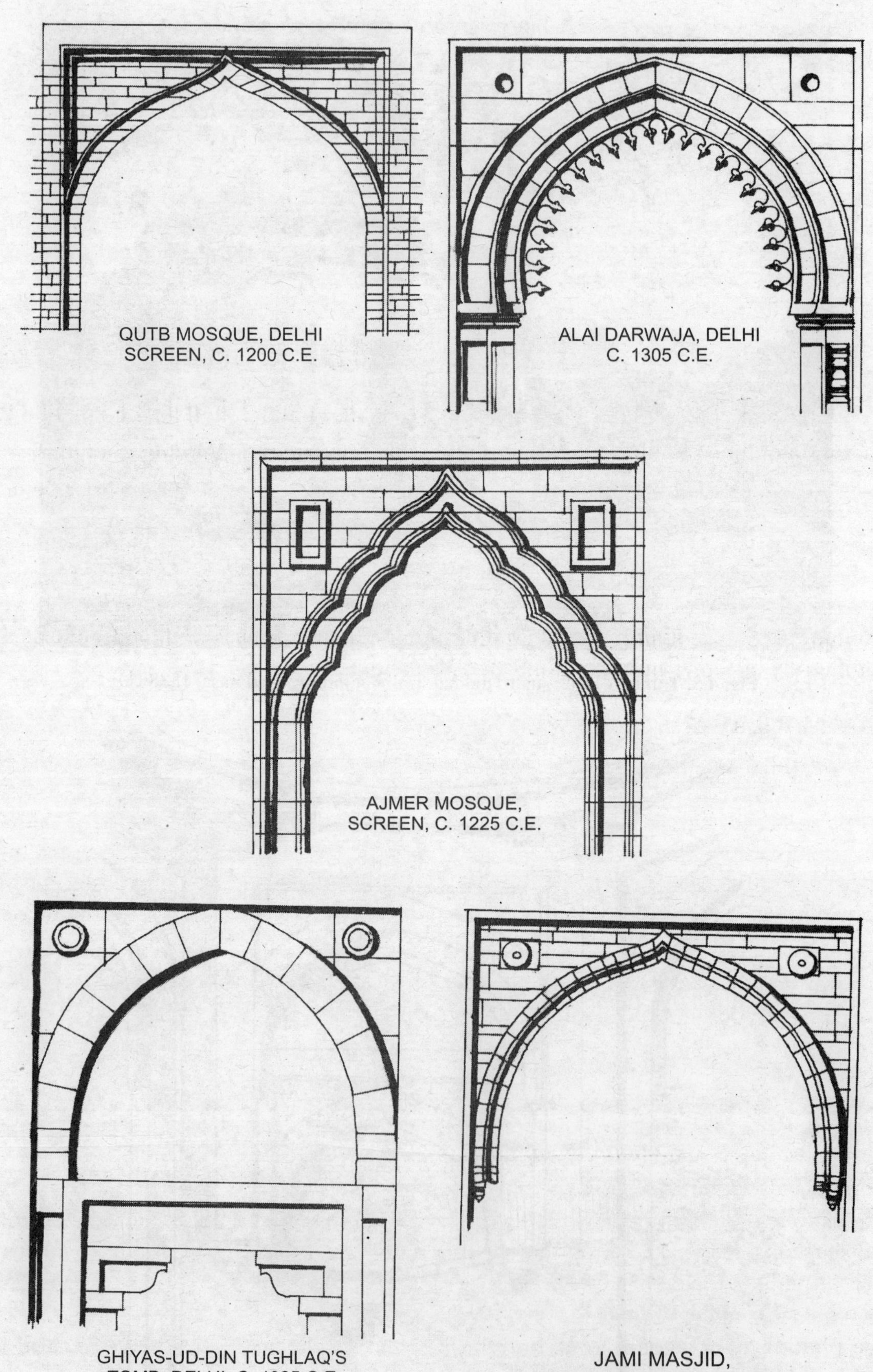

Fig. 4.7. Types of Arches

5

Delhi of Imperial Style

Under Sayyids (1414-1451 C.E.) and Lodis (1451-1526 C.E)

5.1. INTRODUCTION

Delhi has suffered worst after the invasion of Timur and the sack of Delhi. During the course of time in 15th century and in the first quarter of 16th century C.E, under the rule of Sayyids and their successors the Lodis, no great buildings were undertaken. No capital cities, imperial palaces or fortresses have been built except the tomb buildings. The founder of Sayyid dynasty was Khizar Khan and Buhlul Lodi was the founder of Lodi dynasty. South India was under the rule of Vijaynagar emperors during this time.

5.2. PERIOD OF MAQBARAHS

But however, the only monument that appealed to the rulers was the memorial structures to the dead. This was the period of Maqbarahs the cemeteries. Perhaps in no other time have the tomb buildings more raised than during the rule of Sayyids and Lodis. Scores of large tomb structures arose in the neighbourhood of Delhi. In the course of time the area around Delhi was converted into a vast necropolis. No less than fifty sizeable and important tombs were found. They range from simple open pillared pavilions in which the cenotaph is exposed outside to imposing great structures standing in an enclosure entered by tall gateways with an addition of a mosque. Lodis introducted double dome built one above other leaving a gap in between.

Tughlaq dynasty architecture had much influenced the structures of Sayyids and Lodis.

Types of tomb structures

The following two types of tomb structures were built.

– Octagonal tomb structures

– Square tomb structures

5.3. OCTAGONAL TOMB STRUCTURES

These buildings were one storey in height. They are surrounded by an arcaded verandah along with a projecting eave. Octagonal shape is a recognized design for royals and the square shape was meant for nobles and others of higher rank. The origin and the earlier octagonal mausoleum building was the tomb of Khan-i-Jahan Tilangani built during the reign of Tughlaq dynasty.

The average plan of an octagonal tomb building is one third larger in size and one third less in height approximately than the square tomb building.

IMPORTANT EXAMPLES:

1. Tomb of Mubarak Shah sayyid, Delhi, 1434 C.E

2. Tomb of Mohammed Shah Sayyid, Delhi, 1444 C.E
3. Tomb of Sikhander Lodi, Delhi, 1517 C.E

1. TOMB OF MUBARAK SHAH SAYYID, DELHI, 1434 C.E (Fig. 5.1)

This is the earliest tomb of Sayyid dynasty. It is an octagonal tomb building built over the remains of Mubark Shah Sayyid at Kotla Mubarakpur at Delhi. Kotla Mubarakpur got its name after the name of Mubarak Shah Sayyid. The dimensions of this building are 9 metres each octagonal side, 23 metres wide, and 15 metres high including the dome.

The tomb contains the following:

– Internal chamber with a dome above
– Surrounding corridors supported on pillars
– Kiosks one over each side of the verandah roof

The design of this type of structure was still in experimental stage. Hence the proportions of the dome and kiosks are yet to be improved and adjusted. The height of the structure requires to be raised in proportion to the width.

There is a funerary mosque near this tomb. But now the surroundings of this tomb building were encroached closely by modern constructions like shops, houses etc. Hence the building is obscured.

2. TOMB OF MOHAMMED SHAH SAYYID, DELHI, 1444 C.E (Fig. 5.2)

This is the best example of Sayyid tomb monuments located near southwest corner of Lodi garden, Delhi. The design of this Maqbara is an inspiration with some modifications from the earlier tombs of Khan-i-jahan Tilangani and Mubarak Shah Sayyid both built at Delhi. The monument is elegant and some original coloured plaster work is still visible.

This is a royal octagonal tomb building consisting of a central chamber surrounded by verandahs. The chamber measures 7.16 metres in size having door openings into verandahs in each face. The openings are bridged by lintel and arch.

Verandahs

Each octagonal side has three arched openings divided by pillars. The two side openings are slightly narrower than the central one. The pillars at the angles are larger in size than other pillars. They are sloped externally by means of an attachment, which persists throughout the entire series. Eight kiosks are placed above verandah roof one each over octagonal side.

Improved proportions

The dimensions of the tomb are similar to that of the tomb of Mubarak Shah Sayyid. But the drum of the dome and the kiosks (chatris) are elevated relatively improving its proportions. The effect here is satisfying, well proportioned and pleasing.

The width of each octagonal face is equal to the height including basement and ornamental pinnacles at the corners. This height is half the entire height of the building including the finial.

3. TOMB OF SIKANDER LODI, DELHI, 1517 C.E (Fig. 5.3)

This octagonal tomb structure produced after a gap of around three quarters of a century. It is much like the earlier tomb structures mentioned above. The measurements are similar to that of the tomb structure of Mohammed Shah Sayyid built at Delhi. But Sikander Lodi's tomb has no kiosks over the verandah roof.

Double dome

All the earlier tomb structures had the dome of one thickness. But here in this tomb, a change and an innovation is made. Here a double dome was built consisting of an inner and outer shell of masonry with a void space left in between. This is the first application of a double dome in Indian architecture. The intention is to raise the height of the structure and the dome to present an imposing appearance. And at the same time the deep void space inside the dome is to be concealed from inside. Hence a two shell dome is made. This has improved the proportions of the structure. Based on this principle of double dome, larger and greater domes were built later.

Though the tomb building is impressive in all its aspects, but the kiosks are missing over verandah roof. This building would have been still better, if it has the kiosks.

5.4. SQUARE TOMB STRUCTURES (Fig. 5.4, 5.5)

The other class of tomb buildings are square type tomb buildings built at Delhi. Square tomb building is a recognized design to the nobles and other persons of higher rank other than royals. These buildings are square in plan and had no verandahs. Out of many of such tombs some seven are larger and imposing in the neighbourhood of Delhi. These structures hardly bear the names of those to whom they were built. Now they are called by local names. The word Gumbad used in the name of these structures denotes the dome. The exterior of these structures is in two or sometimes three storeys in height surmounted by a dome.

Interior:

Inside, the building consists of a square room with sunken archways on all sides and that on the west contains a mihrab. At each corner of the square is a squinch arch above to support the dome.

Exterior

The buildings had no sloping walls and were elevated in floors. The vertical middle portion of wall on each face is projected into a rectangle up to the height of the building similar to Firuz Shah Tughlaq's tomb built at Delhi in 14th century C.E. A large recessed archway takes place in this projected wall. Within the arch is a doorway containing beam and bracket order. The upper storeys contain arched recesses each sunk in a rectangular panel with openings to allow light inside the hall. Parapets are solid merlon type.

The average size of the square tomb structure is one third less in plan and one third more in height than the octagonal tomb structures.

Important Examples:

1. Bada Khan ka Gumbad (Fig. 5.4)
2. Chota khan ka Gumbad (Fig. 5.5)
3. Shish Gumbad (Fig. 5.6)
4. Bara Gumbad
5. Tomb of Shihab-ud-din Tajkhan
6. adi ka Gumbad
7. Poli ka Gumbad

The above structures are now standing isolated without any enclosure walls.

8. Isa khan tomb–This is an elegant building but slightly lacking in height. This is somewhat adjusted in the tomb of Adham khan. The intermediate storey and the dome were raised, which has 16 arched recesses skillfully adjusted. But the kiosks over the verandahs were not added. (Fig. 5.7)

5.5 NAMES OF IMPORTANT MOSQUE STRUCTURES

The following are mosque structures built during this period.

– Mosque attached to Bara Gumbad, 1494 C.E

– Moth ki Masjid, Delhi, 1505 C.E

– Jamali Masjid, Delhi, 1529 C.E

Conclusion

The Delhi or Imperial style of architecture of Sultans ends now paving a way to Mogul architecture.

QUESTIONS

1. Explain the plan and construction of Octagonal and Square type of tombs of Sayyid and Lodi dynasties.
2. Describe the plan and elevation of Mubark Shah Sayyid's tomb, Delhi.
3. Describe the plan and elevation of Mohammed Shah Sayyid's tomb, Delhi.
4. Explain the structure of Sikander Lodi's tomb, Delhi.
5. Name any five important tomb structures of Sayyids and Lodis built at Delhi and list the building elements in these structures.
6. Sketch the view of any Octagonal tomb of Sayyids built at Delhi and mention the name of the building.
7. Sketch the view of any Square type of tomb of Sayyids or Lodis built at Delhi and mention the name.

Fig. 5.1. Octagonal type tomb—Mubarak Shah Sayyid tomb, Delhi

Fig. 5.2. Tomb of Mohammed Shah Sayyid, Delhi

Fig. 5.3. Sikander Lodi tomb,Delhi

Fig. 5.4. Square type tomb—Bada Khan ka Gumbad, Delhi

Fig. 5.5. Square type tomb—Chota Khan ka Gumbad, Delhi

Fig. 5.6. Shish Gumbad, Delhi

Fig. 5.7. Tomb of Isa Khan, Delhi

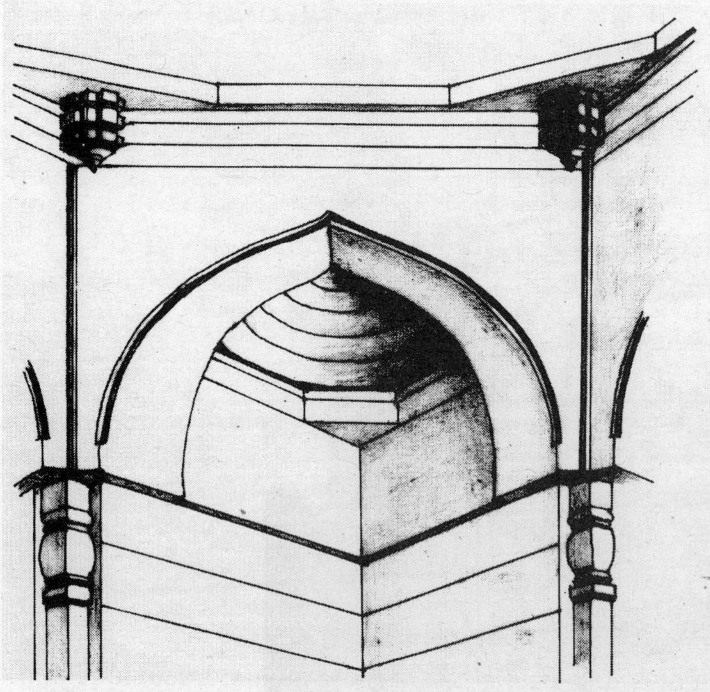

Squinch arch in Shamsuddin Altmush tomb, Delhi

Squinch arch in Alai Darwaja

Fig. 5.8. Squinch arches

6

Islamic Architecture of Provinces

Bengal (1203 to 1573 C.E.)

6.0. INTRODUCTION

The architectural development at Delhi under Sultan rulers was described earlier. This development does not restrict only to the capital Delhi, but it took part in the outlying portions of the country *i.e.* in the provinces which are self-contained developments of great importance. Here the structures of remarkable beauty displaying original indigenous architectural characters were produced. The influence of Imperial architecture of Delhi on the provincial style depended on the distance of the province from Delhi and the association of the rulers of the province with that of Delhi. Also this building art varied by the reasons like availability of local materials, building techniques and even climatic conditions.

These buildings were spread in different parts of the country. Therefore description of this development is made according to regions and are divided into some seven divisions as follows.

Names of Provinces and Period:

1. Bengal province – 1203 to 1573 C.E
2. Jaunpur province – 1360 to 1480 C.E
3. Gujarat province – 1300 to 1572 C.E
4. Malwa province – 1405 to 1569 C.E
5. Deccan province – 1347 to 1617 C.E
6. Bijapur province – 1490 to 1656 C.E
7. Kashmir province From 1410 C.E

Punjab province in Pakistan was also important where construction of tombs was initiated. The period of this province is from1150 to 1325 C.E. The fine example of tomb built here is Tomb of Shah Rukn-i-Alam at Multan, 1324 C.E. But this province is not considered here for description as it is now in Pakistan.

BENGAL PROVINCE

6.1. GEOGRAPHICAL AND POLITICAL POSITION

Bengal is a province situated far and remote on southeast side to Delhi. It is more a humid deltaic region of Ganga river with diversified life and activities. Earlier this was the seat of two Hindu dynasties of the Palas and the Senas with their capital at Lakhnauti. The Islamic conquest, penetration and occupation of this area took place in 1202 C.E. Muhammad Bakhtiar Khilji, a Turkmansthan general of slave dynasty from Delhi Sultanate defeated

Lakshman Sen of Sena dynasty and conquered Bengal. Bengal was ruled by feudalists under Delhi Sultanate. But the structures in this province are not much impressive or elegant. They are more solid and closed.

Art of construction here was different from the arid plains of Punjab. Majority of buildings were grouped in Malda District in West Bengal state in between the rivers of Ganga and Mahananda in the towns of Gaur and Pandua.

6.2. EXAMPLES

Out of several buildings, the following two important are described here.

1. Adina Masjid, Pandua, 1364 C.E
2. Dakhil Darwaja,Gaur, 1465 C.E

1. ADINA MASJID, PANDUA, 1364 C.E.

Adina masjid is located some 20 kilometres north of Malda town in West Bengal state built by Sikandar Shah of Ilyas dynasty. It was mostly ruined in earthquakes. This is one of the largest mosques in India. The design of this mosque is based on 8th century mosque of Damascus. Carved Basalt masonry stones obtained from earlier Hindu temples were used in building this mosque. This was built by Sikander shah II, Sultan of Ilyas dynasty.

It is a large mosque measuring externally 155 metres long and 87 metres wide. This is planned on conventional mosque design with a large open courtyard in the centre measuring 130 metres by 43 metres. This is enclosed by ranges of pillared aisles, five bays on the western or sanctuary side and three bays on the other sides consisting of 260 pillars in all. (Fig. 6.1, 6.2)

Courtyard

The expansive Quadrangular courtyard shows endless archways many of them had fallen. Surrounding the courtyard are continuous ranges of arches numbering to 88 surmounted by parapet up to 6.7 metres high from the ground. Each bay was carrying a cupola numbering to a total of 387 in all.

Gateways

A fine lofty gateway in the middle of eastern side to this large impressive mosque would have been better. But in an unusual manner these arches are opened outside. It may be to serve the purpose of using it as Baradari. Three other small doorways are provided in the western wall in the sanctuary in northwest corner and two of these lead to upper storey.

Nave of the Sanctuary

Sanctuary is divided into central nave and side aisles of 5 bays. The nave is the most impressive portion of the mosque containing no pillars inside. It is a large hall measuring 21 metres by 10 metres and the height from the pavement to the ridge of the roof is 15 metres. On each side on north and south there are tall pointed arches giving access into the bays of aisles, showing the perspective row of piers. The nave is now roofless. The huge brick vault over the nave might have collapsed due to its heavy weight. The front screen of the nave also is disappeared now. Nave still retains some of its appearance. (Fig. 6.2)

Mihrab

The treatment of the western wall is exceptional. It shows a Mihrab in the center and a supplementary one on one side and contains a mimber or pulpit on other side. The central Mihrab is in the form of a trefoil arched alcove set within a rectangular frame delicately inscribed with arabesques. (Fig. 6.2)

Upper storey and pillars

This is the earlier mosque in India to have upper floor for its use by royals and women as a private worshiping hall. In the ground storey the pillars took the form of piers, abnormally thick, short and square surmounted by massive bracket capitals. The upper storey pillars are graceful fluted shafts with expanding lotus capitals, removed from the same pre-existing Hindu structure. Within the royal chapel in the western wall, 32 alcoves (Miharbs) have been sunk, each one opposite the centre of each bay. These are exquisitely designed and ornamented. (Fig. 6.3, 6.4)

Use of stone and brick

Both materials of stone and brick were used in construction. The substructure was built with basalt stone brought from pre-existing temples of Lakhnauti. The arches, domes and upper parts were built in brick.

2. DAKHIL DARWAJA, GAUR, 1465 C.E (Fig. 6.5, 6.6)

This is a triumphal arch aligned to face the citadel of Gaur produced to the order of Barbak shah. This is also called Salami Darwaja situated in Malda district in West Bengal state. This is a remarkable and immense structure measuring nearly 23 metres wide in front and 34 metres from front to back with a height of 18 metres. This has a central arched opening and a passage 7.3 metres high having guard rooms on each side. This bulk structure carries projections and recesses with prominent rounded bastion at each corner. This provides a deep and wide portico containing arched openings. The circular bastions at the corners were built tapered and surmounted by rounded cupolas. The projections and recesses produced light and shade effect. The surfaces were enriched by ornamentation consisting of rosettes, hanging lamps, fretted borders, niches and other patterns. Most of the structure had fallen and is now unimpressive. The skyline shows the grouping of pyramidal roofs, domes and merloned parapets.

6.3. NAMES OF OTHER MOSQUES

Most mosque structures at Gaur were collapsed and are unimpressive. They are:

- Tantipara masjid, 1475 C.E
- Chamkatti masjid, 1475 C.E
- Daras Bari masjid, 15th cent. C.E
- Lotan masjid, 1480 C.E
- Chota sona masjid, 1510 C.E
- Rasul mosque,1530 C.E

QUESTIONS

1. Explain the Geographical and Political position and Art of construction developed in Bengal Province during Islam rule. Mention the name important mosque of Pandua.
2. Describe the famous mosque built at Pandua of Bengal.
3. What is Dakhil Darwaja and where it was built and explain its physical features.

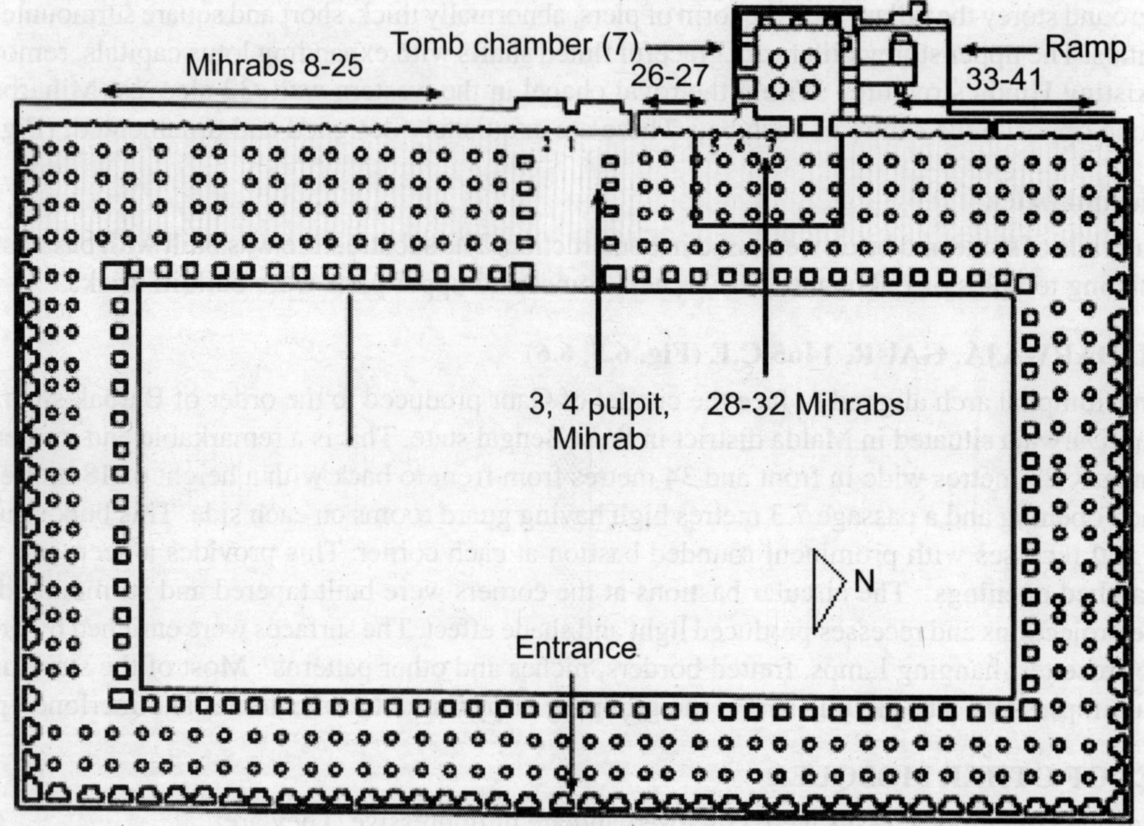

Fig. 6.1. Adina Mosque—Plan

Fig. 6.2. Adina Masjid, Pandua—Main PrayerHall (roof colapsed)

Fig. 6.3. Adina masjid, Pandua—Inside

Fig. 6.4. Adina masjid, Pandua—Mezzanine floor

Fig. 6.5. Dakhil darwaja, Gaur, 1465 C.E

Fig. 6.6. Dakhil darwaja, Gaur

7

Islamic Architecture of Provinces

Jaunpur (1360 to 1480 C.E)

7.1. GEOGRAPHICAL AND POLITICAL POSITION

Jaunpur was a large and important eastern strong hold of Delhi. Its governor was called by the title of Malikush-sharq (king of east) afterwards known as Sharqi dynasty. The city of Jaunpur stands on the river Gumti, some sixty kilometers northwest of Varanasi in Uttar Pradesh state. This was one of the strong capitals established by Firuz shah Tughlaq, the sultan of Delhi in the middle of 14th century. Hence Jaunpur structures had some similar features of Tughlaq dynasty structures. But due to the enmity shown towards the Sharqi kings of Jaunpur by the Delhi sultan Sikander Lodi at the close of 15th century, many monuments of this dynasty were ruthlessly destroyed and mutilated.

Jaunpur state assumed independence after Timur's invasion and capture of Delhi. Shams-ud-din Ibrahim had taken position at Jaunpur.

Centre for literature and Arts

Jaunpur became a resort for literature and variety of colleges. It became a university town. Arts and architecture were also encouraged. Hence in a course of short time the palaces, mosques and tombs have grown up.

7.2. EXAMPLES

The prominent structures were the mosques. Three important mosques are described here. They are.

1. Atala masjid, Jaunpur, 1408 C.E
2. Lal Darwaza masjid, Jaunpur, 1450 C.E
3. Jami masjid, Jaunpur, 1470 C.E

1. ATALA MASJID, JAUNPUR, 1408 C.E

Atala masjid was built on the site of a Hindu temple of Atala devi at Jaunpur during 1408 C.E. Hence its name came as Atala masjid. The stone materials of Atala Devi temple and other nearby temples were utilized in the construction of this mosque.

Layout of the mosque

The mosque plan is as per the convention with a central large open courtyard of 54 metres square. There are cloisters on three sides and the sanctuary on western side. The cloisters are five aisled and are spacious with a breadth of 13 metres rising up to two storeys. The two aisles of the lower storey are separated for its use as Baradari consisting a row of cells and a pillared verandah facing outside to the street to provide accommodation to visitors, piligrims and others. (Fig. 7.1)

Gateways

In the middle of each of three sides and interrupting the cloisters are impressive structures forming gateways. The two on north and south are prominent and the domes surmount them.

Sanctuary

The sanctuary is the most striking structure of the mosque. This occupies the whole width on western side. The sanctuary has its nave and the aisles. The nave is a rectangular hall of 11 metres by 9 metres with pillared transepts on either side. The nave has three stages vertically.

The lowest one is a compartment containing three Mihrabs and a high pulpit with steps on western side. The nave is flanked by transepts on both sides by arched openings.

Above this, the second stage has eight decorated arches, four of which are squinch arches at angles changing the square to an octagon. Light is admitted through perforated screens fitted in these arches.

The third or uppermost storey is converted into a sixteen-sided form by means of brackets fitted in each corner. At the top, it is roofed by a hemispherical dome. The dome at 17 metres high is placed over this drum. The centre of the transepts opened into an octagonal bay roofed by a smaller dome.

The end transepts are two storeyed. The upper storey was enclosed by perforated stone screens reserved for Zenana (Women's chamber). Many of the elements like recessed arch with its fringe ornamentation, the shape of the arch and the sloping side of its supports were derived from the buildings of Tughlaqs of Delhi. The arch is absolutely simple and it is just a straight line and a gentle curve and there is no ogee curve at top.

Sanctuary façade

The sanctuary façade has most prominent features like pylons- a larger one in the center and two smaller ones on sides. The main pylon is a commanding structure with sloping sides recalling Dravidian temple Gopurams and the pylons of Egyptian temples. Its height is 23 metres and width at the base is 17 metres. This pylon contained a great arched recess of 3.3 metres deep and contains the entrances to the nave. This also has arcaded window openings on its top. Similar pylons in a smaller scale are repeated on either side to the transepts. These pylons are the most striking features of this mosque with their recesses, projections, solids and voids well disposed and catching strong light and dark shadows. (Fig. 7.2)

Solid rear side

The rear sidewall on west side shows plain wall with no openings and has three projections. At each corner of these projections tapering turrets were added. The rear side shows the solid parts like retaining walls, turrets and domes and had no voids and arches.

2. LAL DARWAZA MASJID, JAUNPUR, 1450 C.E

Lal Darwaza mosque (Red Door mosque) was built around 1450AD. It is a royal mosque within the palace. This was planned and executed by Bibi Raja, the Queen of Mahmud shah. The approach to the mosque is through a distinctive high gate painted in red colour, hence its name as Lal Darwaza. The mosque is a simplified version of Atala masjid, Jaunpur and about two-thirds in size.

This mosque is of conventional design with an open court of 40 metres square. In its interior, Zenana is placed adjoining the nave in the upper floor enclosed with stone grill screens. Here Zenana means a secluded area or a chamber for women. The influence of the Queen lady worked out here in this Jaunpur mosque. The religious needs of women were taken into consideration and given special attention.

3. JAMI MASJID, JAUNPUR, 1470 C.E

The largest and ambitious mosque of Jaunpur is the Jami masjid constructed about 1470 C.E during the reign of Hussain shah. He was the last king of Sharqi dynasty. This is more similar to Atala Masjid in its design and other features. The entire structure was raised on a large terrace to some 4.80 to 6 metres above its surroundings to give impressive elevated appearance. Its entrances are approached by steep flight of steps. The cloisters surrounding the courtyard are two storeys in height. They are only two aisles in width, unlike the five-aisle width of Atala masjid. In the middle of each side is an entrance hall, each with a dome over. In the western end of the quadrangle the great pylon raises high giving access into the sanctuary. It is 26 metres high and 23 metres wide at its base. On each side of this pylon are the arcaded aisles (transepts). A vaulted roof covered these two large halls. (Fig. 7.3)

Sanctuary

The nave of the sanctuary is 11.6 metres in square designed in the same lines of Atala masjid. But here the clerestory arcade is open in order to light the inside of the dome. The central hall is flanked by aisles (transepts) on its both sides connected by arched openings. These transepts contain spacious hall on its upper floor, which is the private chapel for the royal family ladies (Zenana). Each hall measures 15 metres long, 12 metres wide and 14 metrs high having openings filled with perforated stone grilles, opening into the courtyard. The spacious halls are skillfully designed and daringly built with no support obstructions within the halls. There are three mihrabs in the opposite wall on west side. (Fig. 7.4)

Pointed vaulted roof

The roof of nave of sanctuary is a pointed vault. This is unique in its design. Construction of such large interior space with no supporting interruptions is rare and uncommon. Similar attempt was done in the nave of the Adina mosque at Pandua, Bengal a century ago, which was built in brick but has fallen. And in Jami Masjid of Jaunpur the great vaults are still intact. This is due to the sound and scientific method employed in construction. For achieving this, along the 12 metres width, four pointed arches or ribs consisting of two transverse ribs in the middle were laid. This system has become permanent centering. On this the flat stones are filled on the back of the ribs. This formed a solid stone shell of large blocks. To counteract the heavy outward thrust, the exterior walls were built strong and solid of some 3 metres thick.

The façade design and the pylons of Jami masjid, Jaunpur is undoubtedly remarkable in its design and style. The pillars of the mosque are square monolithic shafts with a moulded band across the middle. Similar band forms the capital above, from which the brackets spring.

The building art of Jaunpur came to an end with this Jami Masjid. This independent state was absorbed into the kingdom of Lodi Sultans of Delhi at the end of 15th centuary.

7.3. NAMES OF OTHER MOSQUES

- Khalis Mukhlis mosque, Jaunpur, 1430 C.E
- Jahangiri mosque, Jaunpur, 1430 C.E

QUESTIONS

1. State the Geographical and Political position of Jaunpur province of Islam rule and explain its excellence.
2. Describe the layout and architectural characters of great Atala masjid, Jaunpur.
3. Explain the layout and construction features of Jami masjid, Jaunpur.
4. Sketch the Sanctuary façade of Atala masjid, Jaunpur.

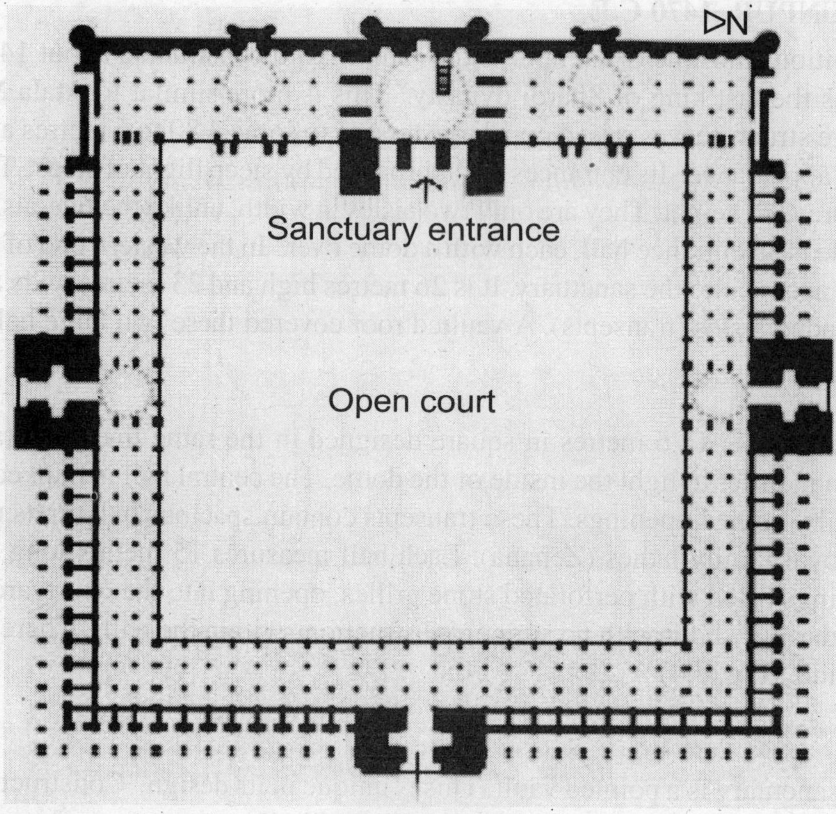

Fig. 7.1. Atala masjid, Jaunpur, 1408 C.E—Plan

Fig. 7.2. Atala masjid, Jaunpur—Sanctuary facade

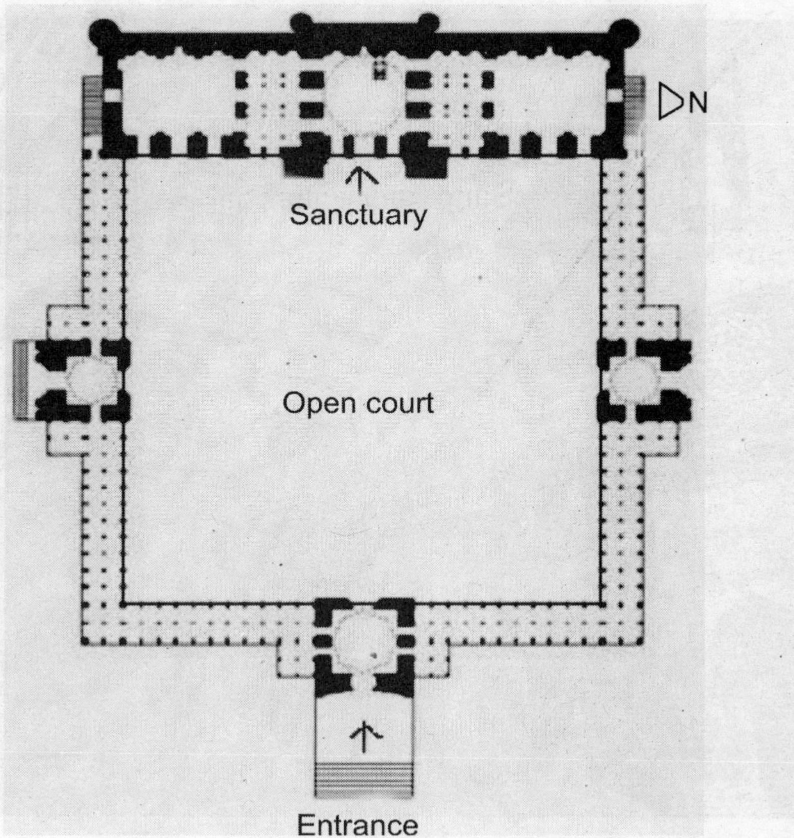

Fig. 7.3. Jami masjid, Jaunpur, 1470 C.E—Plan

Fig. 7.4. Jami masjid, Jaunpur—Sanctuary facade

Fig. 7.5. Atala masjid, Jaunpur—Facades

Fig. 7.6. Jami masjid, Jaunpur—Sancuary Facade direct

8

Islamic Architecture of Provinces

Gujarat (1300 to 1572 C.E)

8.1. GEOGRAPHICAL AND POLITICAL POSITION

The largest and important of the provincial styles is that of Gujarat in west India with its capital city at Ahmadabad. This development flourished in this area for a period of some 2 ½ centuries. Early in 14th century Gujarat was under the rule of Governors appointed by Khalji sultans of Delhi. Later it came under the independent rule of Ahmed Shahi dynasty. It was absorbed into the empire of Moguls in the second half of 16th century.

The contemporary rulers in south India were Hampi Vijayanagar emperors and Vijayanagar temples were under construction.

Much decorated and ornamented buildings were built during this period. The strong influence of Gujarat and Rajasthan Hindu craftsmanship are seen in these structures in the form of fine and intricate carvings.

The two causes for the development of good architecture here are:

– Patronage and building ambitions of the rulers

– Artistic skills and building techniques of local craftsmen.

8.2. EXAMPLES

During early period, construction of Islamic buildings is in the formative and experimental stage. Hence the earlier structures built here have not yet attained a definite shape. The best example of the early period is the Jami masjid of Cambay (circa 1325 C.E).

Later the style progressed and attained perfection during the period of Ahmed Shah in 15th century. The finest example of this period is the Jami masjid at Ahmadabad.

The same vigour was carried in 16th century during the power and patronage of the ruler Mahmud Begarha (1458 to 1511 C.E) and his successors. The typical and important example of this period is the Jami masjid at Champanir.

These three mosque structures are described here under.

1. JAMI MASJID, CAMBAY, 1325 C.E (Fig. 8.8)

This was built at ancient seaport town of Cambay about the year 1325 AD. The mosque has an arched screen in front of its sanctuary as was built in Qutb mosque, Delhi and Arhai-din-ka Jhompa mosque at Ajmer. As Gujarat province was under the rule of Khalji dynasty kings, hence the structures built here had the influence of contemporary Delhi architecture. Hence this Jami masjid building is similar to the buildings built during Khalji dynasty at Delhi. Group of artisans who were working in building construction at Delhi were recruited to work with indigenous builders at Cambay.

Intoduction of engrailed arch

The foliated arch is a modified variant of arch containing spear heads hanging from the intrados of arch. This became more prominent in the architecture of Gujarat. The sanctuary façade has three arches of horseshoe type with wider and higher opening in the center. The arched openings were fitted in a projected rectangular frame, which is common in most instances. The remainder of the scheme is usual.

2. JAMI MASJID, AHMADABAD, 1423 C.E

Jami masjid Ahmadabad was built during the reign of Bahmani ruler Ahmed shah I, completed in 1423 C.E. The mosque design was considered as perfect and complete in Western India. It is conventional in its design containing central open court, sanctuary on west and cloisters on three sides. The central court measures 78 metres long and 67 metres wide. (Fig. 8.1)

Sanctuary interior

The sanctuary has its nave and aisles. The nave is a hypostyle hall of 64 metres long by 29 metres deep and consists of some 300 tall slender pillars, closely set, that the distance between the pillars is less than 1.5 metres. Whereas the naves of Adina masjid, Pandua, West Bengal and the mosque of Jaunpur are spacious halls containing no pillars inside. There are 15 square bays each covered by a dome. The central nave rises to three storeys, the side aisles into two storeys, while the remainder is one storey in height. (Fig. 8.2)

Nave and Rotunda

The nave contains two pillared galleries one above the other. These galleries enclose a central open area extended to top, called here as 'rotunda'. The lower gallery is square and the upper octagonal. A dome covers this rotunda on top. At each stage is a platform with a balcony overlooking the rotunda and provided with Asana (sloping seat backs) in the manner as built in temples. Around the exterior of these galleries are pillared verandahs. These galleries are enclosed by perforated stone screens in between pillars for ventilation. The same design of the galleries is repeated in the transepts, but one storey less than the central nave. The increased height and better ventilation with an upward sweep was artistically solved in the sanctuary. (Fig. 8.3, 8.4)

The arches excel in their beauty with their fine curves. The pillars, beams, bracket capitals and interior show the workmanship of indigenous temple builders.

Sanctuary facade

The whole architectural effect is concentrated in its sanctuary. Especially there are two different conventions in the facade.

– The screen of arches placed in the center

– The pillared portico placed on the wings

– The volume of sanctuary wall was well relieved by the skillful adjustment of deep vault arched recesses, buttresses, simple pillared porticos at both ends and geometrical decorative inscriptions. The facade is superb in composition of solids and voids and it has three main arched openings. The large central archway supported by the richly moulded buttresses of minarets, the upper parts of which are now disappeared. The graceful curves of arches against inner dark background, interplay of light and shade in the front columns, the slender shafts, the fanciful engrailed arches all superbly composed giving a perfect composition and beauty. The transepts at the far end are simple pillared porticos containing five arches on each side. (Fig. 8.2)

3. JAMI MASJID, CHAMPANIR, 1485 C.E

The Jami masjid, Champanir is within the citadel at Champanir. Champanir was the capital city captured by sultan Mahmud Begarha from the Hindu king Jaysingh Patai Rawal in 1484 C.E. Champanir is situated some 117 kilometres southeast of Ahmedabad. These monuments are now UNESCO's world heritage site. (Fig. 8.5)

Layout

In plan and general arrangements, the mosque is more similar to Jami Masjid, Ahmedabad, built some 60 years before. The size of the mosque is about three fourth of the area of Jami Masjid of Ahmadabad. The mosque measures a rectangle of 82 metres by 55 metres and the sanctuary occupied less than half of this area. The courtyard is surrounded by cloisters only one aisle deep.

Sanctuary

The sanctuary is a pillared hall measuring 82 metres across and 40 metres deep and containing 176 pillars. The pillars of the sanctuary are soft in their design than the pillars of Ahmadabad mosque. The nave is in three storeys and there is a mezzanine gallery for the zenana at the northern end. The sanctuary façade contains five pointed archways with two slender minarets on each side of the larger central opening. These towers are well ornamented at the bottom level and the remaining top five stages are left unadorned. The front screen is rather more enclosed and the walls are plain and unadorned. (Fig. 8.6)

Oriel windows

There are prominent oriel windows one above the central archway, and one each by the side of two minarets. These projecting windows supported at the bottom by a row of brackets. The oriel windows are the charming features of buildings of Gujarat and Rajasthan, whether they belong to Hindus, Jains or Islams.

Rotunda and upper floors

Similar to Jami masjid of Ahmadabad, here also the rotunda is carried up and roofed by a dome. Stairs in the minarets provide access to each upper floor. The first floor is continuous with wide terraces and with rotunda opening in the centre of the nave. The second floor is a pillared gallery with the oriel window above the main arch of the facade. The balcony in this floor is octagonal with ribbed and richly fretted dome rising on pillars immediately above this storey. Around these balconies are the sloping seat backs of stone.

Gujarat craftsmen have well executed these buildings in every feature. The pillars, arches and other decorative elements in these mosques of Ahmadabad and Champanir are unique, indigenous and appreciable.

8.3. SECULAR STRUCTURES

In addition to mosques and tombs, there are other important structures, which are of secular nature. These are briefly described here.

1. Tin Darwaza, Ahmadabad, 1425 C.E

This is a triumphal archway in the city of Ahmadabad. It was the central feature of Ahmed shah's processional route, connecting the palace and the Jami Masjid, Ahmadabad. The archway is known as Tin Darwaza or triple doors. It contains three archways. It is now encroached by shops and is now a commonplace bazaar.

2. Wavs or Step wells (Fig. 8.7)

The other secular structures are the step-wells or wavs. These wells were common in the towns of western India. The practice of construction of step-wells was there even earlier to Islams ruling. Muslim rulers also continued the tradition. As the region is hot and nearer to desert, hence public wells were built to meet people's water needs. In no other parts of India, have these commonplace objects been enlarged or embellished to such an extent. The Wavs of Gujarat were not merely constructions over the well shaft, but took the form of extensive subterranean galleries of a high architectural value.

Eg: Bai Hari wav, Ahmedadbad, 1494 C.E

Wav at Adalaj, near Ahmedabad

8.4. NAMES OF OTHER IMPORTANT STRUCTURES

Mosques:

– Ahmed shah's royal chapel mosque within the citadel, 1411 C.E

– Haibatt Khan's mosque, Ahmadabad, 1412 C.E

– Sayyid Alam's mosque, Ahmadabad, 1412 C.E

– Sidi Sayyid's mosque, Ahmadabad, 1515 C.E famous for its shaking minarets

– Rani Rupmati's mosque, Mirzapur 1440 C.E

– Rani Sipri mosque, 1505 C.E

Tombs:

– Tomb of Ahmed Shah, 1440 C.E

– Rauza of Rupamati, Ahmadabad, 1440 C.E

QUESTIONS

1. State the Geographical and Political position of Gujarat province of Islam rule and explain its influence on buildings.
2. Describe Jami masjid of Ahmadabad with respect to its Layout, construction and decorative elements.
3. Explain the architecture of Jami masjid of Champanir.
4. What are the Wavs built during Islam rule near Ahmadabad and explain them in brief.

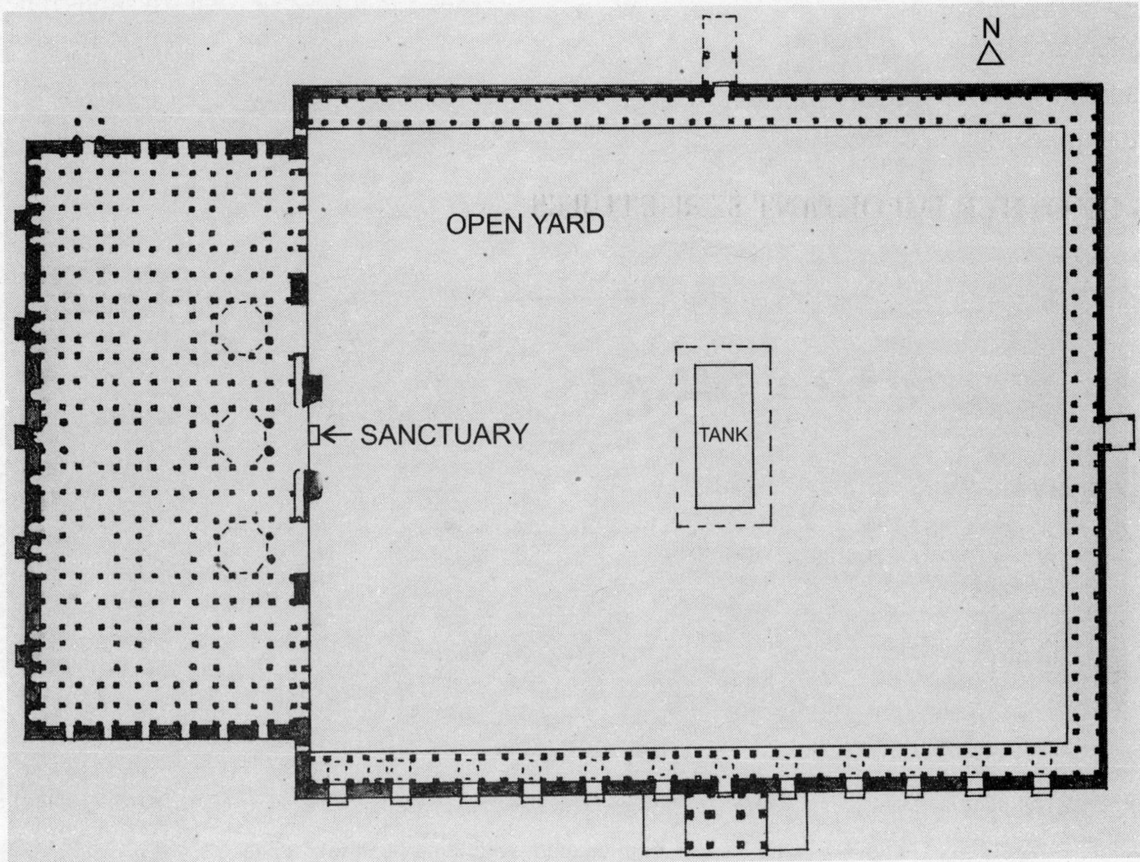

Fig. 8.1. Jami Masjid, Ahmadabad—Plan

Fig. 8.2. Jami Masjid Ahmedabad—Full facade

Fig. 8.3. Jama Masjid, Ahmadabad—Sanctuary central facade

Fig. 8.4. Jama Masjid, Ahmadabad Sanctuary—Entrance top details

Fig. 8.5. Jami Masjid, Champanir

Fig. 8.6. Jami Masjid, Champaner—1485 C.E

Fig. 8.7. Wav at Adalaj Ahmadabad, 15th cent.

Fig. 8.8. Jami Masjid, Cambay, 1325 C.E

9

Islamic Architecture of Provinces

Malwa (1405 to 1569 C.E)

9.1. GEOGRAPHICAL AND POLITICAL POSITION

Malwa region exists towards the west centre of the country, having connections with two cities of Dhar and Mandu situated in Madhya Pradesh state. Dhar was the ancient capital city for several centuries during the early mediaeval period under the stronghold of Paramaras, a Hindu powerful dynasty.

It was conquered by Delhi Sultan Alla ud din Khalji in 1305 C.E. After the decline of power in Delhi by the sack of the city by Timur, Ghuri governor Dilawar Khan declared himself as Shah and Mandu as independent state. His son Hushang Shah shifted the capital to Mandu from Dhar. The Ghuri dynasty invaded and established their hold in Malwa.

9.2. DESIGN AND CONSTRUCTION

As the political relations with neighbouring rulers were not amicable, hence Malwa rulers had imported and depended on imperial capital Delhi for construction designs and artisans. Hence the buildings of Malwa region are more similar to the buildings of Khaljis, Tughlaqs and Lodis of Imperial Delhi. The features of the buildings are:

- The battering walls
- Pointed arch decorated with spearhead fringe
- Arch-lintel-bracket combination
- Pyramidal roof
- High raised plinths
- Long and stately flight of steps leading to entrances

Use of colours

A striking feature found in these buildings is the use of colours. Coloured stones, coloured marble and tiles were used for colour effect. The principal material employed here was red sandstone. Strong and harmonious colours in borders and panels are applied throughout the buildings. Glazed earthen ware was the flourishing industry at Mandu in 15th century. Probably the craftsmen might have got connections with earthenware industries of Multan, Punjab where the earthenware and brick industries were flourished earlier. Due to various causes these colours are now disappeared, except some few patches.

Later the capital was moved from Dhar to Mandu some 33 kilometres away from Dhar.

9.3. EXAMPLES

1. JAMI MASJID, MANDU, 1440 C.E

Jami masjid, Mandu is a large and most impressive congregational mosque begun by Hushang Shah Ghuri and completed by sultan Mahmud Shah Khalji-I about the year 1440 AD. The mosque has exceptional features.

Layout of mosque

The mosque covered a spacious square area of 88 metres side. On eastern side it is prolonged by 30 metres forming an entrance hall roofed by a dome approached by wide flight of steps. Two subsidiary entrances on north side are one for priesthood and the other a private doorway for Zenana. Both are elegant in their features.

The design of mosque is conventional containing a central open courtyard and surrounding cloisters. Arched cloisters surround on all sides of the open courtyard 49 metres square with eleven openings on each side. The north and south side aisles are three aisles deep and that on the east has two aisles. On the west it was elaborated into a sanctuary of five aisles making it spacious. The sanctuary carries three large domes. All other bays carry cylindrical cupolas each one placed over each bay, numbering to 158 in all. There are no minarets in the mosque. (Fig. 9.1)

Interior

The interior of the sanctuary and the colonnades produced stately appearance by the repeating arcades of arches. The pointed arches are plain and simple. There are 17 Mihrabs at regular intervals decorated with Hindu delicate patterns and carvings in black polished stone. The Mimber has a chatri (kiosk) having 'S' shaped brackets richly ornamented. The architectural effect is simple, broad with graceful lines, curves and planes. The wall surfaces are unadorned. It may not be the intention of the builders to leave the surfaces unadorned, as it is often the common practice of artisans, builders and the rulers showing much desire in exquisite decoration, carvings and ornamentation. But the simple unadorned surfaces, graceful lines and simple curves are showing modern beauty to the architects of today and fitted into order of this day. (Fig. 9.2)

Exterior

The exterior is relatively plain and simple. The building is raised on a high plinth and the arcaded chambers of the basement are used as a Sarai. The gatehouse still retains some of the coloured borders and panels in glazed tiles.

9.4. NAMES OF OTHER IMPORTANT STRUCTURES

– These structures denote the prominent architectural features similar to Imperial structures of Delhi. But the roofs are collapsed.

– Ashrafi mahal

– Mausoleum of Hushang Shah

– Hindola mahal

– Jahaz mahal—120 metres long ship palace built between two lakes (Fig. 9.3, 9.4)

– Shahzadi-ka-Rauza at Chanderi

QUESTIONS

1. Explain Geographical, Political position and Design and Construction of buildings of Dhar and Mandu of Malwa Islam province.
2. Explain the Layout, interior and other parts of Jami masjid, Mandu.

Fig. 9.1. Jami Masjid, Mandu—Sanctuary showing fine simple pillars, cupolas and domes, 1440 C.E

Fig. 9.2. Jami masjid, Mandu—Sancuary interior showing Mihrab and Mimber

Fig. 9.3. Jahaz Mahal, Mandu, 15th cent.

Fig. 9.4. Jahaz Mahal, Mandu

10

Islamic Architecture of Provinces The Deccan

Gulbarga (1347 - 1422 C.E) Bidar (1422 - 1512 C.E) Golconda (1512 to 1687 C.E)

10.1. INTRODUCTION

The Deccan area refers to the country towards south covering the dominions of Karnataka state and Nizam state areas in the present Andhra Pradesh state. The building art having a definite character began here after the Delhi Sultans occupied this territory in 14th century and it continued up to 17th century until it was absorbed into Mogul empire.

10.2. EXOTIC PEOPLE AND IMPORTING ARCHITECTURE

The rulers of Deccan have ignored the presence of existing art of the country, which they occupied. They proceeded to produce an original and independent style of their own. The building art here consisted of two styles, one is the forceful influence from Delhi and the other entirely a distant source from the country of Persia.

The influence of Delhi architecture is due to Sultan Mohammed Bin Tughlaq's forced migration of inhabitants of Delhi to the new capital of Daulatabad in 1340. The exodus of masons, artisans, workmen and their successors laid foundations to Deccan architecture.

The Islam rulers who were migrated from Afghanistan, Persia and Turkey were settled permanently in India. But they look instinctively towards their motherland for solutions. Hence military adventurers, engineers, artisans and skilled workmen came in Arab ships from Persian Gulf to the lands of western India. There were strong overseas travels mainly the Persians to this Deccan capital. The first independent ruler of the Deccan was a Persian adventurer from the court at Delhi, Alla-ud-din Hasan Bahman shah who served as an official under Mohammed Bin Tughlaq who established Bahman dynasty at Gulbarga, in Karnataka state in 1347 C.E.

The Deccan area resolves into three periods according to the capital city of administration.

DIVISION OF THREE PERIODS

Gulbarga

The first period was from 1347 C.E when the city of Gulbarga was founded under Bahman dynasty rulers.

Bidar

The second period begins from 1422 C.E when the capital was transferred to the city of Bidar. This was first ruled by Bahman shahis and later by Barid shahi kings.

Golconda

The third period starts from 1512 C.E from the city of Golconda under Qutb shahi kings until 1687 till the country was conquered by Moguls.

Architecture developed under these three periods is described here capital city wise.

GULBARGA, 1347 TO 1422 C.E

10.3. INTRODUCTION

Alla-ud-din Bahman after thrown off his loyalty to Delhi established his capital at Gulbarga situated in Karnataka state in 1347 C.E. He immediately commissioned the fortress buildings. Most of the structures of this fort were disappeared and the remains show that it was an example of military architecture and immensely strong. Within the fortress is the Jami masjid which is now intact.

10.4. EXAMPLES

1. JAMI MASJID, GULBARGA, 1367 C.E

This is a rare mosque in India having no usual central open courtyard. The whole structure was covered by a roof. The design is not as per custom. This was built under the direction of a hereditary architect named Rafi from north Persia. The building was finished in plaster. (Fig. 10.1)

It measures 66 metres by 54 metres in plan. The central area was filled by rows of 68 bays each roofed by a cupola. Around three sides of the central rectangle are wide cloisters. On western side is the sanctuary.

Sanctuary

The sanctuary contains spacious nave roofed by a high dome. The main dome was mounted on a lofty square clerestorey with additional height. The same type of domes were repeated at corners to a smaller scale. The dome over the nave was supported on a clerestorey by means of squinch arches of graceful foliated type.

Cloisters

The design of the cloisters is remarkable, as they are not the usual multi aisled type with number of rows of pillars. But here it is only one row of an archway of extremely wide span supported on lower height posts. (Fig. 10.2)

Interior

The interior opens into square bays after passing through the receding arches. The interior has solid piers, vaulted ceilings and plain plastered surfaces with solemn dignity. The surfaces are absolutely plain without any decorations, bands, inscriptions or so. The construction is bold and daring in its abnormally wide arcades of cloisters. Though the covering of the central court in a mosque presents advantages in having a large central hall, but it was never practiced. The main reason is that the design is unorthodox and is not in accordance with tradition.

Exterior

The exterior of this mosque shows plain solid surfaces marked by dark shadowed archways in the enclosing walls. The stilted dome on a sub-structure has light and aerial effect by its fine proportions. The main entrance to this mosque is not on eastern side as per convention, but it is in the center of northern side. (Fig. 10.1)

2. TOMBS OF GULBARGA

The other structures at Gulbarga are the royal tombs of the rulers seven in number including the tomb of the founder. These are known as Haft Gumbaz or seven domes.

BIDAR, 1422 TO 1512 C.E

10.5. INTRODUCTION

The capital was shifted from Gulbarga to Bidar in Karnataka state by Ahmed shah (1422 to 1436 C.E), the ninth ruler of the dynasty. The chief building productions are

– Fortress, Palaces,

– Two mosques within the fort,

– Madarassa (college)

– Royal tombs

10.6. EXAMPLES

1. Fortress at Bidar (Fig. 10.3)

The fortress at Bidar is larger than the Gulbarga fort. The imperial buildings within the fort are

– Mahals or palaces,

– Rang mahal or painted palace- a large structure with coloured decoration

– Zenana mahal- a fine edifice

– Takt mahal or throne room, also called Durbar hall or Diwan-i-am or Public audience hall

Other amenities within this fort were:

– Water palaces,

– Tank,

– Fountains besides ornamental gardens,

– Hammams- the bathing areas of large and luxurious kind with running water facility

2. MADARASSA, BIDAR, 1481 C.E (Fig. 10.4)

A building of exotic character is the Madarassa, or college found by Mahmud Gawan, a Persian scholar and minister under Mohammed shah III in 1472 AD. This is an Islam college built with complete lecture halls, library, mosque, and accommodation for teachers and students.

The design of this stately college building is an inspired replica of the buildings at Samarkhand. This covers a rectangle of 62 metres by 55 metres. It has a quadrangle in the centre and the halls and chambers surround it. In the middle of three sides are semi-octagonal projections rising up and surmounted by Tartar domes. While on fourth side is the main entrance and has two tall minars in three stages one at each corner. The building is in three storeys with arched window openings and overall above is the parapet.

The surfaces are well treated with brilliant coloured glazed tiles. There are many inlaid decorations in patterns, floral, conventional and arabesques. Colours of green, yellow and white are predominant. Other part of the building was finished in plaster coating.

3. TOMBS

The other monuments at Bidar are the tomb structures of the rulers. They are twelve in number and all are of same type. These are large square buildings with tiers of arched arcades in walls and three turrets at each corner. Above the center rises an octagonal drum on which a massive stilted dome stands.

GOLCONDA, 1512 TO 1687 C.E

10.7. INTRODUCTION

The last place of Deccan architecture was from the city of Golconda situated near the city of Hyderabad in present state of Andhra Pradesh under Qutb shahi dynasty from 1512 to 1687 C.E.

Qutb Shahis were Shia muslims belonged to a tribe from Turkmenistan in Armenia region. Sultan Quli Qutb ul Mulk was the founder of the dynasty. Golconda became a rich and powerful state at that time. This is the first Muslim rule in Telugu speaking state of Telangana region. The ruling continued up to 1948 till the state joined in Indian nation.

The important structures of this period are scattered within the fortified city of Golconda and some in Hyderabad. Most structures are now ruined and deserted. A distinct style of architecture is seen in mosques and tomb structures. Important examples are described here.

10.8. EXAMPLES

1. GOLCONDA FORT

The fort was built by Ibrahim Quli Qutb Shah Wali, fourth king of the dynasty. Earlier this was under the control of Hindu Kakatiya kings in 12th century. Golconda is a hill of 120 metres high. It was surrounded by massive ramparts and had splendid built areas and palaces all built in massive stone walls. The fort is highly defensive and has a special kind of acoustical system by which the claps from a spacious portico are audible at the royal palace on the cliff some 100 metres away. But most of this is now in ruins.

2. MECCA MASJID, HYDERABAD, 1694 C.E (Fig. 10.5)

The largest and oldest mosque of Hyderabad is Mecca masjid located near Charminar. It was begun by Mohammad Quli Qutb Shah in 1597 and was completed by Aurangzeb. It is believed that some bricks brought from Mecca were used in construction of arches. Hence it is called Mecca masjid. The mosque has mainly a huge sanctuary hall and a large front open court containing a large artificial water pool having fountains. The sanctuary measures 67 metres long, 55 metres deep and 23 metres high. The sanctuary façade contains five huge size 4 centered pointed arches. The hall can accommodate some 10000 persons at a time. Holy text from Quran has been depicted on the arches.

Names of other important mosque structures:

– Mushirabad mosque, Hyderabad

– Toli masjid, Hyderabad which is small but well finished

3. QUTB-SHAHI TOMBS

There are a group of tombs located in Ibrahim Bagh situated to the north west side of the Golconda fort at Hyderabad. These monuments are some seven royal tombs, while others are of the members of the royal family within the vicinity. All the tomb buildings are square in plan and finished in plaster.

All are much in same type of design. Some large tombs are in two storeys. The tomb building consists of an inner mortuary chamber (cenotaph) and a surrounding arcaded verandah of one storey. The cornices of verandah are supported on brackets. This gave much effect to the exterior of the building. The mortuary chamber was built in two storeys. The lower storey was covered by a curved ceiling. Over this the upper storey rises into the drum and dome visible externally. Thus a large void was left above the ceiling and under the dome.

Decorative elements

These structures display decorative elements like—

– Moulded patterns,

– rnamentation in stucco,

– Fanciful pinnacles.

Examples:

Tomb of Abdullah Qutb Shah, 1672 C.E: This is an immense royal tomb built near Golconda fort in Ibrahim Bagh in Hyderabad. It is a square building of two storeys having a mortuary chamber and an arcaded verandah. Verandah is one storeyed containing fine row of arches surrounded by bracketed cornice. Mortuary chamber is covered by a curved ceiling and over this the drum and the dome were built leaving a great unused void in between. Its upper portion surrounded by a hanging balcony. The pleasing architectural elements of this tomb are the perforated panels, merlons and numerous finials. (Fig. 10.6)

Other such notable tomb structures are:

– Mohammed Quli Qutb shah

– Hayat Bakshi Begum

10.9. CHARMINAR, 1591 C.E (Fig. 10.7)

Charminar is neither a mosque nor a tomb. It is a triumphal monument built in 1591 C.E. Undoubtedly this is a remarkable structure built by Mohammad Quli Qutb Shah, 5th ruler of Qutb Shahi dynasty. Charminar means four towers. This was built in the centre of crossing of two royal avenues, i.e. in the center of four road junction.

It is a symmetrical pavilion structure looking same on all sides and is square in plan measuring 30 metres side with chamfered corners. A minar (tower) raises one at each corner rising up to 57 metres in height. On the ground it is a large square hall having rooms at all corners accommodating spiraling stairs rising into the tower. The hall is roofed by a vault supported on intersecting of arches, which are skillfully planned and executed. The hall is open on four sides by means of a huge size pointed arch joining into vaults inside. At the top of the hall a circular surrounding balcony opens into the hall, to which access is made from the four towers through door openings. The vaulted roof of the hall is made flat on its top accommodating a mosque at that height.

The facade consists of four huge archways, one on each side spanning 11 metres. Especially noticeable are the minars, which diminish in size stage by stage while they ascend. Its storeys are demarcated by projecting balconies at intervals having arcaded parapets. The minars have arched window openings ventilating the tower inside. Hemispherical cupolas crown these minars. Entire building was finished in thick plaster coat.

The following architectural elements made the structure strong, stupendous and graceful.

– Four-centered pointed arches with slight ogee curve

– Soaring minars

– Graceful row of arches in upper floor

– Bracket supports

QUESTIONS

1. Explain the Geographical position and Influence of Persia on buildings in Deccan region.
2. Describe the specific features of Jami masjid, Gulburga.
3. Explain briefly the building elements of Madarassa of Bidar.
4. Name and describe the important mosque built at Hyderabad.
5. Describe Qutb Shahi tombs of Golconda. Mention the name of an important tomb.
6. What is Charminar and describe the construction and decorative elements.

Fig. 10.1. Jamimasjid, Gulbarga, 1367 C.E—view

Fig. 10.2. Jami masjid, Gulbarga—Plastered unadorned pillars and arches in cloisters

Fig. 10.3. Bidar fort entrance, 15th cent.

Fig. 10.4. Madarassa at Bidar—View, 1481 C.E

Fig. 10.5. Mecca Masjid, Hyderabad, 1694 C.E

Fig. 10.6. Tomb of Abdulla Qutb Shah, Golconda, 1672 C.E

Fig. 10.7. Charminar, Hyderabad—close view

11

Islamic Architecture of Provinces

Bijapur (1490 to 1656 C.E)

11.1. GEOGRAPHICAL AND POLITICAL POSITION

Bijapur province situated in northern Karnataka state. This is relatively a province established late. It stands on gently rising ground without any natural protection.

Bijapur came under the supremacy of Adil Shahis. Yousuf Adil Shah was the founder of the dynasty. Adil Shahis have much influenced Architecture and allied arts. Within the limited area of this city, there are the remains of scores of structures of high importance and artistic excellence. These buildings are of three kinds numbering to over fifty examples.

– Mosques

– Tombs

– Fortress

11.2. DESIGN AND CONSTRUCTION

Well developed and elegant structures were built in Bijapur. A definite and different order of construction principles are seen in these structures. The planning, structural system, the piers, elevation elements, applied decoration were all well in marked dignity and maturity. The solutions were indigenous mixed with past experience of construction. Architectural beauty and utility are achieved through structural elements. The spacious arches, the clerestorey, the domes, intersecting arches were all both structural and architectural elements. Here the buildings were finished in plaster.

Pillars

The pillars are rare. Their place was substituted by substantial masonry piers, usually rectangular in section.

Shape of Arches

The arch here is distinctive. It has lost the angularity and the ogee outline of the early prototype. The typical Bijapur arch is of four-centered variety.

Cornice and brackets

The most remarkable feature in the facades is the inclined cornice or chajja. It is supported on closely set decorated brackets, catching dark shadows.

Intersection of Arches method

The halls are square and a dome is to be placed over the square hall. The dome requires a circular base as a support. For this a device of converting the square into a circle by means of corner vaults is required. This was done by means of squinch arches in the structures at Delhi. But in Bijapur structures, this is made by means of intersection of arches. As the walls rose in height, the square was made to change to an octagon and then to a circle. This was achieved by arranging each arch, so that its feet stood within the sides of the square, but its plane of arch stands at an angle. The intersection above produced an eight-sided figure from which a circular frame was made.

This is further described here in detail. If one side of a square is divided into three equal parts, it gives two points on each side. Such division on four sides of the square gives total eight points. A square is formed by joining the first consecutive points. Another square is formed by joining the second consecutive points. Arches rise above from each side of these two squares making a total of eight arches. The intersections of these eight arches make an octagon above. Additionally long narrow pointed arches like Gothic arches were also formed by this intersection. The volume behind these arches was filled to make vaults. By this a solid vaulted base is made above to place the dome. All the superstructure loads are transmitted to the ground through vault and arch legs. (Fig. 11.2, 11.5)

Geometrical use of square to form a stellate (star) plan in the temples of Hoysala period during 11th to 13th century was already well in practice in Karnataka. Such experiences might have helped in making the design of intersection of arches.

Dome

In the average buildings the dome is spherical in shape and rises out of a band of conventional petals at its base. The same spherical domes were repeated to small scale in the turrets as an ornamental finish. The spherical dome rising from petals is like Kalasha, i.e a coconut placed over lotus in a Kalasha.

Symbol of crescent

Adil Shahi kings of Bijapur claimed to be of Turkish origin. Hence accordingly the symbol of crescent appeared on the finials of their monuments.

Embellishments

The embellishments are either carved in stone or moulded in stucco. They are:

– Medallion in the spandrels
– Rosettes
– Conventional hanging lamps
– Running borders

11.3. EXAMPLES

Out of many structures of deserted capital of Bijapur, four important examples are selected here for description. They are

1. Jami masjid, Bijapur, 1570 C.E
2. Ibrahim Rauza, Bijapur, 1615 C.E
3. Gol Gumbaz, Bijapur, 1660 C.E
4. Mihtar mahal, Bijapur, 1620 C.E

1. JAMI MASJID, BIJAPUR, C. 1570 C.E.

The earliest monument of Bijapur is the Jami Masjid built by Ali shah I. This is considered as fine and classical example. But the building was not completed. It lacks two minars to flank the front of its eastern entrance and the ornamental merlons above the parapet surrounding the courtyard are missing. Even with these omissions, the mosque presents an imposing appearance. This is a large structure occupying a rectangle of 137 metres by 69 metres.

Courtyard

The internal courtyard is a square of 47 metres side, which contains superb range of arches on its three sides, seven on each side. The middle arch on sanctuary side was emphasized by foliations to make it prominent from others. Over these arches projects a wide and deep cornice supported on closely set brackets.

The Sanctuary

The sanctuary hall is spacious and impressive. It consists of large hall 63 metres by 33 metres divided into five aisles by means of arches supported on masonry piers.

The nave is a square compartment of 23 metres side and contained 12 arches, three on each side. The beauty of the interior was an outcome of structural and architectural order, mainly the intersection of arches. The square shape was converted into an octagon and then into a circle by means of intersection of arches to place the dome over the nave. The arches intersect above producing an octagon to support the dome above (Fig. 11.2). The bays of the aisles are square and the roof was built on the same principle of the nave, modified to suit to its small size.

The masonry surfaces are simple and plastered. There are inscriptions from holy Quran in gold on the walls of sanctuary.

The nave of the sanctuary rose into a square arcaded clerestory supporting a great dome and the parapet above is of refined merlons. Above this, a hemispherical dome was placed. It has bold foliations at its juncture with the drum. Its apex is a massive metal finial crowned by the symbol of a crescent. (Fig. 11.1)

Exterior

The exterior presents two rows of arcades within the walls, one above the other. The lower is merely ornamental, and the upper row opens into an arched corridor. As a whole the mosque is a good example of architectural dignity.

2. IBRAHIM RAUZA, BIJAPUR, C.1615 C.E. (Fig. 11.3)

This is the mausoleum of Ibrahim Adil Shah I (1580 to 1627 C.E) situated outside the city of Bijapur on the west. This consists of two buildings, a tomb and a mosque standing within an enclosure of 137 metres square. The buildings are more ornate, perfect and moderate in size.

Within the walled enclosure these two buildings stand on an oblong platform of 110 metres by 46 metres. The tomb was placed on eastern side and the mosque on western side. The open court in between was developed into an ornamental tank and fountain. The tomb building is more impressive out of these two. The buildings were finished in plaster coat.

Interior

The interior is an arrangement of double arcade around the central chamber with a row of pillars within the arched verandah. Every portion of the outer wall of the tomb chamber is profusely embellished with carvings. Each wall of the tomb chamber has three shallow arches enclosed by borders and panels. At each of the corner are finely ornamented piers. The surfaces are finished with arabesques, repeating patterns and tracery inscriptions. All these designs are distinctive and the artisans have created a whole series of new designs.

Tomb Chamber

The tomb chamber is a small room of 5.5 metres square, to which a graceful and coffered ceiling was added giving a fine appearance. A hanging ceiling was built using great structural techniques. The ceiling was well devised by means of masonry being joggle-jointed and hence it shows no visible supports. The dome was built above this ceiling, leaving a large void in between.

The whole work whether structural, technical, ornamental or utilitarian was carried out most meticulously.

Exterior

The mausoleum building is usual in its plan comprising a central chamber with encircling arcaded verandah. The façade consists of seven arches in which two of the arches are narrower than the others which are skillfully adjusted, thus presenting a variety in the voids. The same space alteration was carried in the parapet and ornamental finial, presenting a pleasing uniformity. Tall turrets rise from each corner. Wide projecting cornice supported on ornamental brackets had added much beauty to the building. The crowning glory is the shapely bulbous dome carried on elaborately bracketed and battlemented upper storey.

Mosque

The mosque building is an associate structure within the mausoleum enclosure. It corresponds in mass and architectural treatment to the tomb building and disposed in perfect harmony with the tomb and with the whole composition.

3. GOL GUMBAZ, BIJAPUR, 1660 C.E (Fig. 11.4)

A great monument in Bijapur is the mausoleum of Mohammed Adil shah II (1627 to 1657 C.E) normally called Gol Gumbaz means Round dome. This is the largest and most remarkable mausoleum ever constructed. The building is larger than Pantheon, Rome. The dome is second largest pre modern masonry dome after S. Sophia, Constantinople. Construction of such large dome was remarkable and adventurous. It took many years for construction. It was built in dark grey basalt rock and finished in plaster work. The height of entire building is some 61 metres. Other such higher structures built earlier are:

- Sikhara of Brihadeswara temple, Thanjavur, 1010 C.E- 60 metres high
- Sikhara of Jagannath temple, Puri, 1100 C.E- 61 metres high
- The surfaces of Gol Gumbaz structure are severely plain both inside and outside. This is a square building with chamfered corners.

The other buildings within the walled enclosed are

- A mosque
- A Naqqar khana or Drum house
- A Dharmasala or Rest house
- A Gateway
- Other amenities associated with mausoleum

The building is vast in size but its architectural forms are simple.

Interior

The interior is only one large chamber of majestic proportions and is the largest chamber in India. Tall pointed arches formed the sides. Intersection of arches gave support to the circular platform above and over which the dome was placed. It has underground chambers possessing the main cenotaph. There are no pillars inside. A 3.5 metres wide gallery projects in the hall all round at a height of 33.5 metres at the periphery of dome.

Exterior

Externally the building is a large cube with a tower placed at each corner. The main wall surface of the building is solid consisting of three shallow arches of elegant shapes sunk in each wall. The central arch is wider in size divided into panels to reduce it to the size of a normal doorway. The projecting octagonal towers at each angle are striking in appearance. They are vertical and no slanting in walls. These towers are divided into seven tiers. All of them are of same size with small arched openings and above each tower is a hemispherical graceful domical kiosk having carved leaves at its base.

The other supplementary elements are

– Fine projecting cornice supported on closely set brackets catching deep dark shadows

– Above this is the arcade of small arches

– Ornamental parapet

– Bold foliations at the base of the dome

A large hemispherical dome stands on top in the center. The proportions of the square mass below and the rounded dome above have achieved excellent appearance. The dome has no complex curves. It is simple like an inverted bowl.

Dome

Intersection of arches method: The square base of the chamber was converted into eight-sided figure by means of an innovative construction method of intersection of arches, which was described in detail in Design and Construction of this chapter. The dome is set back by some 3.6 metres from the edge of the circle, so that its weight is transmitted directly downwards on to the walls and a circular balcony is formed inside. The dome is only one layer of thick masonry and hence its appearance is same inside and outside.

Construction of Dome

The dome is a plain plastered vault with six small openings at the drum. It was built of horizontal courses of brick with a thick layer of mortar between each course. The average thickness of masonry is three metres. It seems that in the construction of this vast cupola no formwork was used except for the central section near the crown. It was built by a system of over sailing courses of brickwork laid in lime. The technique of supporting the dome by means of intersection of arches is surprising. This construction technique definitely was indigenous. There are six openings at the base of the dome giving way into the gallery.

Size and scale

The mausoleum unquestionably is one of the finest structural triumphs of the Bijapur builders on account of its magnificent size and proportions. The total external width of one of its square sides is equal to the entire height of the building, which is about 61 metres and outside diameter of the dome is 44 metres. The hall measures 41 metres side and is 54 metres high, while the gallery is 33.5 metres from the pavement. The hall covers an area of some1700 square metres and the Pantheon of Rome measures 1472 square metres only. Hence this mausoleum of Mohammed Adil Shah may claim to be the largest domical building in existence.

As a whole, this monumental mausoleum is a grand production, creating awe and amazement by means of its bulk and immense scale. The architectural elements like arches, cornices, arcades, foliated parapets and fluted drum were all harmoniously combined and disposed in an effective manner.

4. MIHTAR MAHAL, BIJAPUR, 1620 C.E (Fig. 11.6)

Though this building is called Mihtar Mahal, it is not a Mahal or a palace. It is a small remarkable entrance structure to the courtyard of a mosque. It appears to have been built about 1620 C.E during the reign of Ibrahim Adil shah II.

This has an upper storey and an open terrace above it, surrounded by a wall with oriel windows and perforated

Fig. 11.1. Jami masjid, Bijapur—Sanctuary facade

Fig. 11.2. Jamimasjid, Bijapur—Sanctuary Nave showing intersection of Arches

Fig. 11.3. Ibrahim Rauza, 1615 C.E

Fig. 11.4. Golgumbaz, Bijapur, 1660 C.E

parapet. The façade contains two slender buttresses rising up into graceful turrets. The outstanding feature is the window, its balcony projected on brackets and shaded by an eave. The other architectural elements all intricately well rendered are:

- Doorway of pointed arch recessed within a rectangle
- Buttresses
- String courses and mouldings.

The stone in this building is handled and treated skillfully as if it is plastic clay.

QUESTIONS

1. Describe the Design and Construction of Bijapur Islam province structures.
2. Explain the Layout and construction elements of Jami masjid, Bijapur.
3. What is Ibrahim Rauza, Bijapur? Explain its plan and exterior features.
4. What is Golgumbaz and where it was built? Describe its plan, elevation and construction features.
5. Sketch the Intersection of Arches and explain its principle.
6. Sketch the elevation or the view of Golgumbaz of Bijapur.
7. What is Mihtar mahal of Bijapur? Explain its features.

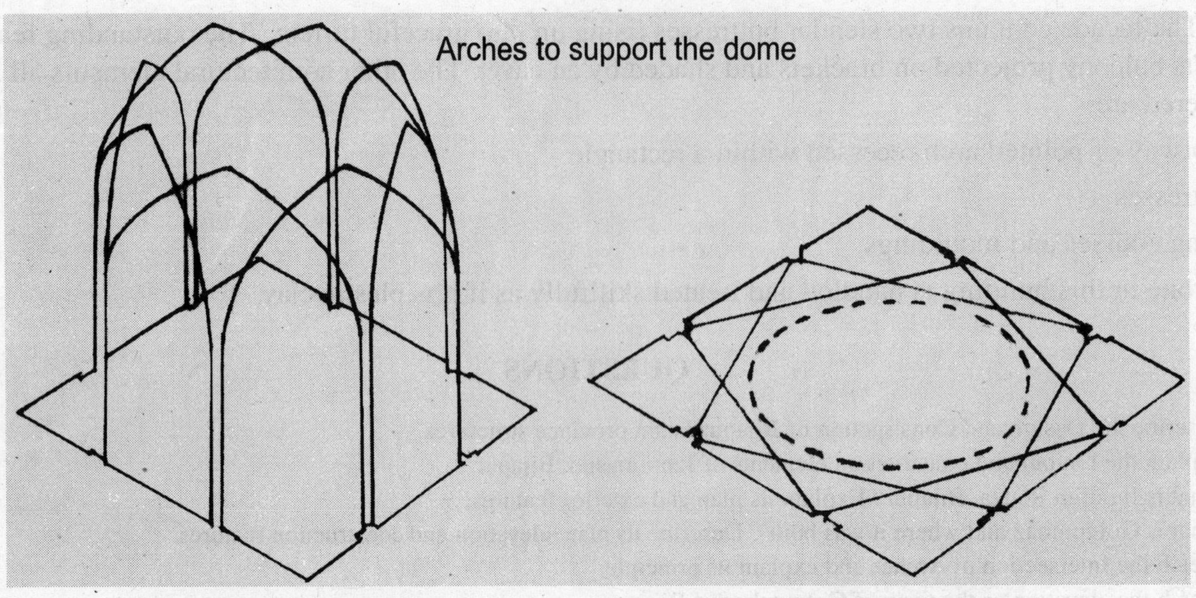

Intersection of Arches

Plan of arches

Fig. 11.5. Intersection of Arches method

Fig. 11.6. Mihtar mahal, Bijapur, 1620 C.E

12

Islamic Architecture of Provinces

Kashmir (From 1410 C.E)

12.1. INTRODUCTION

Kashmir's position and situation is different with respect to its geography, resources and climate. It is situated far in north India. It is bordered by present day Pakistan on west, China on north and east and India on south. It is mountainous situated at high altitude and filled with thick green forests. Natural resources like water, timber and stone are abundant. Its high altitude made the climate too cool and chilled. For most of the year the mountains are filled with ice and snow. It is described as heaven on earth. The population is less when compared to plain areas of India. As the country is bounded in mountains, hence movement of people is not easy and is restricted. It may be the reason that it was not much influenced by the developments taking place outside Kashmir. The early people of Kashmir were Hindus. There was the influence of outsiders on this part of the country.

12.2. DESIGN AND CONSTRUCTION

The structures of Kashmir are different from the rest of areas of India. Though the early structures in Kashmir were built in stone, but timber replaced stone in later structures. Kashmir presents contrasting characters of architecture by the use of two materials of wood and stone. In the first millennium here, the Buddhist and Hindu period flourished with stone structures. But in the middle period it is all timber constructions. But Mogul emperors turned back to stone structures in Kashmir as they were already well experienced and habituated in building stone structures at Delhi and Agra.

Use of timber

Timber is available and is used much as it is suitable to the cool climate to keep insides warm. The matter of economy of material did not arise as it is available plenty. Single tree trunks were employed in case of pillars. A variety of Cedar and Deodar are mainly used. The logs were floated and transported down the rivers.

Timber bridges

A simplest method of log construction was found in a series of bridges, which span the river Jhelum in Srinagar, the capital city of Kashmir state. Several of these bridges are still built on cantilever principle. The practice was in existence for many hundreds of years. The main supports or piers take the form of a massive wooden structure, resembling an inverted pyramid with its truncated apex resting on masonry platform. Each pier is built up of layers of logs in alternate courses placed transversely at right angles. It was a pile up of timber logs. The timber bridges are called kadals.

Construction method

Timber buildings were produced on the same lines, but refined and elaborated to suit their appearance. Logs are made to square section. The spaces between each course filled with neat brickwork on glazed tiles. In the interiors, these spaces are converted into recesses, for their use as lockers or cupboards. There is no good knowledge of woodwork or of the joinery. Simple dovetail joint is occasionally found. The logs are fastened to one another by stout wooden pin. There are no struts, trusses or diagonal members to secure lateral rigidity. The sole system is that of the dead weight bearing directly downwards. Due to these unscientific methods, the structures frequently collapsed. Also they were destroyed by fire. Hence little of the original structures remain. Most of them contain later replacements. The basement of masonry, the upper portion in wood and brick are the characteristics of Kashmir Islamic structures as a whole.

12.3. EXAMPLES

1. Mosques and tombs

These structures were built in brick and wood. The timber structures and the tombs are called Ziarats. Both mosques and Ziarats are same type in their architectural elements. The main elements are three in number, consisting of

– Lower cubical portion or main body of the building containing a hall or a chamber,
– A pyramidal roof in tiers
– Slender spire above the whole

Names of examples:

Mosques:

– Mosque of Shah Hamadan, Srinagar (Fig. 12.1)
– Jami masjid, Srinagar, 15th cent. C.E (Fig. 12.3)
– Hazratbal mosque,17th cent.

Tombs:

– Zain-ul-Abidin's mother's tomb
– Pir Haji Mohammed sahib's tomb

2. Moguls' Stone Buildings

Mogul emperors forced their efforts to revive the art of stone building in Kashmir in 16th and 17th centuries. The design of these Mogul structures was that which was flourishing at that time at Delhi and Agra. The Kashmir workmen lost the art of handling the stone, as they were accustomed to work only in wood. Hence the emperor Akbar was compelled to import two hundred Indian master builders to carry out his projects as per an inscription.

The following are the three buildings all built in grey limestone, available in the nearby area:

– Fort of Hari parbat (Green mountain) (Fig. 12.4)
– Pattar masjid (Stone mosque), 1623 C.E.
– Mosque of Akhun Mullah Shah, 1649 C.E.

The fort built on the peak of the hill of Hari parbat (Green mountain) is usual in its design and much of it was recent replacement. The two gateways, the Kathi Darwaja, and the Sangin Darwaza are of the original Mogul period. The other buildings show the style in temperate manner with minimum decoration.

The masonry buildings, whether in stone or brick are impositions only to satisfy the alien rulers. These intruding productions did not make any mark on the indigenous style of using timber. It continued its course uninterrupted and unaffected.

3. MOGUL GARDENS:

The landscape designs and the Gardens laid by Moguls were described separately in the chapter of Mogul architecture-Jahangir.

QUESTIONS

1. Explain the Design and Construction method of Kashmir structures.
2. Explain the Mogul structures built near Srinagar.

Fig. 12.1. Shah-Hamadan-mosque, Srinagar

Fig. 12.2. Patthar masjid, Srinagar

Fig. 12.3. Jami Masjid, Srinagar

Fig. 12.4. Hari parbat fort—Srinagar, 16th cent.

13

Buildings of Sher Shah Sur

Sasaram and Delhi (1530 to 1545 C.E)

13.1. GEOGRAPHICAL AND POLITICAL POSITION

Sasaram is a small town in the Shahabad district of Bihar state. Sher Shah came to power and established his independent kingdom at Sasaram. In 1539 C.E he defeated Humayun in a battle and captured the throne at Delhi. He consolidated his kingdom from Punjab to Bengal. Sher Shah's original name was Farid Khan. He was a Pahyan from Afghanistan. He introduced new administrative, economic and welfare schemes some of which were continued by Moguls later.

He reigned for about fifteen years from 1530 C.E. Such a limited period generally can not mark any effect on architecture. But Shershah had been an outstanding and experienced, hence decisive buildings were the outcome.

There are two stages in which Shershah had played his powerful role.

1. The early role was at the lower province at Sasaram, where mausoleums were built.

2. The second stage is at Delhi, after seizing the throne at Delhi from the Mogul emperor Humayun.

13.2. STRUCTURES AT SASARAM

It presents a group of three tombs belonging to the ruling family and a memorial to the architect Aliwal khan, who built these. Here it is ridiculous and strange that the finest example of Lodi type of tomb was produced not at Delhi, but on this relatively remote site in the province, some 750 kilometres distant. Shershah's tomb at Sasaram though is a monument in a province, but it is far superior to the structures built at the capital Delhi. This is due to the reason that the ruling power at Delhi approaching its decline and on the other hand, Shershah Sur showed his great vigour and courage throughout his brief career. These buildings were built under the supervision of the master builder Aliwal khan who trained in Imperial tradition. His first commission at Sasaram was the construction of the tomb of Hasan Sur Khan, father of Shershah, about 1535 C.E.

13.3. EXAMPLES

TOMB OF SHERSHAH SUR, SASARAM, 1540 C.E (Fig. 13.1)

This is one of the grandest and most imaginative architectural productions in whole of India built at Sasaram in Bihar state. The designer Aliwal khan's efforts bore rich fruit. Lodi type of octagonal tomb design was conceptually implied, modified, filtered and transformed into a fine model. The entire structure stands in the centre of a large artificial lake of size of 305 metres side. Access to the tomb building is by means of a causeway, which was connected to a guardroom on northern side of the lake.

The tomb building is in five stages. The lowest is the basement rising directly from above lake water. Above this is the large stone terrace. Both these are square in plan. A terrace of 9.15 metres high is enclosed by a parapet wall containing octagonal pillared pavilions placed at all corners.

Plan and interior

Occupying the centre of the terrace is the tomb building. The building consists of an octagonal tomb chamber and a surrounding verandah. The tomb chamber is entered through the verandah by doorways, one on each side except on west, which is closed to accommodate the mihrab. The compartment is 20 metres in diameter. The interior walls are plain and the Qibla wall was decorated by graceful inscribed letters.

Beam and bracket method was used over void spaces. The lintels supported on projecting corbel were placed at angles in each stage. Light is entered through doors and perforated screens fixed above doors.

Exterior

Externally the structure is in three diminishing stages.

The lowest storey is an open verandah of 3.10 metres wide having triple arches in each of its eight sides with a small projecting eave above. Over this rises a parapet with loopholes. Eight kiosks with cupola roofs were placed over the roof of verandah placed at corners.

The second stage is a plain wall similar to the tomb of Hasan Khan. Above this again pillared kiosks are placed at each angle.

The third stage above is the circular drum of the dome. The brick dome is a broad low dome crowned by lotus finial. It is raised directly to a height of 27 metres from the pavement and the dome is not a double dome.

Proportions

The proportions of its diminishing stages, the harmonious transition from one form to other, the variety, simplicity, breadth and scale of each element and skillfully adjusted mass show high aesthetic capacity of the designer at its greatest.

Use of sandstone

Fine sandstone collected from local quarries at Chunar was used, giving an appearance of uniform grey mass. Striking colour schemes are added to most of the surfaces.

Adjustment of orientation

It was intended to place the building exactly to the compass, but on completion of the stepped plinth, error was found to some degrees. Therefore the remaining upper part of the building was carried out at an angle with its basement.

As a whole, the mausoleum of Sheıshah Sur at Sasaram is a great-inspired monument and a sober creation.

13.4. STRUCTURES AT DELHI

Shershah seated on the throne at Delhi in 1540 C.E, after seizing the empire from the Mogul king Humayun. Immediately he proceeded to build a new fort, which is now known as Purana Qila or old fort. This is more a concentration of military and palatial structures mostly ruined now. Within this fort a Royal chapel Qila-i-kuhna masjid was built.

13.5. EXAMPLES

QILA-I-KUHNA MASJID, DELHI, 1545 C.E

A prime example and a gem of architecture is Qila-i-kuhna masjid, the royal chapel of Sur rulers built within

Purana Qila at about 1545 C.E. This mosque is much like Jamala Masjid, Delhi built some 15 years earlier during the reign of Humayun.

Sanctuary

The mosque contains only the sanctuary and occupies an oblong of 48 metres by 14 metres with a total height of 20 metres. Private entrances on north and south sides are for the use of royal family. Interior of the structure has five bays of elegant arches, broad mouldings and plastic ornamentation on the Qibla wall. The bays are roofed by low dome which has finely modeled squinch arches at the corners. Interior shows striking lines and curves in recessed arches, mihrabs and squinch arches. (Fig. 13.4 to 13.7)

Facade

The mosque facade is novel in its arrangements. The facade has five archways. The central arch was sunk within an arch fitted in a rectangular frame. Over the nave is the single layer Lodi dome. Each arch gives access to a long hall divided into five bays by lateral arches. To add varied colours, the sandstone surfaces are enriched with inlay patterns of coloured and white marble. The fine and most pleasing elements are the oriel windows placed over main façade arches. There are two substantial stair turrets one at each rear angle. (Fig. 13.3)

Vaulted roof

This shows the great imagination of builders. The construction methods employed in building the roof are

– The Squinch arches to support the dome in the central bay

– Stalactite variety in the next bay

– And cross-rib and semi-vault in the end compartment

Mihrab

The mihrabs in each bay are the finest variety, the elegance of which cannot be described in words. It is the finest combination of recessed arches and vaulted niches contained within each other with decorative imposts.

Unquestionably Qila-i-kuhna mosque is one of the finest productions without a parallel to it. (Fig. 13.5)

Conclusion

The architectural productions of Shershah Sur are so extra-ordinary in their design and fineness of embellishments, that the credit goes much to the emperor that within a limited period, such fine structures were mastered and built both at Sasaram and Delhi.

QUESTIONS

1. Explain the Geographical and Political position of Sasaram province and what structures were built mainly at Sasaram.
2. Describe the plan, elevation and construction of Sher Shah Sur's tomb of Sasaram.
3. Explain the plan and other fine decorative elements of Qila i Kuhna masjid of Delhi. Who built this?

Fig. 13.1. Shershah Sur tomb, Sasaram—Entrance view, 1540 C.E

Fig. 13.2. Shershah Sur's tomb, Sasaram

Fig. 13.3. Quila-i-Kuhna Masjid, Delhi, 1545 C.E—Sanctuary

Fig. 13.4. Qila-i-Kuhna Masjid, Delhi—Interior

Fig. 13.5. Quila-i-Kuhna masjid, Delhi—Central Mihrab

Fig. 13.6. Quila-i-Kuhna Masjid, Delhi—Detail of squinch arch

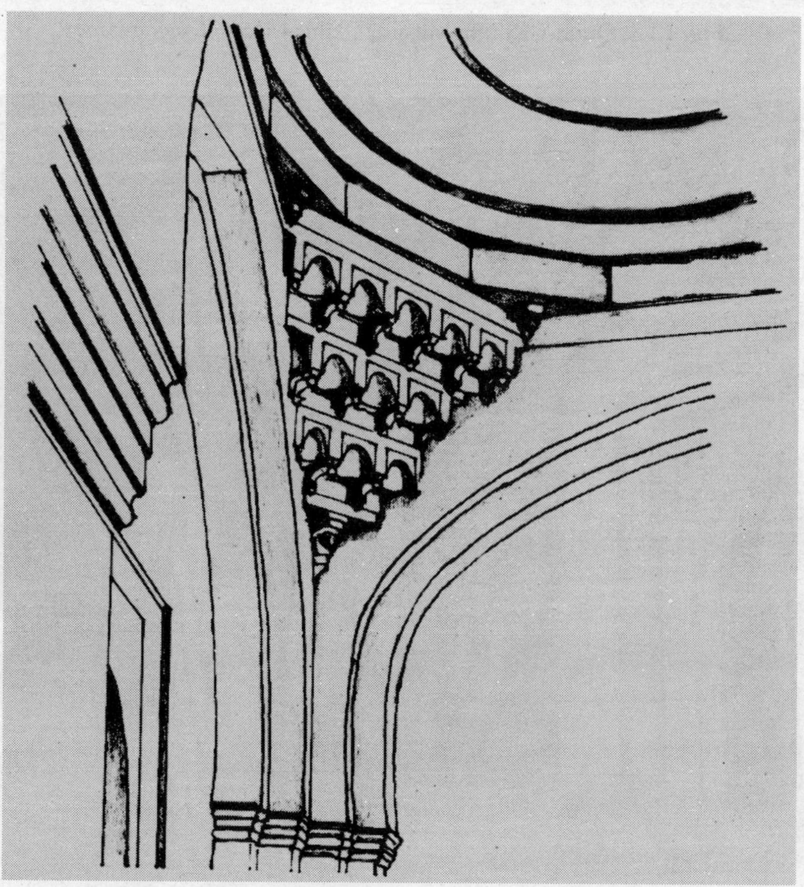

Fig. 13.7. Squinch arch in Quila-i-Kuhna Masjid, Delhi—C. 1545 C.E

14

Mogul Period

Babur (1526 to 1531 C.E) Humayan (1531 to 1556 C.E)

14.1. POLITICAL POSITION

The imperial rule of Sultans at Delhi had declined and Moguls captured Delhi and began to assume control over Northern India. Zahir ud din Mohammad Babur was the founder of Mogul dynasty. He was the descendant of Chenghis Khan and Timur from Mangolia. The word Mogul is the changed form of Mangolia to Magol or Mogul. Moguls were Sunny Muslims. They entered into India through Khyber Pass.

Moguls were passionate towards buildings, which resulted in construction of great buildings. The building art in North India has attained its supreme form under the patronage of Moguls. Excellent buildings were built during this period and the factors responsible for this are:

– Wealth and power of the empire
– Settled conditions prevailing in the country and surroundings
– Aesthetic nature of Mogul rulers themselves

The five rulers of Mogul dynasty responsible for flourishing of building art of this period after Babur were: -

– Humayun
– Akbar
– Jahangir
– Shah Jahan
– Aurangzeb

Hence the building art developed during this period was described emperor wise in different chapters. During the early years of Mogul rule, the country was in unsettled condition. Babur's ruling is a short period of five years and hence no remarkable buildings were built. Moreover Shershah Sur, an Afghan usurper has expelled Humayun away from Delhi to live in Persia for fifteen years.

The following are the mosques built in 1526 C.E during Babur's period.

– Mosque in Kabuli Bagh at Panipat
– Jami masjid at Sambhal in Moradabad district in Uttar Pradesh, which was Sikandar Lodi's provincial capital.

Mogul architecture may be divided into two phases.

Red sandstone phase

The first phase in which the buildings were principally constructed in red sandstone during the reign of Humayun and Akbar.

Marble phase

The second phase, when white marble was largely employed to the luxury taste of Shah Jahan.

The important building of this period is Humayun's tomb built at Delhi around 1565 C.E.

14.2. EXAMPLES

1. HUMAYAN'S TOMB, DELHI, 1565 C.E (Fig. 14.1 to 14.4)

The mausoleum of emperor Nasiruddin Mohammad Humayun at Delhi is one of the important and outstanding landmark structures in Mogul architecture. This is UNESCO's world heritage site.

The construction of this tomb building appears to have begun in 1564 C.E, eight years after Humayun's death. Hamida Banu Begum, the wife of Humayun and a most devoted consort has commissioned the tomb for her husband. As per some records, the mausoleum was designed by Mirak Mirza Ghiyas, a Persian architect. The monument presents an Indian interpretation of Persian conception. Hence it stands as an example of two great building traditions, the Persian and the Indian.

Site plan

The mausoleum was built in an immense square open garden with the tomb building placed in the centre. Humayun's tomb structure ranks as first spacious tomb built symmetrically in a spacious garden having entrance gate ways. Some Lodi tombs built earlier have gardens, but were not up to the mark. In the middle of each of four sides of enclosure, a large entrance structure was built through the archway of which the view of the tomb is presented. The garden is laid into an arrangement of squares and rectangles divided by paths and pavements well laid in harmony with the main structure.

Main building

The central building stands on a wide and lofty sandstone terrace, of some 7 metres in height. The sides of this basement are arcaded, each archway opening into a small vaulted chamber numbering to some 124 in all used to accommodate visitors or attendants. The tomb structure occupies the middle of a spacious upper platform of some 48 metres side and square in plan, except certain projections and chamfered angles.

Interior

The interior is not a single compartment, but is a group of cells. The largest in the centre is the cenotaph of the emperor with smaller rooms at each angle for those of his family. All the rooms are octagonal in plan and connected to the central hall by radiating or diagonal passages. Light is admitted through clerestorey perforated screens fitted within arched recesses in the walls.

Exterior

In elevation all the four sides are alike except some changes in the main central part. Each face consists of a central rectangle containing an arched recess flanked by wings each possesses a similar but smaller arched alcove. Above all hangs the noble marble dome rising to a height of 43 metres. Pillared kiosk having a cupola roof rises over smaller rooms at each angle. The shape of the arches and their curves are finer and the arches are four-centered arch variety.

Double dome

A well designed double dome appears here in this structure. The dome instead of consisting of one thickness of masonry, it contains two separate shells, one an outer dome and the other inner ceiling leaving a void space in between. The outer shell supports the white marble casing of the exterior. The inner dome forms the vaulted ceiling of the main hall in the interior. This device enabled the ceiling placed at lower level in relation to the size of the hall and the outer dome rising to the desired height. The construction of double dome was already in practice in India. An attempt of double dome was already made in the tomb of Sikander Lodi, Delhi.

Conclusion

The fine visual effect of this monument is due to the skillful and admirable blending of red sandstone and white marble. There is perfection in its proportions, the interplay of its surfaces and planes, the shapes and distribution of voids, the graceful and bold curves of the arches and above all the grand volume of the dome. The building is shorter in height in proportion to its width. However these proportions were well realized and adjusted in the building of Tajmahal at Agra built some seventy years later.

Humayun's tomb stood as an inspiring example for forthcoming great monument of Tajmahal built at Agra.

QUESTIONS

1. Describe the Political position and type of structures built during Moguls in general.
2. Explain the plan layout, elevation and other decorative elements of Humayun's tomb of Delhi.
3. Sketch the elevation or view of Humayun's tomb of Delhi.

Fig. 14.1. Humayun's tomb—Corner view

Fig. 14.2. Humayun's tomb, Delhi—Other Side elevation, 1565 C.E

Fig. 14.3. Humayun tomb—Arch and Vault details

Fig. 14.4. Humayun's tomb—Sketch view

15

Mogul Period

Akbar (1556 to 1605 C.E)

15.1. INTRODUCTION

Jalal ud din Mohammad Akbar ascended the throne in 1556 C.E at the age of 13, when his father Humayun died. He keenly studied the local traditions, Hindu culture and grew into a most powerful and ideal emperor. Akbar became a man of culture, wisdom and sense of fairness. His political vision, policies and principles are democratic and encouraged indigenous practices.

Akbar's empire was the largest after Asoka. He lived in Red fort at Agra in early years and established his rule at Agra, as the capital city. He built great architectural monuments which were unparalleled.

15.2. DESIGN AND CONSTRUCTION

A settled form of building art emerged and developed into a significant architectural style in India during Akbar's reign. The buildings were mainly built in red sandstone readily available nearby. Important elements were emphasized by insertions in white marble for the purpose of beauty and clarity. Construction was mainly trabeated style and the Tudor arch was used as decorative element. The dome was of Lodi type in the early period. The pillars are many-sided carrying bracket capitals. Carved designs, inlaid patterns, painted designs were introduced in the interior walls and ceilings.

Fine buildings were produced during the reign of Akbar. The important buildings are as follows.

1. Fort at Agra, 1566 C.E
2. Fort at Lahore, 1575 C.E
3. Fort at Allahabad, 1583 C.E
4. Capital city of Fatehpur Sikri, Agra, 1565-80 C.E

The above examples are described here under.

15.3. EXAMPLES

1. FORT AT AGRA, 1566 C.E

Fort of Agra also is called Lal Qila (Red fort). It has got long political history and was captured by many kings for its great treasure including Kohinoor diamond. Earlier it was a brick fort built and used by Rajput kings. Lodi sultans captured the fort and lived here. Babur defeated Ibrahim Lodi in 1526 C.E and captured the fort. Shershah who interrupted Humayun's ruling also lived here. Moguls finally defeated Afghans and captured the fort in 1556 C.E. All the Mogul emperors lived here and added distinguished structures of their taste. Akbar dismantled the earlier brick structures and built new structures including the enclosure walls, entrances, palaces in red sandstone.

The fort is now UNESCO's world heritage site. It has won Aga Khan Award of architecture in the year 2004.

It is an irregular semi-circle with its chord measuring some 825 metres in length lying parallel to right bank of Yamuna river measuring a land of some 38 hectares and has wide and deep surrounding moat. The fort is a large complex containing office buildings, courts, luxurious fortified palaces and service buildings. (Fig. 15.1)

Enclosure wall

The massive enclosure wall is most remarkable. It consists of solid sandstone rampart of 21 metres high and nearly 2 ¼ kilometers in circumference built in dressed stone in such large scale. The wall is a fine work of architecture containing features like battlements, bastions, kiosks, stringcourses all carefully designed and executed.

Gateways

The enclosure wall has two gateways.

– Main gate called Delhi gate on west side

– Lahore gate on south side called Amar Singh Rathore gate intended for private use.

The main gateway is notable for its design. It consists of two octagonal towers joined by an arched vault. The rear side of this gate also presents an elegant façade containing arched terraces above surmounted by cupolas, kiosks and pinnacles. The structure provides accommodation to the guards. The string courses and borders in white marble had greatly relieved the mass of red sandstone and is most effective (Fig. 15.2). Within this fort, there are number of structures like—Diwan-i-am, Khas Mahal, Jahangir Mahal and other luxury palaces.

Jahangir Mahal

A most completed building is Jahangir Mahal. This is an extensive arrangement of compartments. The brackets under the eaves, the inclined struts supporting the roof beams of northern hall, all of which are fine works of art in stone inspired from timber carving works.

As per some records, there were some 500 different structures of red sandstone built in fine styles of Gujarat and Rajasthan within this fort. Unfortunately most of these earlier structures were demolished to make way for construction of marble pavilions by his grandson Shah Jahan. Most of these were built along the parapet on eastern wall overlooking Yamuna river.

2. THE FORT AT LAHORE, 1575 C.E (Fig. 15.5)

The Fort at Lahore is smaller and similar to Agra fort in many respects. This fort forms an irregular parallelogram of 366 metres long by 320 metres wide contained within a high bastioned wall. It contains official buildings, royal palaces and service buildings.

Picture gallery

There is a remarkable display of a mural made on north enclosure wall of the fort. This is a unique picture gallery in coloured glazed tiles extends from the Elephant gate (Hathi Pol) now the main entrance upto the eastern tower of Jahangir's quadrangle. This covers a large wall space of around 440 metres long and 16 metres in height. The decoration mainly covered the subjects of sports such as elephant combats, polo game, hunting and some floral fillings.

3. THE FORT AT ALLAHABAD, 1583 C.E

The fortress stands near the cross junction of rivers of Ganga and Yamuna called Triveni Sangamam at Allahabad. This is the largest fortress built by Akbar, measuring some 915 metres as its longest dimension. This formed into an irregular segment of a circle. Most of its parts are now in damaged state.

Baradari

Among the structures remained is a 'Baradari' or pavilion known as Zenana palace. This explains the architectural characters as a whole. Trabeated order of construction and the peristyle are the main features. The halls are surrounded by a colonnade with pairs of pillars except at the corner, where a group of four pillars were made presenting an elegant perspective of columns. Above this there are perforated parapets surmounted by kiosks with lattice screens.

4. FATHEPUR SIKRI, AGRA (1565 – 1580 C.E)

Introduction: The village was earlier called Khanswa. Babur named it as Shukri meaning thanks. Fatehpur Sikri is an entirely a new capital city built by Akbar at Sikri village, some 39 kilometres west of Agra. This is a most remarkable building achievement and was the conception of emperor Akbar. The fort was built on a rocky outcrop of sandstone lies from southwest to northeast. This covered an irregular rectangular area of 3 kilometres long and 1 ½ kilometers wide surrounded by a bastioned wall. The city is an arrangement of broad terraces, stately courts, paved paths, numerous palaces, pavilions, offices and utilities. The fort has extremely planned town planning. This is now UNESCO's world heritage monument and site.

This is an imperial city of Moguls used in between 1572 to 1585 C.E. The buildings are unique and a blend of different architectural traditions. It shows strong Hindu architecture of Gujarat and Rajasthan. The exquisite architectural splendor of Fatehpur has left permanent impression in the legendary of Indian architecture. A uniform architectural style is seen in these structures.

Approaches and layout (Fig. 15.7)

The main approach to this fort was from Agra through Agra gate leading to Naubat Khana or a Drum House, where distinguished visitors were called. This leads straight to Diwan-i-am or a public audience hall. Here the public had the right of admission. This is a place where celebrations, public prayers and court transactions take place and hearings are announced. It has open courtyard surrounded by cloisters on three sides and emperor's pavilion on west side. From here a road leads to Jami masjid. The southern side of the fort is made accessible to the people. The large area behind Diwan-i-am to the northern side is catered for private use, where on the cliff royal palaces, pavilions and similar structures were built. Extending to downwards on northern side are the supplementary and utilitarian structures like offices, Sarais, gardens, stables and baths etc. The palaces are connected by pillared corridors, paved open spaces and gardens. Efficient system of water supply and drainage was also made.

Architectural characters

The secular buildings are mainly trabeated and the religious buildings of the city are arcuated. The architecture is mainly of Hindu style of western India of Gujarat and Rajasthan. There is adequate uniformity in every aspect. It shows that the work is well coordinated by a chief designer. The main building material used here is the rich red coloured sandstone quarried on the spot from the ridge of the hill itself. The earliest structure on this site may probably be the Stonecutters mosque, a small mosque on western side built by stone workers for their worship.

The buildings of this fort may be resolved into two classes:

– Secular structures

– Religious structures

SECULAR STRUCTURES

These buildings are meant for emperor, his family members and other connected royals. Hence this is more a secured zone. The buildings are:

– Palaces

– Administrative buildings

– Miscellaneous buildings

These are spacious buildings connected by paved paths, terraces and corridors. These are briefly described here under.

Palaces

The following are the Residential Palace buildings

1. Jodh Bai's palace
2. Mariam's house
3. Sultana's house
4. Birbal's house
5. Panchmahal

1. Jodh Bai's Palace (Principal Harem Sara) (Fig. 15.8 to 15.10)

An important building of high security, privacy and luxury is Jodh Bai's palace. Jodh Bai is the Rajput queen wife of Akbar. She was renamed as Mariam-uz-Zamani Begum Sahiba. But as per some records the name Jodh Bai is a misnomer and her actual name is Hira Kunwari, alias Harkhabai. It is believed that this palace is meant for all the wives of Akbar to live. The palace is complete in its design and arrangements. There are high plain outside walls 10 metres high with principal apartments attached to its inner side opening into the courtyard. The palace measures 98 metres by 66 metres. Entrance is through a guarded single monumental gatehouse on east. It has staggered doorways to keep privacy.

Interior

Within this palace there are living rooms, corridors, private chapel for devotions and roof terraces with screened parapets. It contains symmetrical range of buildings surrounding an open quadrangle square. Middle of each side and the corners are formed into separate blocks rising into two storeys. Each is a self-contained suite of living rooms with stairs to first floor. There are corridors in the ground floor in between these living rooms. The first floor contains living rooms, corridors, open and semi open terraces at regular intervals and has chatris. Heating system was arranged for the ground floor halls in cold winter weather. It contains several decorative Hindu motifs like swan, parrot, elephant, lotus, ghatmala etc.

The exterior is simple and plain. Superstructure comprises hemi spherical domes and pyramidal roofs.

Architectural Characters

The design of Jodh Bai's palace resembles the architecture of Gujarat and Rajasthan containing the elements like pillars, niches, ornamental brackets, wide inclined eaves and volute forms. Blue glazed tiles are applied to some of the roofs and cupolas. The ceiling in one of the upper room is made of wagon-vault with groins.

The following are accommodated near this palace.

– Hawa Mahal (palace of air) on north

– Service rooms and bath rooms on south

2. Mariam's House (Sunahra Makan)

The Golden House: Mariam does not mean the Chrisitian Queen of Akbar. But as per the Archelogical survey of India, Akbar's mother is Hamida Banu Begum, who was called Maryam Makhani (equal in rank of Mary). Mariam Makhani lived here.

Mariam's house is less in size by one-sixteenth part of Jodh Bai's palace situated on northeast corner to Jodh

Bai's palace. The house is called Sunahra Makan means Golden house. It is so called that the rich frescoes of large mural paintings of Persian subjects were inlaid and painted in gold in the manner of that country.

This is a perfect little abode consisting of an arrangement of rooms in two storeys with no central courtyard and other extra amenities. Stone eaves surround the building supported on heavy brackets. On the front of these are the carvings of Lord Sri Rama attended by Hanuman probably added later. Other carvings are elephants, geese and rosettes.

3. Turkish Sultana's House (Anuptala'o Pavilion)

This is smaller and is a single storeyed pavilion with only one compartment contained within a pillared verandah. On the west is the portico as high as the roof of the main chamber. Though it is smaller in size, but is richly carved and decorated. Every surface is carved into delicate and refined patterns. This house is described as 'superb jewel casket' with its elaborate carvings on its brackets, friezes, cornice, columns, pilasters and dado panels. It appears like the work of wood carvers from Punjab.

4. Birbal's house (Fig. 15.11)

Birbal's house is more complex in its arrangements. This is a two storeyed building having four rooms, each with 5 metres side and two porches in ground floor. The first floor contains only two rooms in northwest and southeastern corners placed corner to corner leaving the remainder of the upper storey into open terrace. The house is totally enclosed. It has two flights of stairs, one in northeast and the other in southwest corner. There are cupolas over the upper rooms and pyramidal roofs over the porches, all are double layers in roof leaving open space in between, thus keeping inside the rooms cool.

Rich bracket supports

The exterior of the building presents richly treated pilasters and wide projected massive eave brackets. These brackets are lavishly decorated and are the chief attraction of this building. The design and the workmanship of this house is entirely of Hindu craftsmen.

Some of the records say that this is not Birbal's house.

5. Panchmahal-Palace of Five Storeys (Badgir) (Fig. 15.14, 15.15)

This is an open pillared hall of five storeys. The building is meant for women of royal household for living, playing, time passing etc. This is a notable structure entirely columnar and open with no enclosing walls. It is in five storeys diminishing in size while ascending. The building is unusually asymmetrical. The ground storey contains 84 columns, the first storey 56 columns, the second 20, the third 12 and the top storey is a single domed kiosk supported on 4 pillars making 176 columns in all. No two columns of the first floor are alike. Some are circular, some octagonal and the others twisted. The pillars show the workmanship of Hindu temple pillars of western India.

ADMINISTRATIVE BUILDINGS

1. Diwan-i-khas or private hall (the Jewel house) (Fig. 15.12)

The purpose of this building has not been clearly established. Some believed that the building was used for religious discussions or to look the exhibited jewelry or so. Hence this building also called the Jewel house.

This is a moderate size building conceived in an unusual manner. It is rectangular in plan and is in two storeys having a flat terraced roof with a pillared kiosk rising above the parapet at each corner.

Bracket pillar (Fig. 15.13)

The interior is only one chamber containing a massive and richly carved pillar in the centre of the chamber. The pillar is supporting a fantastic spreading capital ever produced. The capital is a circular arrangement of brackets branching out into a series of 36 closely set volute and pendulous brackets carrying a circular platform above, to which small bridges span from each corner of the hall.

The building is unique in its design. There is no such arrangement anywhere in the whole of the world.

Miscellaneous structures

There are numerous other structures built to serve for different purposes. The important are as follows.

– Diwankhana-i-khas (Khwabgah) or House of dreams

– Anup Tala'o – A water tank containing a platform in the center connected by four bridges

– Astrologer's seat

– Daftar khana (Record room)

All the structures have much the same architectural characters. The exterior of these structures is remarkable with their wide, striking, horizontal eaves casting deep shadows. The structures are connected by pillared corridors and stone spreaded open spaces which is excellent.

RELIGIOUS STRUCTURES

Undoubtedly the most marvelous splendour of architecture of Fatehpur fort is the group of religious buildings. They are:

1. Jami masjid
2. Buland Darwaja or Triumphal Gateway
3. Saint Salim Chisti's tomb

Buland Darwaja and Salim Chisti's tomb are a part of Jami masjid. But they have been separately described here.

1. Jami Masjid

Dominating the scene and occupying the highest point on the ridge of Fatehpur Sikri is the Jami masjid. This covers a rectangular area of 134 metres north and south and 165 metres east and west making this the largest mosque of the country. The mosque is as per true traditions and conventions, consisting of a large open courtyard (Sahn) with pillared cloisters on its three sides and the western end occupied by a sanctuary. The quadrangle presents a great effect of dignity and spaciousness.

Sanctuary facade (Fig. 15.16)

Here the facade of the sanctuary consists of large rectangular portico in the centre containing a spacious arched alcove. The pillared arcades on each side form the wings. A large dome rises over the nave behind the central portico. There are smaller domes over the wings. The remaining is covered with flat roof. The range of pillared kiosks over the parapets presents an excellent look of skyline. The architectural and decorative elements are most elegant and completely finished.

Sanctuary interior (Fig. 15.17)

The sanctuary is entered by three doorways through an arched portico. The three side archways give access to the aisles. The nave and the aisles were covered by domical roof. Mural decoration was carried over most surfaces of the walls of sanctuary hall. All types of embellishments like carved, painted and in-laid ornamentation were applied to the surfaces.

Mihrabs

The western wall of this sanctuary contains the principal 'Mihrab'. There are three Mihrabs in each of the seven bays. The central one recessed by some 1.3 metres from the face of the wall, pentagonal in shape. This was covered by a little semi-dome and is splendid in its beauty and decoration. To the north of this central Mihrab is the pulpit, a simple marble structure of three steps.

Pillars

The flat roofs are supported on pillars carved in pure geometric shapes. The shafts are first square in section, then octagonal and finally sixteen-sided with an octagonal section at the very top.

Badshahi Darwaja

There is an entrance to the mosque in the centre of east side, which was used by Akbar. It projects from the wall of the mosque in the form of a half-hexagonal porch, 13 metres broad by 19 metres high. This is called the Badshahi Darwaza.

2. Buland Darwaza

This is a great Triumphal archway to the Jami masjid in Fatehpur Sikri commemorative of the conquests of Akbar over the Deccan, built on southern side after some twenty-five years of completion of Jami masjid.

Size and scale

The gateway is a most imposing structure of 41 metres high, approached by steep flight of steps of 13 metres high from the roadway. In its front, it measures 40 metres in breadth and from front to back it is 38 metres, thus presenting a great form of masonry of immense proportions, making all other buildings smaller in its vicinity.

Front facade (Fig. 15.18)

The most notable in its front façade is its huge portal structure containing a large main face in the centre and chamfering side faces. The central main face is 26 metres wide with its great arch and half domical vault. The side faces are in three storeys with varying openings in each stage. The most striking feature is the large arched recess in the centre, the semi-dome of which is carried on five surfaces in the form of half-decagon. Above this is the perforated parapet behind which raises a range of kiosks. The stately structure is decorated in rectangular frames with marble inlaid borders, emphasizing its beauty.

Rear facade (Fig. 15.19)

The rear portion of the gateway is joining into open court of the mosque and is a fine mass of masonry containing three arched entrances. The rear side façade consists of recessed tiers backed by fine-pillared kiosks joining and matching with the features of the mosque.

The Buland Darwaza is a work of great force, presenting awe and inspiring view, especially when viewed from the ground below.

3. Saint Sheik Salim Chisti's tomb (Fig. 15.20, 15.22)

The marble Dargah of Sufi saint Shaik Salim Chisti is one the most famous examples of marble work in India. This was placed within the open courtyard of Jami masjid of Fatehpur Sikri in northwest corner. This is an edifice presenting most delicate chiseled, polished and fretted lace work of great grace. This building is a square measuring externally 7.3 metres side. Entrance is through a porch projected on pillars from south side. Inside is a square mortuary cell of 4.8 metres side. A wide verandah is carried round the cell. A low simple dome covers the cell. Verandah carries a flat roof on pillars and the spaces in between the pillars are filled with marble perforated screens.

Brackets and Pillars

There are carved brackets all-round to carry the extremely wide eaves. The chief beauty lies in the elegant material and the fine ivory type carvings. The brackets or struts are unique in their design. They consist of long serpentine volutes with the spaces between the curves filled in with perforated foliations. Structurally these supports have little value. They are almost decorative. The marvelous work of this tomb building is certainly a produce of temple builders.

Conclusion

Though this royal capital city was built ambitiously, but the life of this stately city was extremely short. Its glory lasted for little less than a generation. This was abandoned due to the reasons like lack of water, hot climate and its location not being Delhi. It is now remaining as a mute testimony, exhibiting the greatness and supremacy of its designers, builders and the great royal patronage. The great buildings have not lost their charm even now.

QUESTIONS

1. Describe the buildings, enclosure walls and gateways of Agra fort.
2. List the names of important structures built in Fatehpur Sikri, Agra.
3. Explain general layout, Approaches and architectural elements of Fatehpur Sikri, Agra.
4. Describe the great Residential palaces of Fatehpur Sikri, Agra.
5. Sketch the view of Birbal's house.
6. Explain Diwan I Khas and its special features in Fatehpur Sikri, Agra.
7. What is Panch mahal of Fatehpur Sikri, Agra? Explain its features.
8. Describe the architecture of great Jami masjid of Fatehpur Sikri, Agra.
9. What is Buland Darwaja? Describe its construction features.
10. Sketch the view of Buland Darwaja.
11. Where Salim Chisti's tomb located? Explain its decorative elements.
12. Explain the Brackets, Chatris, Shades and the roofs of the structures of Fatehpur Sikri, Agra.
13. Sketch the layout of Fatehpur Sikri fort of Agra.

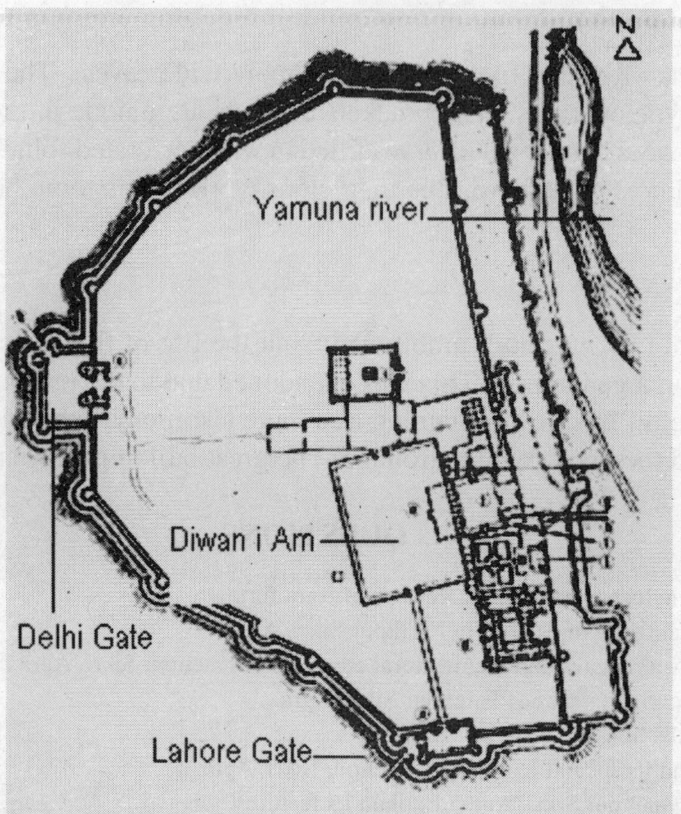

Fig. 15.1. Agra fort layout

Fig. 15.2. Agra fort-Entrance, 1566 C.E

Fig. 15.3. Agra fort—Jahangir palace

Fig. 15.4. Agra fort-Khas mahal, 1566 C.E

Fig. 15.5. Lahore fort, 1575 C.E

Fig. 15.6. Agra fort—Diwan-i-Am

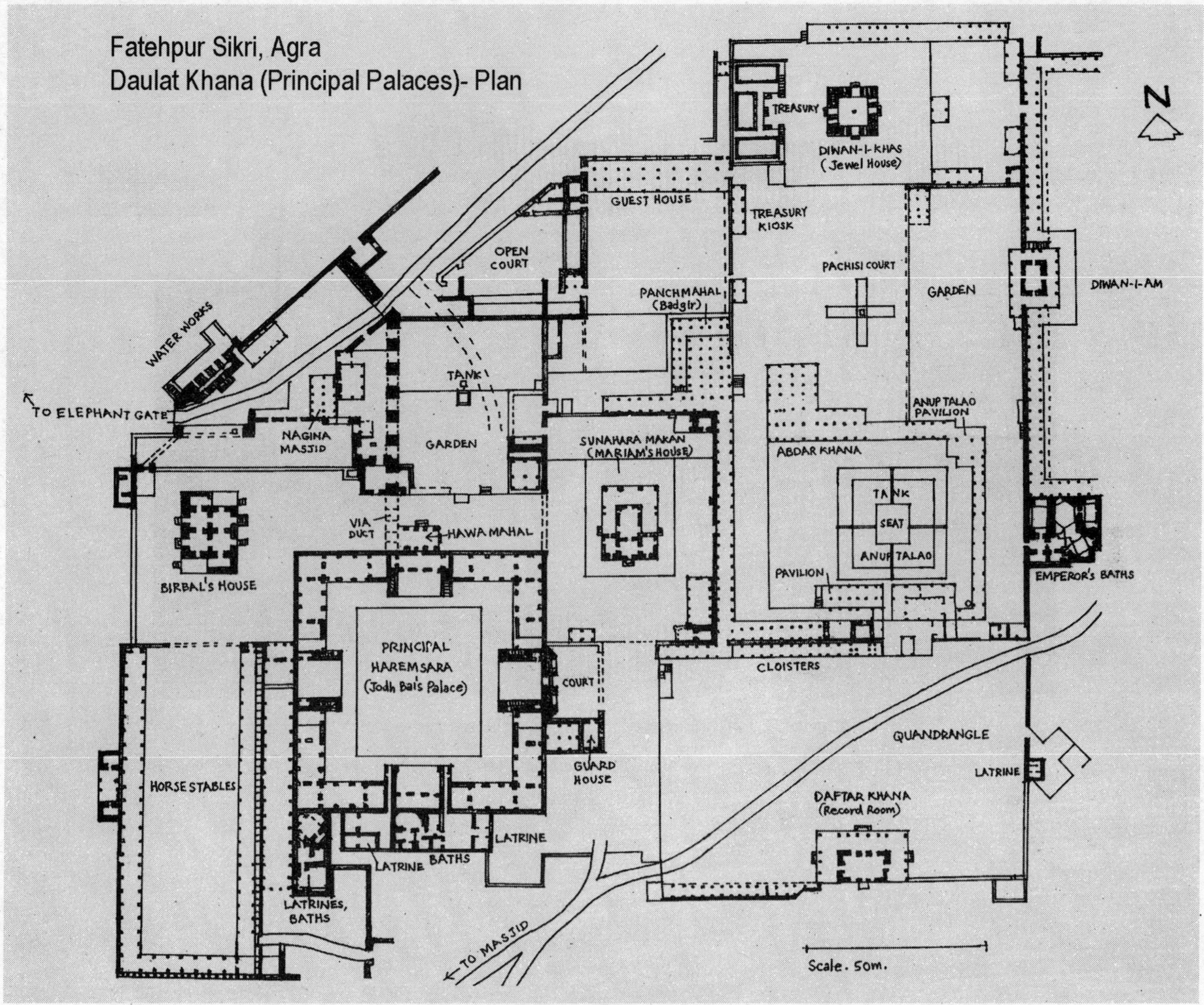

Fig. 15.7. Fatehpur sikri, 1565-80 C.E—Principal Palaces—Plan

Fig. 15.8. Fatehpur Sikri, Jodhbai's palace—Entrance

Fig. 15.9. Jodhbai's palace—Open court

Fig. 15.10. Jodhbai Palace—Inside

Fig. 15.11. Fatehpur sikri, Birbal house

Fig. 15.12. Fatehpur sikr, Diwan i Khas

Fig. 15.13. Fatehpur sikri, Diwan i khas-—Interior pillar

Fig. 15.14. Fatehpur sikri, Panchmahal and other pillared halls

Fig. 15.15. Fatehpur Sikri, Panch Mahal

Fig. 15.16. Fatehpur Sikri, Jama Masjid—Sanctuary facade

Fig. 15.17. Fatehpur Sikri, Jama Masjid—Sanctuary interior

Fig. 15.18. Fatehpur Sikri—Buland Darwaza

Fig. 15.19. Fatehpur Sikri, Buland Darwaja—Inner face into Mosque court

Fig. 15.20. Fatehpur sikri—Salim Chisti's tomb

Fig. 15.21. Fatehpur sikri, Salim Chisti's tomb—Brackets details

Fig. 15.22. Salim Chisti's tomb—Front view

16

Mogul Period

Jahangir (1605 to 1627 C.E)

16.1. INTRODUCTION

Nuruddin Salim Jahangir the son of Akbar succeeded the throne after Akbar. Jahangir devoted much of his time in Kashmir landscapes.

The construction of buildings by Jahangir is low, when compared to his predecessor and father Akbar. Remarkable structures built during this period are described here.

16.2. EXAMPLES

1. Mausoleum of Akbar at Sikandra near Agra
2. Tomb of Itmad-ud-Daulah, the father of Jahangir's Queen Nurjahan at Agra built by the queen.
3. Kashmir gardens

1. MAUSOLEUM OF AKBAR AT SIKANDRA, AGRA, 1613 C.E

Akbar commenced the construction of his mausoleum during 1600 C.E. Jahangir completed it in 1613 C.E. The scheme of Akbar's mausoleum was conceived on a large and grand scale set in 48 hectares of land in a square of 690 metres side. Its perimeter walls enclose a large garden with the tomb building placed in the centre measuring 98 metres side and over 30 metres in height.

Gateways (Fig. 16.1)

Four gateway structures were built in enclosure walls and each was placed in the middle. Three structures are false and were added for symmetry and beauty. The south gate is the main entrance. The entrance structure is magnificent and elegant in its proportions and decorated with bold in-laid ornamentation. It contains four graceful white marble Chatri topped minarets rising above at each corner. The design of these minarets is original and new in their design and form.

Garden and water pools

The gateway leads to a well laid ornamental garden having pathways suitably expanded at intervals to accommodate water pools and fountains. The garden is symmetrically and geometrically laid with green lawns, bushes, trees and flower plants.

Tomb Building (Fig. 16.2)

The tomb building takes the shape of a low truncated pyramid, built in three storeys. The first is the large and wide lower floor. Above this is an arrangement of red sandstone pavilions forming the middle portion. The upper storey is an open court surrounded by marble screens.

The ground storey is over 91 metres side and 9 metres in height having a series of arched recesses in its four sides. In the centre of each side rises a tall rectangular portico structure containing arched alcove and above the parapet is a graceful marble kiosk. Access is provided to the tomb chamber inside by a doorway from south side. This lower portion was completed during last years of Akbar's reign.

Some of the upper portions built were demolished, altered and reconstructed. The middle storey consists of arcades of low height and row of kiosks. The top most storey is of white marble, light in appearance with range of perforated screens. And above this, at each corner are the tall and graceful kiosks. The interior of this storey is an open court surrounded by arcaded cloisters, with cenotaph in the centre exquisitely carved. A dome over this would have certainly enhanced its beauty and elegance. But the building does not have any dome on its top. It is in its truncated appearance. The interior of tomb was heavily decorated in patterns of floral, geometric and calligraphy in stucco. (Fig. 16.3)

Conclusion

The mausoleum is one of the ambitious productions, but as a whole it lacks its effectiveness. History says that the ideals of father and son differed and there were clashing of temperaments, of which this building also may be the result of the effect. When compared to the great buildings of Akbar and that of Humayun's tomb, which were built some fifty years ago, the mausoleum of Akbar is retrogression. Had Akbar lived and supervised this building, it would have been a great monument to his stature.

Unfortunately Akbar's tomb did not rank in merit. Mohammad Adil Shah's tomb called Golgumbaz built in Bijapur achieved the merit of largest tomb of India.

2. TOMB OF ITMAD-UD-DAULAH, AGRA, 1628 C.E

Itmad-ud-Daula is a title meaning Lord of Treasure or pillar of Government. Actual name is Mirza Ghiyas Beg, the father of Jahangir's Queen Nurjahan by whom this tomb was built in 1628 C.E. This is small but an elegant structure more refined and more delicate. The mausoleum stands in a square enclosure of 165 metres side with picturesque green garden against gateways of red sandstone. The white marble building fits like a gem within the green garden of lawns, pathways, tanks and fountains. The design of the building is original in its conception.

Interior

This is square in plan and is only 21 metres in size. The interior of the lower storey is an arrangement of rooms and passages with a central chamber containing the cenotaph. The square pavilion in the upper floor was built of screens of fine marble tracery. There are two yellow cenotaphs on its patterned and polished pavement.

Exterior (Fig. 16.5, 16.6)

The exterior of the building is too fine. It is a fine symmetrical marble edifice consisting of broad octagonal minarets at each angle crowned by fine pillared kiosks. A pavilion of appropriate size rises above the roof in the center. There are arched openings on each side producing voids in appearance. A wide eave supported on ornamental brackets at a higher level provide horizontal lines and shadows. The wall surfaces are decorated in horizontal and vertical inlaid stone patterns dividing the plain surfaces into panels.

Use of Colour Stones

Its exquisite white marble enhanced the fineness and beauty of the structure. Hard and rare stones such as lapis, Onyx, Jaspera, Topaz, Cornelion and the like were embedded in the marble in decoration work.

The tomb of Itmad-ud-Daulah figured as fine, elegant and variety monument in the architectural productions of Moguls. The Queen Nurjahan had built a fine monument to her noble father.

3. KASHMIR GARDENS

Kashmir is mountainous and is cool in climate. It is already a natural garden laid with trees, forests and springs. Within this natural landscape man made gardens were laid in its sloping grounds. The Mogul emperors Jahangir and Shahjahan re-laid some gardens. The popular gardens are:

– Shalimar garden, Srinagar, 1630 C.E

– Nishat Bagh, Srinagar, 1633 C.E

Shalamar Garden, Srinagar, 1630 C.E

This is located on northeast side of Dal lake some 15 kilometres from Srinagar city in Kashmir state laid by Mogul king Jahangir around 1630 C.E. This is a celebrated royal garden of Kashmir. Shalimar means an abode of love. Early in 6th century C.E this site belongs to Hindu king Pravarsena II who built a sacred structure here.

The site of this garden is approximately 12.4 hectares. It measures 587 metres long and 251 metres wide. It is oriented from southwest to northeast with the higher point located on northeast side. The topography and the contours of the site were well exploited in making the design of this pleasant garden.

The design of this garden is similar to Persian 'Chahar bagh'. The main stream is flowing in the center axially and other channels are crossing the axial stream, which divide the garden into four parts. The central water channel is the main feature. The water flow of the stream from top is channelised downwards into terraces through Baradaries (pavilions) in the garden. The stream water flows into a larger pool at each terrace highlighting the Baradari.

The total garden is laid on three large terraces.

– First lower level terrace is a public garden

– Second middle level terrace is Emperor's garden

– Third higher level terrace is Zenana (Harem) garden

The two small pavilions at the entrance lead to the public garden on first terrace. A large Baradari or Diwan-i-Am (Public audience hall) is located in this terrace, where daily court transactions of the people were conducted by the king when the king was in camp at Srinagar. A black marble throne is the central feature of this hall. Water cascades surround this throne.

The second terrace accommodates the Diwan-i-Khas (Private audience hall) where the distinguished guests, noble men of the court had access. Only the basement remains now.

Up above this second terrace the Zenana garden houses a Baradari of black marble called Black pavilion built by Shah Jahan. This is surrounded by a fountain pool. Behind this at the end there are two octagonal pavilions and a cascade wall in which small niches (Chini khana) were cut into it. Once, oil lamps were placed in these niches.

The Shalimar garden in it's enliven cool and natural surroundings with its Chinar row trees, water pools, fountains, flower beds, baradaries is a heavenly garden in Kashmir.

Nishat Bagh, Srinagar, 1633 C.E (Fig. 16.8)

This is situated on the banks of Dal lake in Srinagar in Kashmir state. This is the largest Mogul garden in India built by emperor Jahangir. It was also named as Garden of Bliss. It is designed by Asaf Khan, the brother of Nurjahan, wife of emperor Jahangir in 1633 C.E. The garden has the background of Zabarwan mountains. It has the splendid view of snow filled Pir Panjal mountain range and Dal lake.

The garden is built in different levels. There is a small spring behind the garden known as Gopi Tirth. This is the source of supply of pure water to the garden. The water stream is channeled axially in the center of the garden with water flowing down to the lower terraces. The channel is widened to form a pool at the place where Baradari (pavilion) was built. Green grass lawns, walking passages, flower beds, trees, fountains are laid symmetrically in the garden.

There are ruins of some buildings, one is a double storey pavilion enclosed on two sides with latticed windows.

QUESTIONS

1. Describe the Layout, gateways and tomb building of Mausoleum of Akbar, Agra.
2. What is Itmad ud Daula and where it is situated? Explain its interior, exterior and fine ornamental features.
3. Explain the layout and contents of Kashmir gardens. Name any two important Kashmir gardens.
4. Sketch the layout of a typical Kashmir garden.

Fig. 16.1. Akbar's Tomb, Sikandra—Entrance

Fig. 16.2. Akbar Tomb, Sikandra—Front, 1613 C.E

Fig. 16.3. Akbar's tomb, Agra—Panels and inlaid decoration in interior

Fig. 16.4. Akbar Tomb, Sikandra—Cross section

Fig. 16.5. Itmad-Ud-Daulah Tomb, Agra—Front

Fig. 16.6. Itmad-Ud-Daulah, Sikandra—Surface decoration

Fig. 16.7. Itmad-Ud-Daulah, Tomb, Agra

Fig. 16.8. Nishat bagh, Kashmir

17

Mogul Period

Shah Jahan (1627 to 1658 C.E)

17.1. INTRODUCTION

Shah Jahan's name as prince was Shahib-ud-din Muhammad Khurram. As emperor he was called Shahenshah Shah Jahan. He was the son and descendant of predecessor Jahangir. New range of marble structures were built in place of red sandstone making it Marble era.

17.2. ARCHITECTURAL CHARACTERS

Transition from red stone to marble

Shah Jahan's reign is termed as marble era. Architecture has reached highest form of expression with exceptional splendour. In place of sandstone, marble was largely employed. Hence a new expression was achieved in its fine and smooth form. As the marble used here is of white colour, hence it became necessary to carefully decorate the surfaces by means of inlaid patterns in coloured stones in lines to emphasize the boarders.

New forms in buildings

New and fine design forms are filtered and a whole series of new designs were created.

Arches

A noticeable change was found in the shape of arches. The curves of arches are foliated by means of nine cusps. These engrailed arches have become distinguishable feature of Shah Jahan's structures.

Domes

The dome has assumed a new shape. The curve of Persian type bulbous dome was pressed inwards at its neck.

Pillars

The pillars are square or twelve-side type. In some instances they are double pillars of circular cross-section.

Shah Jahan's predecessors' sandstone structures were removed to replace them by new structures of marble. At the fort of Agra, the following structures were added at different times.

– Diwan-i-Am

– Diwan-i-khas with double columns

– Moti-masjid or pearl mosque

The marble palaces and pavilions are:

– KhasMahal

– Shish Mahal

– Nagina masjid

In the same manner, at Lahore within the fort, Akbar's sandstone structures were removed to accommodate new structures.

17.3. EXAMPLES

1. SHAHJAHANBAD (DELHI RED FORT), 1639 to 1648 C.E

Shah Jahan built a new royal city in 1638 C.E on a site situated on right bank of Yamuna river at Delhi. Hence there arose a series of palaces and other structures on a large scale within a high and strongly fortified walled enclosure. Most of common structures were built in red sandstone, hence the fort was called Red fort. Shah Jahan renamed Delhi as Shahjahanabad. This is now UNESCO's world heritage site.

The buildings reflect a fusion of elements of Persia, Mongolia and Hindu architecture.

Layout of fort

The area is an oblong of 945 metres long and 503 metres wide and is aligned to south north direction. The layout of this fort is regular and formal laid in squares and rectangles.

Entrances (Fig. 17.1)

There are two entrances:

1. The main entrance in the middle of longer western side is called Lahore gate. This takes the form of a broad vaulted arcade with strongly built octagonal bastions on either side.
2. The other gate on southern side was used for private purpose. From these gateways, two thoroughfares pass into the fort, each meeting the other at right angles towards the center at a large rectangular area. The area beyond this towards east side overlooking the river accommodates the whole royal and private apartments. The remaining areas are the service quarters, such as army barracks, servants' quarters and other miscellaneous structures.

Important buildings are here described.

Diwan-i-Am (Fig. 17.3)

This is a place for public meetings, gatherings and other transactions with people. This originally consisted of a square open court surrounded by a colonnade with a pillared hall on its eastern side. But now all these surrounding structures disappeared and the pillared hall remained. The hall is a sandstone structure of 56 metres by 21 metres. Its façade is formed by an arcade of nine arches with twin pillars and a group of four pillars placed at corners. In the interior there are three aisles making 27 bays and 40 pillars in all. Engrailed arches bridge the spaces above pillars.

The stone masonry structure was fully covered by shell plaster and ivory polished. Its application was a technical process carried by the craftsmen from Rajasthan to great perfection. The entire complex of buildings was standing in brilliant white. The significant feature of the interior in the opposite back wall is the alcove, where the emperor sat. Here on ceremonial occasions the famous peacock throne was placed for the emperor to sit. The wall surfaces of this alcove have a series of designs. (Fig. 17.4)

Behind this Diwan-i-Am the royal apartments exist.

Royal apartments

A series of marble pavilions were built along the eastern wall above the ramparts. Their balconies, oriel windows and turrets crowned by cupolas are giving a pleasing picturesque appearance. These pavilions were closed on eastern outer side by screened windows and their frontages enriched by architectural elements looking into the gardens inside the fort enclosure. In between these buildings, there are wide terraces and courts separated by balustrades and perforated screens on the rampart side. The large open area in front of these structures was developed into gardens.

The palace enclosure consists of the following important structures in a line from south.

– Zenana
– Rang Mahal or Painted palace
– Khas mahal
– Diwan-i-khas (Hall of Private Audience)
– Hammam (Bath)

2. Rang Mahal

This is a crowning jewel in marble and is a lavishly ornate structure in the fort of Delhi. It measures 47 metres by 21 metres in plan. It consists of a main hall with compartments at each corner. This is a single storey open pavilion or loggia of elegant proportions with their parts well placed. In the basement of this structure, there are summer rooms which stay cool in hot summer. These were used by ladies.

Interior (Fig. 17.10)

The central hall is divided into fifteen bays, five bays in the longer side and three bays in the shorter side, by means of ornamental piers. Each bay measures six metres side square. The piers are square twelve sided type over which graceful engrailed arches spring up.

The ceilings in the interior are flat and richly decorated. It appears that the spaces were originally filled in with perforated marble screens for want of privacy.

Shallow basin with a fountain (Fig. 17.11)

A notable setting in the Rang Mahal is a shallow marble basin with a fountain sunk in the floor occupying the central bay. The perfumed water was bubbling out of a silver lotus flower fixed on a slender stem rising from the centre. The basin is a design of a large lotus flower of finely modeled petals contained within a square bordered frame. This is a place of attraction in Rang Mahal laid in perfection matching with the patterns of interior.

Exterior (Fig. 17.8, 17.9)

The façade is simple and graceful. The engrailed arch openings were shaded by a wide eave (chajja). Above this rises a parapet and from each corner a graceful kiosk covered by a cupola roof.

3. Khas mahal

This is a simple stone structure containing sleeping chambers, dining hall and sitting rooms.

4. Diwan-i-khas

This is an open pavilion hall built in marble, well-planned measuring 27 metres by 20 metres. Its façade consists of an arcade of five equal arches in its longer and shorter sides. But the arches on its shorter side are varying in their size skillfully adjusted.

Interior (Fig. 17.6)

The interior is divided into fifteen bays by means of engrailed arches supported on square marble piers. There are window openings with elegant tracery on eastern side. The massive piers were enriched with inlaid flower motifs. The foliated arches decorated in gold and colours. The mirror polished marble flooring is reflecting the objects.

Exterior (Fig. 17.5)

The exterior is decent with its usual elements of eaves, parapets and graceful kiosks at corners. Ornamentation of gilt coloured and inlaid patterns of scrolls or serpentine lines were distributed over every portion. Conventional flowers like roses, lilies and poppies were freely introduced on the walls, piers, arches and traceries. Moguls besides growing flowers in their gardens also introduced the pictures of flowers and foliations in their buildings showing their love towards flowers and greenery.

5. Hammam (Fig. 17.14, 17.15)

Hammam were the luxurious bathing facilities by the side of Diwan-i-Khas on north side adjacent to royal palaces. It consists of three apartments interconnected by corridors. The western apartment had heating arrangement used for hot bath and vapour bath. Marble floors and dados with beautiful floral patterns of multi coloured stones.

An important amenity in such large fort having some bearing on the planning and arrangement is the provision of continuous flow of water throughout the entire portions. This was carried out by means of channels around the marble pavements. They are so devised that each apartment was served with full water supply. This was brought by means of conduits from northeast corner from Yamuna river. Such continuous supply of water not only enabled the Hammam to function, but also beautified the gardens by water pools, fountains and cascades all round the palaces.

2. JAMI MASJID, DELHI, 1644 TO 1658 C.E (Fig. 17.18)

A notable structure built by Shahjahan is the Jami masjid built in Delhi. This is a congregational mosque occupying a large site outside Delhi fort in southwest side to the fort. This is one of the large mosque buildings in the country. On account of its size and scale, the mosque holds a high place.

Plan

As usual adhering to the traditional form, the mosque was raised on a high plinth. Three noble gateways approached by flights of steps had added dignity and height to the structure. North and south gateways are made for entry to public and that on the east reserved as royal entrance. Within these are the cloisters and the quadrangle measuring 99 metres side. The quadrangle is an open place with square tank in the middle for ablutions.

Sanctuary interior

The sanctuary is a great hall divided into bays by massive piers supporting engrailed arches. There are elegant arched Mihrabs sunk in each bay in the western wall. The architectural decoration was set in matching with its large dimensions.

Sanctuary exterior (Fig. 17.17)

The sanctuary on western side is an imposing structure of red sandstone. It measures 61 metres in breadth and 27 metres in depth. Its exterior presents a wide central archway flanked by an arcade of ten engrailed arches, five on each side of the wings. These wings terminate at the end by a tall minaret of four stages. Over the sanctuary rise three bulbous domes of white marble, the central one being larger than others on the wings. The white domes are made more prominent by means of inlaid black upward lines, first of its kind of application in India.

3. TAJ MAHAL, AGRA 1634 C.E

The Tajmahal, a materialized vision of loveliness marks a perfect indelible mark in the architecture of Mogul period. This building stands on a bend on the right bank of river Yamuna at Agra presently situated in Uttar Pradesh state. This is the mausoleum of emperor Shah Jahan's beloved wife, the empress Arjuman Banu Begum also called Mumtaz mahal. Ustad Isa Khan of Turkey was credited to have been the main architect of this building. Tajmahal is now UNESCO's world heritage site.

But as per another version, it is believed that Tajmahal was not built by Shah Jahan to his wife. It is a palace called Tejomahalaya, which was a palace built by Hindu king Raja Man Singh. It was not built meant for the purpose of a tomb. The building was ceased by Shah Jahan. It consists of guest houses, security quarters, horse stables and other edifices which are unconnected to a tomb structure.

Inspirational buildings to the design of Tajmahal

There are two buildings already built and existing at Delhi from which the design of Tajmahal arrived. These buildings are:

- Mausoleum of Humayun, Delhi
- Tomb of Khan Khanan, a Mogul nobleman, a lesser-known structure, Delhi

Site Layout (Fig. 17.19, 17.20)

The main structure occupies relatively a small portion of the whole architectural layout. The site is rectangular measuring 579 metres by 305 metres. A square portion of 305 metres side was set aside on north side in which the white marble building on a raised terrace was built at the extreme north side adjacent to the river in the center. A high boundary wall encloses the site having broad octagonal bastions at each corner. A monumental entrance gateway is placed in the centre of southern side. In the front southern court, the stables, outhouses and other edifices were added.

Entrance and passages (Fig. 17.25)

The southern entrance structure is imposing containing chamfered angles, arches, parapets and vaulted roof. Access is provided into the garden of the main enclosure through this gate. The front perspective view of Tajmahal building and its garden is seen from this point. The garden is laid on the principle of Charbagh. It is totally symmetrical containing paved pathways, lawns, bushes, flower plants, fountains and elevated lotus pools, all arranged to reflect the images. A straight pathway leads to the main structure.

Main enclosure

Significant structures are placed at the northern end of this enclosure consisting of the tomb building in the centre. The two subsidiary edifices also in marble are placed one on each side symmetrically. Of these two, that on the west side is the mosque and the other on the east is merely a replica of the mosque for the sake of symmetry (Fig. 17.26). It might be used as a guesthouse.

Main tomb building

The main white marble tomb building stands in the middle of an elevated large terrace measuring 57 metres square in plan and 6.7 metres high. This is entered by symmetrical stairs built in the center of south side of terrace. The main building over the terrace is square in plan with chamfered corners.

The interior consists of a main octagonal central hall with subsidiary chambers also octagonal in plan placed at each corner connected by radiating passages. The main hall is in two storeys with a cenotaph chamber built under with descending steps (Fig. 17.28). The main hall was roofed by hemispherical vault forming the inner shell of the double dome. Above this the main dome was built leaving a large void in between. Perforated marble screens filled the arched windows in two levels. There are some carvings on the dados inside the corner rooms. Every part of the monument shows fineness, beauty, curves, decorations which attributes to a royal female to whom the monument was dedicated.

This was carried to a height of 33 metres, having a cupola above each corner, while over the centre is the great bulbous dome reaching to height of 57 metres. The facade is same and alike on all its four sides. A minaret in three stages crowned by a kiosk with cupola roof rises from each corner on the terrace to a height of 42 metres. The same Tajmahal building would become an architectural blunder without these four minarets.

Exterior (Fig. 17.21 to 17.24)

The fine marble building has its facades same and alike on all its four sides. The façade has its large central arch and two arched windows one at the bottom and the other at top on each side. Perforated screens fill all the arched openings except the front entrance. A gracefull and finely curved dome takes place over a circular drum in the center rising to a height of 57 metres. Similar smaller domes were placed over corner rooms. Merloned parapets on top of walls decorate the skyline of the building. The fine lines of stone joints not only divided the surfaces, but also enriched the beauty of surfaces.

Proportions

The factors responsible for the beauty of Tajmahal are not only the fine material of white marble, but it mainly lies in its proportions, the grouping of its parts, their sizes, simple curves, rhythmical disposal, interrelation of parts in total. Its proportions are simple as its shape. The entire width is equal to the height and the height of the main vertical lower building body equals to height of the dome. The crowning glory of the facade lies in the volume and shape of the dome supported on a lofty drum.

17.4. NAMES OF OTHER STRUCTURES

The other important structures built during the reign of Shah Jahan were

– Jami Masjid at Agra
– Jami Masjid at Lahore
– Black pavilion at Shalimar garden, Srinagar
– White marble pavilion at Ajmer garden

17.5. MOGUL GARDENS, 17TH CENT. C.E

Mogul emperors laid gardens in the surroundings of their structures. It shows love and interest towards nature and environment. Such gardens are laid in tomb sites and also near palaces in forts.

Few Examples:

– Humayun's tomb, Delhi
– Tajmahal, Agra
– Akbar' mausoleum, Agra
– Red fort, Delhi

Kabuli Bagh

Babur, the founder of Mogul dynasty has laid a large garden at Panipat to commemorate his victory over Ibrahim Lodi in 1527 C.E.

Layout of garden

Garden was laid mainly in symmetrical and geometrical lines. It was an arrangement of squares and it was further subdivided into smaller squares. It contains paved paths, water pools, fountains, plants, trees, green lawns etc. Oblique lines and curves were seldom used. Chinar (Sycamore) tree was prominent in Kashmir gardens. Gardens were laid in sloping ground in descending levels in Kashmir. The flow of water downwards was utilized into pools and fountains. Garden was located where the source of water like a spring or a stream was present.

Pavilions

Pavilions, loggias and kiosks were an integral part of these gardens. High walls enclosed the garden for security and privacy.

Examples:

– Shalimar garden, Srinagar

– Nishat Bagh, Srinagar

These were already described in detail in the previous chapter.

QUESTIONS

1. Explain the general architectural characters of structures built by Shah Jahan.
2. Describe the layout, entrances and Diwan i Am of Shahjahanabad, delhi.
3. Describe the private Royal structures of Red fort, Delhi.
4. Explain the layout and construction of great Jami masjid of Delhi.
5. What is Tajmahal? Describe its layout, entrances and structures.
6. Sketch the layout of Tajmahal and name the parts.
7. Sketch the plan of Tajmahal building.
8. Sketch the elevation or view of Tajmahal building.
9. Sketch the Sanctuary and the court of Jami masjid, Delhi.

Fig. 17.1. Red Fort, Delhi—Lahore gate

Fig. 17.2. Red Fort, Delhi, 1648 C.E, Royal palaces

Fig. 17.3. Red fort, Delhi Diwan-i-Am—Inside

Fig. 17.4. Marble throne in Diwan-i-Am, Red fort, Delhi

Fig. 17.5. Red Fort, Delhi, Diwan-i-Khas

Fig. 17.6. Red Fort, Delhi, Diwan-i-Khas—Exquisitely decorated Interior

Fig. 17.7. Red Fort, Delhi—Diwan-i-Khas inside

Fig. 17.8. Red Fort, Delhi, Rang Mahal—Front

Fig. 17.9. Red Fort, Delhi—Rang Mahal Shorter side

Fig. 17.10. Red Fort, Delhi—Rang Mahal inside

Fig. 17.11. Red Fort, Delhi—Rang Mahal.Lotus water pool

Fig. 17.12. Red Fort, Delhi—Rang Mahal interior water pools

Fig. 17.13. Red fort, Delhi—Ornamental grill showing symbol of justice (Balance)

Fig. 17.14. Redfort, Delhi—Hammam Building

Fig. 17.15. Red fort, Delhi—Hammam Inside

Fig. 17.16. Red Fort, Delhi—Water pools and Fountains in Rang Mahal

Fig. 17.17. Jami masjid, Delhi—Sanctuary

Fig. 17.18. Jami masjid, Delhi—View

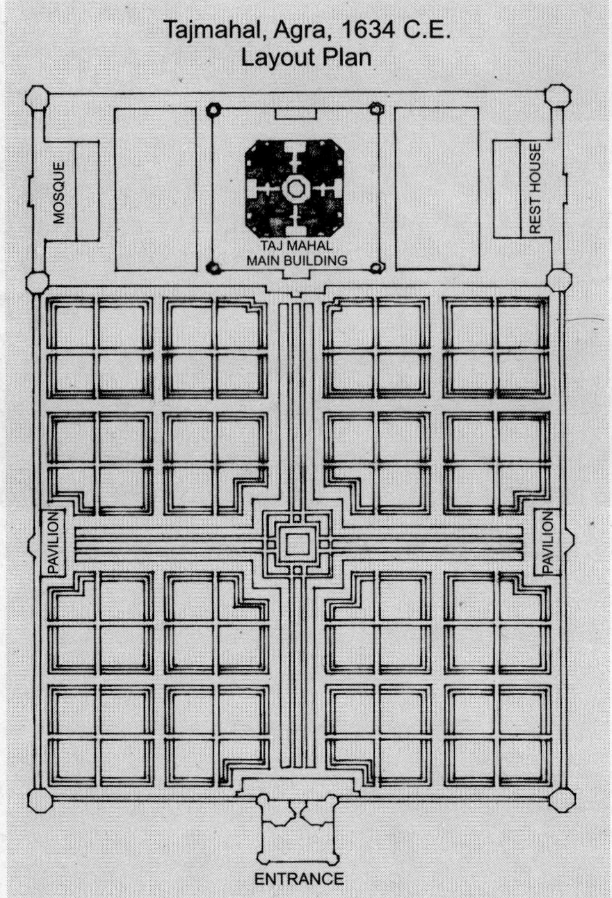

Fig. 17.19. Tajmahal, Agra—Layout Plan

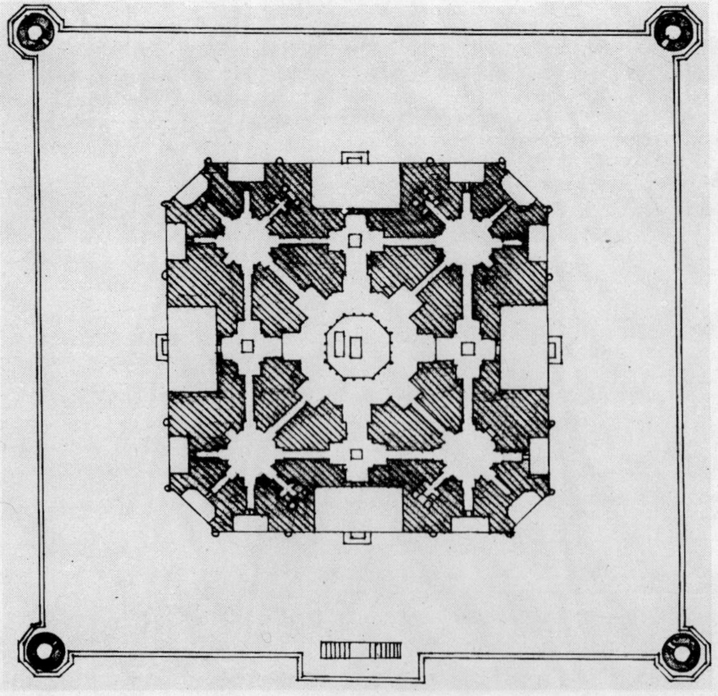

Fig. 17.20. Tajmahal, Agra, 1634 C.E—Building plan

Fig. 17.25. Tajmahal, Agra—Entrance

Fig. 17.26. Taj Mahal, Agra mosque

Fig. 17.23. Tajmahal, Agra-Front

Fig. 17.24. Tajmahal Full view

Fig. 17.21. Taj Mahal, Agra—Front elevation Drawing

Fig. 17.22. Tajmahal—Cross section

Fig. 17.27. Taj Mahal—Octagonal pavilion in enclosure wall

Fig. 17.28. Tajmahal, Cenotaphs of Shahjahan and Mumtaj—Close inlaid carvings

Fig. 17.29. Shalimar Garden, Lahore, 17th cent—Water pools and fountains

Four centered arch of Mughuls 16th, 17th cent C.E.

Foliated arch of Mughuls-Shahjahan 17th cent.

Fig. 17.30. Mogul Arches

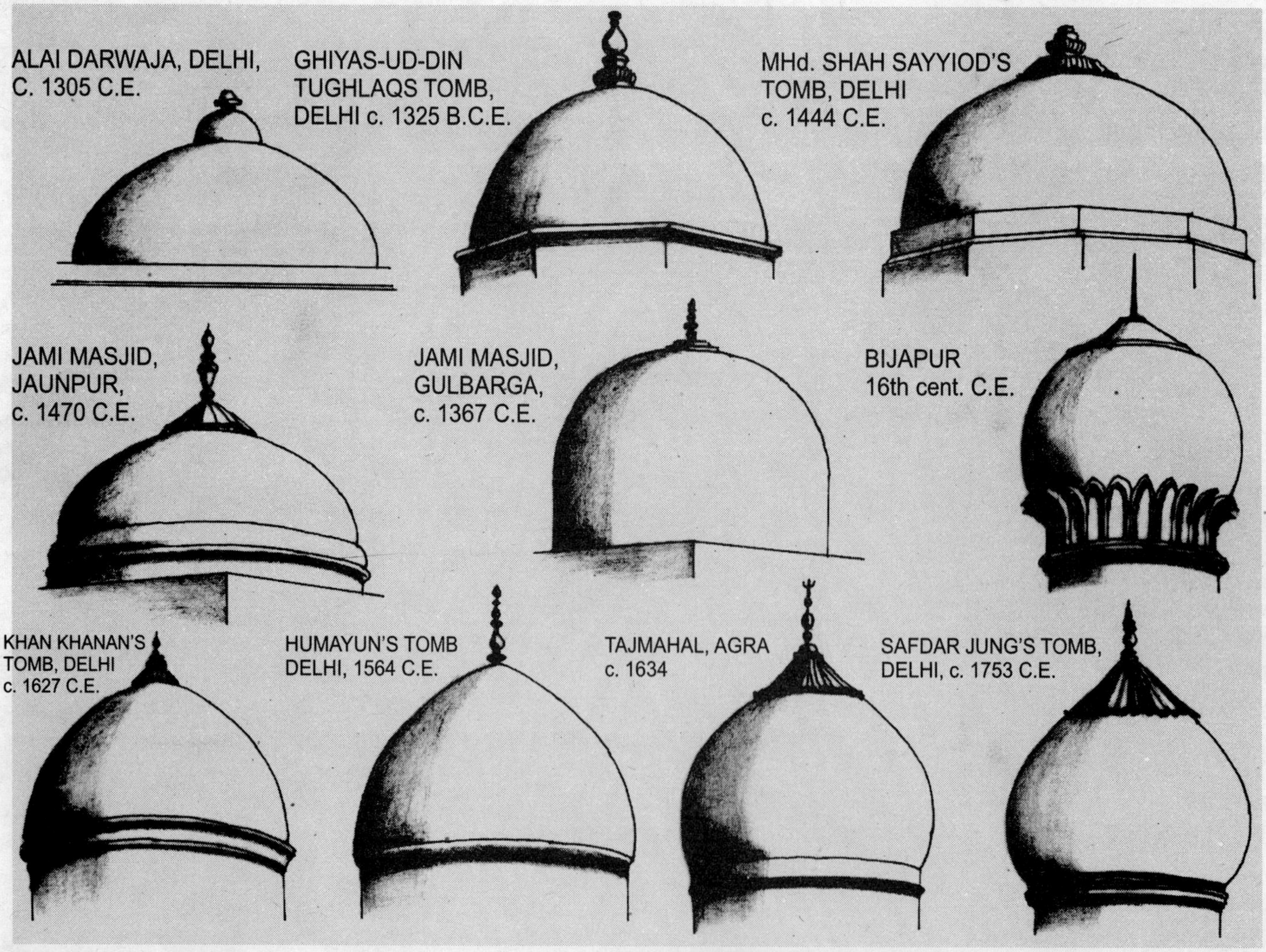

ALAI DARWAJA, DELHI, C. 1305 C.E.

GHIYAS-UD-DIN TUGHLAQS TOMB, DELHI c. 1325 B.C.E.

MHd. SHAH SAYYIOD'S TOMB, DELHI c. 1444 C.E.

JAMI MASJID, JAUNPUR, c. 1470 C.E.

JAMI MASJID, GULBARGA, c. 1367 C.E.

BIJAPUR 16th cent. C.E.

KHAN KHANAN'S TOMB, DELHI c. 1627 C.E.

HUMAYUN'S TOMB DELHI, 1564 C.E.

TAJMAHAL, AGRA c. 1634

SAFDAR JUNG'S TOMB, DELHI, c. 1753 C.E.

Fig. 17.31. Types of Domes

18

Mogul Period

Aurangzab (1658 to 1707 C.E)

18.1. INTRODUCTION

Aurangzeb was the son and successor to emperor Shah Jahan. His full name is Muhiud-din Muhammad Aurangzeb Bahadur Alamgir I. He is one of the longest ruling emperor after Akbar. Aurangzeb extended empire's boundaries and ruled tyrannically. Mogul empire gradually shrunk after Aurangzeb. Muhammad Shah and Bahadur Shah Zafar were the last kings for name sake only after Aurangzeb.

The vigorous construction activity that had been in force during predecessors was now declined. The buildings of Aurangzeb's reign show the same common usual features in a restrained mood. Aurangzeb's buildings changed from stone and marble to brick and rubble structures finished in stucco plaster. Ribbed dome was used. The important buildings that were selected here for brief description are- Moti masjid, Red fort, Delhi

– Badshahi mosque, Lahore

18.2. EXAMPLES

1. MOTI MASJID or PEARL MOSQUE, Delhi Fort, 1662 C.E (Fig. 18.1, 18.2)

The Moti Masjid was added in the fort at Delhi in 1662 C.E by Aurangzeb as royal mosque. This contains sanctuary prayer hall built in polished white marble. There are three cupolas over the sanctuary with a larger one in the center, the contours of which are more curved. Metal finial takes place over these cupolas.

2. BADSHAHI MOSQUE, LAHORE, 1674 C.E (Fig. 18.3)

This large mosque is conventional and was built in 1674 C.E. It has more minarets than usual, one at each corner of the mosque enclosure and other smaller ones at each angle of the sanctuary, making them eight in total. Its sanctuary is designed much similar to Jami masjid of Delhi. The facade contains a large central alcove in the centre with five arches in each wing. Three bulbous domes rise over the sanctuary. The mosque reveals the character of much of the strength and solidity.

18.3. NAMES OF OTHER STRUCTURES

- Jami masjid at Mathura
- Aurangzeb's tomb built at Khuldabad near Aurangabad which is a simple structure in sharp contrast to the magnificent tombs of predecessor Moguls.

OUDE NAWABS

18.4. ARCHITECTURE DURING OUDE NAWABS

After the death of Aurangzeb, the Nawabs of Oude became paramount and the center of power was transferred from Delhi to Lucknow. The British influence increased and Islam domination decreased.

18.5. EXAMPLES

SAFDARJUNG'S MAUSOLEUM, DELHI, 1750 C.E (Fig. 18.4): The last prominent tomb structure built in the city of Delhi is the mausoleum of Safdar Jung (1739 – 1753 C.E), a nephew and the Prime Minister of the first king of Oude, who resided at Delhi. The tomb building is large in size and designed in the usual manner of Mogul structures. The main building was placed in the middle of a large ornamental garden. The building contains common elements like large and small arched alcoves, turrets with kiosks and a central dome all disposed in conventional manner.

With this example the notable and forcible Mogul architectural movement that developed and persisted at Agra and Delhi came to an end.

18.6. LATER STRUCTURES

There are other large numbers of structures especially the palaces built at various places like Udaipur, Jodhpur, Jaipur and Gwalior during 16th and 17th centuries. The planning of these structures and the architectural features are more or less similar and same to the contemporary time. The surfaces of the buildings were not kept plain, but were decorated too heavily leading to confusion, lack of beauty, imbalance and disharmony.

QUESTIONS

1. Mention the names of any two mosque structures built by Aurangzeb and explain them.

Fig. 18.1. Moti masjid, Delhi

Fig. 18.2. Moti Masjid, Delhi—Sanctuary

Fig. 18.3. Badashahi mosque, Lahore—Sanctuary, 1674 C.E

Fig. 18.4. Safdarjung Mausoleum, Delhi, 1750 C.E

Inter Chapter Questions

1. Sketch any three types of Arches used in Islam structures built in India and briefly explain them.
2. What is Squinch arch and explain its purpose, importance and structure. Sketch any two types of Squinch arches and mention the names of buildings where they were used.
3. Sketch any three types of domes built in Islam structures. Name the buildings where they were used and explain their construction features.
4. Describe the construction techniques used in Islam structures to convert Square form to an Octagon to place the dome.
5. Explain the influence of forms and proportions of elements in a building. Describe this by means of any two important tomb buildings.
6. Explain the following
   (*i*) Intersection of Arches
   (*ii*) Double dome
7. How red sandstone and white marble were skillfully blended in emphasizing surfaces and beauty in Islam buildings? Mention any two names of such best examples.
8. How and what created beauty to Tajmahal, Agra. Explain this in detail.
9. Explain the construction of Double dome. Mention any two best examples where it was used.
10. Compare and contrast the planning, interior and other features of the following mosques.
    (*i*) Jami masjid of Ahmadabad
    (*ii*) Jami masjid of Gulbarga

Bibliography

1. Indian Architecture (Buddhist and Hindu) by Percy Brown
2. Indian Architecture (Islamic Period) by Percy Brown
3. The Architecture of India (Buddhist and Hindu) by Satish Grower
4. Fatehpur Sikri by Altar Abbas Rizvi
5. Wikipedia, the free Encyclopedia
6. About.com: Architecture
7. Archeological Survey of India
8. Flickr Photos